# MANAGEMENT IN CHINA
## The Experience of Foreign Businesses

*edited by*
ROGER STRANGE

FRANK CASS
LONDON • PORTLAND, OR

*First published in 1998 in Great Britain by*
FRANK CASS PUBLISHERS
Newbury House, 900 Eastern Avenue, London IG2 7HH

*and in the United States of America by*
FRANK CASS PUBLISHERS
c/o ISBS
5804 N.E. Hassalo Street,
Portland, Oregon 97213-3644

Website http://www.frankcass.com

Copyright © 1998 Frank Cass Publishers


British Library Caataloguing in Publication Data

Management in China : the experience of foreign businesses.
– (Studies in Asia Pacific business)
1. Business enterprises, Foreign – China
I. Strange, Roger
338.8'88'51

ISBN 0 7146 4842 6 (hbk)
ISBN 0 7146 4398 X (pbk)


Library of Congress Cataloging-in-Publication Data

Management in China : the experience of foreign business / edited by
Roger Strange.
p. cm. -- (Studies in Asia Pacific business)
Includes bibliographical references (p. ).
ISBN 0-7146-4842-6 (hardcover). -- ISBN 0-7146-4398-X (pbk.)
1. Management--China--Cross cultural studies. 2. Government
business enterprises--China--Management. 3. Marketing--China.
I. Strange, Roger. II. Series.
HD70.C5M336 1997
658'.049'0951--dc21                                    97-30436
                                                        CIP


The group of studies first appeared in a Special Issue of
*Asia Pacific Business Review*, Vol.3, No.3 (Spring 1997)
[MANAGEMENT IN CHINA: The Experience of Foreign Businesses]

Printed in Great Britain by
Antony Rowe Ltd., Chippenham, Wilts.

4 Week Loan

This book is due for return on or before the last date shown below.

STUDIES IN ASIA PACIFIC BUSINESS
*General Editor: Robert Fitzgerald*

ISSN 1369-7153

Other books in the series:

Greater China: Political Economy, Inward Investment and Business Culture
*edited by* Chris Rowley and Mark Lewis

Beyond Japanese Management: The End of Modern Times?
*edited by* Paul Stewart

Human Resource Management in the Asia Pacific Region
*edited by* Chris Rowley

# Contents

# Operating as a Foreign Company in China: Introduction and Overview

## ROGER STRANGE, SYED KAMALL and HUI TAN

Since its government's dramatic shift in foreign and economic policy in 1978, China has been regarded as a lucrative target for foreign multinational enterprises (MNEs) and international business researchers alike. In the 1990s especially, foreign direct investment (FDI) has been utilized by the Chinese government as a strategic tool for stimulating economic development, and China's success in attracting foreign capital may be contrasted with the ongoing difficulties associated with its many debt-burdened state-owned enterprises (SOEs). China is emerging as one of the most important investment sites around the world, second only to the US in terms of inward FDI flows since 1993. Though more than two-thirds of the realized foreign capital is from overseas Chinese, FDI from the United States, Japan and the European Union is now increasing rapidly, largely due to the strategic importance of the Chinese market and improvements in the business environment. However, the unique features of this business environment and its impact on managing a foreign investment enterprise (FIE) remain unclear to many potential investors. The aim of this essay is to provide an overview of the academic literature on the practice of international business inside the Chinese market.

### FEATURES OF THE BUSINESS ENVIRONMENT IN CHINA

Practitioners and researchers alike are finding that FDI in China presents many challenges to western business practice as well as to current models of FDI strategy. A key issue in international business concerns how to cope with the highly distinctive institutional and cultural characteristics of the host country. While there is no doubt that China has moved dramatically towards a more market-oriented economy, the Chinese market is still very different from western markets in terms of the political, economic and cultural environment. To mention just three of the most important differences:

- the uniqueness of the Chinese socialist market economy;

- the underdevelopment of the social infrastructure;

- the dominance of traditional Chinese culture in business activities.

Roger Strange, King's College, London; Syed Kamal, University of Leeds; Hui Tan, University of Bath

*The Uniqueness of the Chinese Socialist Market Economy*

China has been in the process of developing a 'socialist market economy with Chinese characteristics'. In practice, this means that the current constitution (of a one party dictatorship and mainly state ownership) and the legal regime (with its lack of transparency) will resist political reform even though economic reform has deepened since 1992. The government will attempt to maintain its approach of central planning, intervention and monopoly over certain strategic sectors of the economy, such as railways, post and telecommunications. Furthermore, some of the traditional features of the Chinese business environment will persist, including: changeable economic policy, the important role of internal documentation in economic governance,[1] and market protection as a method for local government to support the development of local economies.

These peculiarities of China's business environment have already created many obstacles to foreign investment. Yip[2] describes how foreign retailers who want to enter the China market must pay particular attention to macro environmental factors, since the market is in rapid transition and is regulated by constantly changing government policy. Seo[3] reports that although the Laws passed by Beijing often look good on paper, there is a wide gap between theory and practice. China's relatively unfavourable investment climate stems from a number of factors, such as unstable political conditions; ambiguous rules and an inadequate legal framework; arbitrary charges and bureaucratic red tape; stiff foreign-exchange balancing requirements and restrictions on profit repatriation; and poor infrastructure. He argues that as long as China remains politically unpredictable, and joint-venture manufacturers are required to export their products in order to balance foreign exchange receipts and expenditures, incentives such as lower land-use fees and tax breaks will be of little use to investors.

It is worth noting that some of the above restrictions, especially the balancing of foreign exchange,[4] have either been eased or changed as a result of the recent deepening of reforms. For example, the government has introduced changes in legislation to make the Chinese economy more transparent to foreign investors, in order to meet the criteria for membership of the World Trade Organization. Also, the *yuan* has been made convertible,[5] paving the way for investors to exchange foreign currency freely, further ensuring that they can reap the benefits of their local operations. This move is regarded as an affirmation of the government's intention to persist with its economic reforms. China's success in maintaining both foreign investment inflows and trade surpluses has resulted in one of the highest levels of foreign exchange reserves in the world, surpassing $100.45 billion (£60 billion) in November 1996.

*The Underdevelopment of Social Infrastructure*

As the largest developing economy in the world, with more than two-thirds of its population living outside urban areas, China is generally ill-equipped to meet the needs of foreign investors in terms of social infrastructure. Although many improvements have been made in the past 18 years, business facilities in China lag behind those of developed economies by decades. This remains a large handicap, especially in the central and the western regions of China. Guo and Akroyd[6] identified several barriers to technology transfer from UK firms to Chinese partners, including: management perceptions, information, communication and infrastructure. Any one of these may threaten the success of international firms in China. Thus UK companies were found to have encountered an information barrier which hindered the promotion of new technology in the Chinese market. One British managing director who had personally been successful in doing business in China commented, 'You can hardly find any Yellow Pages in China'.[7] In the absence of relevant market information, personal contact becomes an effective strategy in the Chinese market. Differences in technological and cultural factors have manifested themselves in communication barriers, which leads to much frustration and misunderstanding. Guo and Akroyd argue that the Chinese communication system is technically-oriented rather than commercially-oriented, in contrast with the UK where information services exist for business use. A number of infrastructural barriers are also identified including: the difficulties of sourcing raw materials, lack of personnel training, as well as problems with the operation and maintenance of the transferred technology. This view is supported by Yip[8] who finds that the market is underdeveloped in a number of important respects which make it less viable for a foreign retailer to directly transfer detailed knowledge from their home country to the Chinese enterprise.

### The Dominance of Traditional Chinese Culture in Business Activities

Some researchers view culture as the critical factor in understanding the differences of operating in China. Five prominent elements of Chinese culture relating to individual behaviour are identified by Child and Lu:[9] respect for age and authority; group orientation; the importance attached to family relationships; close personal connections (*guan xi*); and 'face' (*mian zi*). The most cited of these elements is *guan xi*. While the *guan xi* phenomenon may be found to some degree in almost all parts of the world, commentators seem to be unanimous in the view that it is much more important in the context of China business than elsewhere.

Davies[10] writes that 'the concept of *guanxi*, rendered in English as "personal connections", is all-pervasive in the description and analysis of China business: ... Academic analysts of Chinese business practice identify *guanxi* as a key feature which differentiates business in China from that carried out in the United States or Western Europe'. He argues that *guan xi* seems to be the lifeblood of the Chinese business community, extending into politics and society. Without *guan xi* one simply cannot get anything done. On the other hand, with *guan xi* many things seem possible. Björkman[11] also finds that companies possessing good *guan xi* with the 'right' people are seen to enjoy an advantage over rivals. This has led competitors from different parts of the world to develop friendships with employees of the central ministries in Beijing, with government officials at the provincial and local levels, and with individuals within the buying organization itself. A similar tale is told by other researchers, especially those investigating joint ventures in China. Roehrig[12] proposes that the most important strategy for Sino–foreign joint ventures wishing to elicit favourable implementation of laws, rules, regulations, and policies from local authorities is to establish good, personal relationships with strategically located individuals in business, government, and bureaucracy who may be able to influence outcomes of questions and disputes in favour of the enterprise.

The effective development and use of *guan xi* is seen as a requirement for successful negotiations involving Chinese protagonists, for the effective establishment of new business ventures and for the effective daily management of Chinese enterprises. Examination of the literature suggests considers three facets of *guan xi* which help to explain its importance: *guan xi* as the product of Chinese culture; *guan xi* as a societal response to the economic problems caused by an underdeveloped system of property rights and contract law; and *guan xi* as the (possibly corrupt) response of individuals to the opportunities for personal gain which arise in an economy subject to administrative controls.[13]

It is a fundamental feature of Asian culture in general, and Chinese culture in particular, that one can negotiate a deal most effectively when there is enough trust between the parties and that a verbal agreement is as good as a written contract.[14] However, *guan xi* is not a panacea for overcoming the problems of doing business in China. Björkman[15] found from interviews with enterprises in China that in spite of the perceived importance of *guan xi*, with a few exceptions (usually concerning orders in South China), suppliers who were not able to compete in terms of technical quality and price had little chance of winning business deals in China. McGuinness, Campbell and Lenotiades[16] argue that efforts to gain higher preferences through developing an extremely close rapport based on personal attractiveness may pay off, providing the company's services are also good. For western companies having a limited knowledge of the Chinese language, customs, and systems, however, it would seem mistaken to concentrate on building traditional type 'friendships' with the Chinese. Indeed, the Chinese themselves appear to be taking a more utilitarian approach to commercial relationships. A better strategy for western firms might well be to concentrate on marketing their products or services well, and to let relationships take care of themselves.

## THE MANAGEMENT BEHAVIOUR OF FOREIGN INVESTORS IN CHINA

The 1990s have witnessed a mushrooming of investment in China, accompanied by a surge in interest on the part of international business researchers in China as an emerging market.[17] Setting up and managing joint ventures in China is a challenging and sometimes frustrating commitment for foreign investors, but such investment can also be highly profitable both in terms of financial return and through the acquisition of precious experience.[18] Improved understanding of Chinese culture, value systems, traditions, business customs, and management styles has been widely identified as the key for long-term success in the creation and management of FIEs. However, there is still little empirical research on how FIEs are structured and managed by the partners.[19] Most current research either focuses on the macro political and economic environments in China[20] or provides descriptive accounts of individual joint ventures,[21] typically in their initial stages.

The rest of this section examines the limited empirical research available and presents a brief review of the management issues facing foreign investors in China. This research is discussed under the following headings: entry mode, partner selection, negotiation, corporate governance, human resource management, knowledge transfer, and marketing.

*Entry Mode*

Over the years, there have been three main formats for foreign investment in China: equity joint ventures; contractual, or cooperative, joint ventures; and wholly-owned subsidiaries.[22] Of these, the contractual joint venture was the most favoured format by foreign firms establishing a presence in China between 1979 and 1985,[23] due to the peculiarities of the business environment discussed above. Since then, the majority of research on market entry in China has focused on equity joint ventures.[24] Joint ventures are typically favoured by foreign firms in China, since this format allows them to meet their objectives in terms of acquiring local knowledge and gaining immediate access to local partners' marketing channels, customer and social networks; all of which are extremely important for firms operating in a totally new environment.[25]

In their study of the motivation for US MNEs forming joint ventures in China, Daniels *et al.*[26] compared joint ventures with other modes of foreign market servicing. Some companies found joint ventures superior to exporting as local production avoided relatively high non-production costs (such as high transport costs for cheaply produced goods such as processed foods or cigarettes). There were real cost advantages in producing in or near the market rather than exporting into that market. Furthermore, the protection of the Chinese market through both tariff and non-tariff barriers increased the costs of exporting to China, making joint ventures an attractive alternative. The study also found that joint ventures were preferred to licensing because of China's ineffectual protection of international patents and trademarks.

In another study, Glaister and Wang[27] examined the motivations of UK firms entering joint ventures in China. The broad strategic motivations of these UK companies were as follows: to use the joint venture to facilitate faster entry into the Chinese market; to conform to host government policy; to obtain a faster return on investment; and to compete against a common competitor. This study also revealed that UK companies were particularly motivated to form joint ventures in China if the Chinese partner could provide complementary inputs such as local market knowledge, knowledge of local culture, links with major buyers, distribution channels, labour, materials, natural resources, capital, producers, and production knowledge.

It therefore appears that foreign investors prefer joint ventures as an entry mode when initially probing the Chinese market, in order to utilize their Chinese partner's resources to bridge cultural gaps, to set up local networks, and to avoid potential political and economic risks. Typically, a foreign firm only considers establishing a wholly-owned subsidiary once it has gained confidence in handling the many difficulties and potential risks, as a result of experience gained through joint venture operation.

*Partner Selection*

Li and Shenkar[28] argue that the decision to form a joint venture assumes that one or more of the partners selected will enhance the venture's competitive position. The benefits from a prospective partner's contribution might then outweigh the added costs of inter-firm coordination. In other words, the more skills and assets – such as patents, technical know-how, financial resources, experienced managerial personnel, and access to marketing and distribution systems – that a potential partner can contribute to a venture, the greater the likelihood that it will be selected as a venture partner.[29] Dymsza[30] adds that in manufacturing joint ventures, the major contributions of the MNE typically comprise manufacturing technology, product know-how, patents, business expertise, technical training, and management capabilities. The local partner, in turn, commonly contributes capital, management, knowledge of the domestic market and environment, and contacts with the government, financial institutions, local suppliers, and labour unions.

In their study of UK joint ventures in China, Glaister and Wang[31] found that UK firms looked for Chinese partners with the following skills or characteristics: the ability to negotiate with the host government; related business; appropriate financial status or resources; and an established marketing and distribution system. This list of required assets seems to confirm that MNEs seek complementary resources from their Chinese partners in order to enhance the competitiveness of joint ventures and to make the maximum use of the firm-specific advantages of the parent.

In contrast, the perspectives of Chinese partners in such joint ventures would appear to have been neglected by researchers.[32] It is critical for foreign firms to acknowledge the contribution of Chinese partners, their strategic intent, and the assets they have sought to acquire via the establishment of a cooperative relationship in the course of seeking partners. The Chinese government views joint ventures as crucial in achieving the following major objectives:[33] the attraction of foreign capital;

the import of advanced foreign technology; the promotion of exports and the earning of foreign exchange; the import of modern management experience; and the creation of job opportunities.

Chinese companies share many of their government's objectives and they also obtain the following benefits by entering into joint venture arrangements:[34] improvement of competitiveness in both the international and domestic market; improvement of their image and status, as foreign (especially western) companies usually have a reputation for making technically-superior products of a higher quality; and access to preferential treatment from the Chinese government. Therefore, technology, international experience, and management skills are the most important criteria for Chinese companies when selecting foreign partners, since these factors help Chinese partners to achieve their major objectives of obtaining advanced technologies and management skills, and entering the international market. In addition, other factors such as financial status, mutual trust, and reputation are regarded as crucial characteristics of foreign partners.[35]

*Negotiation*

Once a venture partner has been chosen, the next step is negotiation. 'Though complex, difficult and 'painful' (that is, tough and time-consuming), negotiations are unavoidable as part of the process of establishing ventures in China'.[36] Early work on Sino-foreign negotiations[37] focused on ventures involving China trade rather than FDI in China. Further research over the last ten years draws on the earlier work in considering FDI in China.[38] Wagner[39] presents a review of this literature and identifies a list of variables influencing the outcome of Sino-Western joint venture negotiations:

- businesslike attitude: an attitude which facilitates continuing negotiations and is characterized by friendliness, frankness, and fairness;
- cultural awareness: an awareness of the other side's cultural norms, and the adoption of a long-term view of the venture by the western partners;
- good interpretation: presence of excellent translation skills, usually one or more people who understand both Chinese and western cultures and negotiation goals;
- strategic planning: being prepared for negotiations, and knowing one's objectives in the negotiations;
- strong commitment to successful negotiations.

Based on a case study of knowledge transfer in OTIS's joint venture in Tianjin, Hendryx[40] lists the key bargaining points in joint venture negotiations: joint venture contracts (contribution of the parties, profit remittance, foreign exchange, management and control); technical cooperation agreements (transfer of product technology, transfer of know-how, duration, compensation for technology); and operations-related technology transfer. The latter includes product technology transfer (identification and organization of data, assimilation and localization, tooling and prototyping, manufacturing systems, software); production technology transfer (factory renovation hardware and software, quality control); and management technology transfer (personnel management, motivation, job assignment, financial management, marketing and sales).

Finding an appropriate approach to Sino–foreign negotiation lies at the core of the debate on negotiations research. Lee and Lo[41] believe that a careful selection of negotiating teams, cautious handling of persuasion, concessions and disputes during and after the negotiation, should enhance the quality and atmosphere during the course of negotiations. Foreign negotiators should regard so-called 'behind the scenes' or informal activities as a very important aspect of Sino–foreign negotiations. Shenkar and Ronen[42] argue that traditional Chinese culture, especially Confucian-derived culture, has a great impact on the communication patterns and social obligations of Chinese, and affects the beliefs and behaviour of Chinese partners. An appreciation of Chinese culture would greatly contribute to the success of China venture negotiations.

*Corporate Governance*

Cadbury[43] describes corporate governance as the system or process by which companies are directed and controlled. Tricker[44] proposes that corporate governance ought to be the process for ensuring that a company performs in a responsible and responsive way to the interests of its stakeholders. Internal governance issues in foreign firms in China have received relatively less attention from international business researchers. The limited case studies available[45] reveal that changes in government policy over the last 18 years have ensured that corporate governance structures in FIEs are based on 'international practice', and differ greatly from those in Chinese SOEs.[46] Usually, a two-tiered management system is employed in equity joint ventures: the first tier comprises the board of directors, while the second tier consists of management staff who are 'responsible for the daily operational and managerial work'.[47] Led by a CEO, the management team of FIEs usually enjoy a degree of autonomy under the Board.

Although communist ideology dictates that workers are 'masters of the house', there is no provision for workers' congresses in joint ventures in China. Unlike their western counterparts, the 'management' of a joint venture is supposed to 'positively support' the work and activities of its trade union. Union representatives have the right to attend board meetings in order to air workers' opinions, although they do not have the right to vote. Chinese partners tend to emphasize the cooperative and conciliatory nature of trade unions in joint ventures.[48] Apart from trade unions, other mass organizations such as the Communist Youth League, Youth Federation, and Women's Federation may also exist in the joint ventures just as in many 'units', including SOEs, in China. However, these other mass organizations play a minor role in comparison to trade unions, usually limited to organizing and supporting social functions.[49]

*Human Resource Management (HRM)*

HRM issues in FIEs have been tackled in a piecemeal fashion by international business scholars. Issues of recruiting, firing, and pay policy have been addressed, whilst other issues such as motivation, leadership skills, job assignment, and corporate culture have been largely ignored.

The National Council for US–China Trade[50] reported that the main personnel problem during 1979–87 was the inability to staff joint ventures with skilled employees due to skill shortages and the difficulties of transferring employees. While these problems still exist, their impact has decreased over recent years, especially in the southern part of China where Hong Kong investors have employed over three million workers, while adopting capitalist labour management methods.[51]

Since 1980, Chinese labour legislation has responded to foreign concerns in several ways.[52] First, substantial autonomy has been granted to joint ventures in the areas of recruiting, hiring, disciplining, and firing employees. Also, conditions under which employees may or may not be dismissed have been clarified. Such decisions now require the approval of Chinese management, labour unions, and local labour officials, thereby prohibiting foreign representatives from unilaterally deciding these issues. The legislation has also sought to systematize the level of wages and benefits paid to employees. However, the implementation of regulations more favourable to foreign entrants depended largely on bargaining between foreign joint venture representatives and their Chinese counterparts, within the enterprise as well as in government at local levels and other Chinese state enterprises. The staff of joint ventures may be hired either through an officially-sanctioned labour service company with the approval of the local labour bureau, or as a result of the joint venture advertising any vacancies. Successful candidates typically undergo a three-to-six month probation period, in common with enterprises in developed economies. Therefore, it would appear that joint ventures are well placed to recruit qualified workers or staff previously engaged in other enterprises. A joint venture also has the right to lay off staff and workers whose jobs have become redundant, and to dismiss any staff with a bad disciplinary record or who have committed serious offences. In practice, none of these measures has been opposed by trade unions, since where dismissals have taken place they have been considered justified.[53]

There is no single 'model' for wage payments to staff and workers of FIEs in China. In general, the wage level can be broken down into the following five components: basic wage, floating wage, position wage, piece-rate wage, and bonus. Each FIE enjoys autonomy in deciding a wage pattern which suits them best. A survey conducted in Shenzhen reveals that employees of joint ventures were generally satisfied with the level of wages they received.[54] This can be explained by the fact that employees received higher wages than their counterparts in SOEs, which might reflect the greater efficiency of joint ventures or might indicate that financial reward is an effective means to elicit greater efforts from employees. In contrast, the remuneration of expatriate staff in China is based on contracts signed between the employees and the joint ventures, subject to approval by the board of directors. In general, foreign employees receive a wage comparable to that in their home country with additional hardship allowances and other benefits.[55]

*Knowledge Transfer*

After establishing an affiliate in the Chinese market, MNEs typically seek to exploit their competitive advantages by transferring knowledge to the affiliate in order to develop its capabilities. Knowledge transfer is often a package including both the tangible embodiment of the technology and the associated tacit managerial know-how; and the two often cannot be successfully separated.[56] Key elements of the knowledge transfer process have been discussed by Rimington[57] and include: the development of the organization along western lines; effective communication and performance measurement; training and development of human resources; development of effective Quality Management Systems; localization of material supply; and solutions to problems arising in the development of a joint venture. Additionally, key factors during the conception stage include the creation of an atmosphere of trust between partners and adherence to project time scales.

Guo and Akroyd[58] suggest a five-stage model for the actual knowledge transfer process in the Chinese market: motivation; capitalization; negotiation; execution; and exploitation. A study by Li and Shenkar[59] reveals that existing local partner skills largely determine the types of skills sought from foreign partners. While it is to be expected that a foreign parent will transfer those skills lacking in a Chinese affiliate, there needs to be at least a certain level of existing skills in the affiliate for the successful transfer of knowledge. Chinese firms that completely lack a given skill are less likely to have the particular skill transferred from the parent, unless it is absolutely necessary for local operations. In other words, transfer of a foreign firm's technology, management and marketing skills will be less successful if the local affiliate does not possess the necessary skills base or absorptive capability. In addition, management capacity and cultural appreciation are important factors for the success of knowledge transfer. In order to overcome transfer barriers, all parties involved should share a common map (that is, a common perception of the stages in the transactional voyage); should exercise compatible or complementary functions; and should practise interdisciplinary communication at all levels.

In considering the transfer of knowledge, the evolution of an affiliate should be considered at different stages.[60] In other words, different types of knowledge will be transferred during the various stages of an affiliate's development. Initially, it is usual for key technologies and some management skills to be transferred from the parent to the affiliate. This is usually followed by the transfer of social knowledge which is critical in ensuring that the new affiliate achieves and maintains a competitive advantage by fully utilizing the transferred knowledge as well as creating new knowledge incrementally. This 'different stage–different knowledge transfer' model has been validated in several case studies provided for FIEs in China – see, for example, GPT's successful knowledge transfer to its Shanghai branch.[61]

The study by Li and Shenkar[62] also shows that Chinese state-owned firms were more likely to seek the transfer of managerial (but not marketing or technological) skills than non-state enterprises, possibly because of their dominance in the local market.

*Marketing*

As discussed earlier, the main motive for many foreign companies in establishing a presence in China is to gain entry to its potentially large market. Once foreign entrants gain a foothold in China, decisions relating to the organization of sales and marketing functions becomes increasingly critical. Companies may choose from a variety of operational modes, ranging from company–external modes (such as using various external distributors or agents) to company–internal modes (for example, own sales personnel who only occasionally visit the market in question; or the establishment of a local unit). However, intermediate forms may also be employed such as jointly-owned distributors or agents.[63] In fact, most foreign entrants prefer to establish their own sales teams.[64] Though it is common for Chinese partners to provide distribution channels to the local market, distribution may be limited by the fact that only a few enterprises in China operate on a national scale. The market share of many SOEs is less than ten per cent.[65] This forces FIEs to establish their own nationwide distribution networks.

It is clear from the extant research[66] that western companies selling industrial goods in China face at least three different challenges: how to obtain information about potential orders in China; how to influence the Chinese decision-makers so as to win business deals; and how to handle the implementation of the orders that they receive in China. As a result of the underdeveloped social infrastructure, many FIEs are unable to 'obtain a satisfactory list of Chinese companies operating in the industry in question'.[67]

However, the reforms of the Chinese economic system have led to a decentralization of purchasing. McGuinness *et al.* suggest[68] that the final users of products now tend to be actively involved in the purchasing process. Contrary to popular belief, price-cutting and special offers do not appear to be the best way to influence consumers. The most important factors in winning sales in China are product quality, promotional effort and quality of service. Chinese plant managers seem to demand only that prices be in keeping with the quality of product on offer. This suggests that there is much more to doing business in China than simply being skilful at negotiations. Although China's cultural traditions may suggest that relationships between customers and suppliers may be more important than they are in western markets,[69] gauging the importance of relationships in China becomes more difficult when the effects of other marketing variables are considered. It has been argued that the Chinese concept of 'face' may encourage them to buy only products with a well-known brand name or reputation.[70] Chinese culture tends to rank everything hierarchically so that it is highly desirable to buy what is considered to be 'at the top'. Should buying the best product come in conflict with the desire for friendship, then buying the best will generally win out, especially since Chinese officials leave themselves open to criticism if they do not.[71]

*Summary*

While many pertinent issues relating to foreign enterprises operating in China have been considered by international business researchers, a number of other issues have yet to receive adequate attention. For example, most researchers appear to have ignored or underemphasized the importance of finance for operating successfully in China; a market that lacks both capital and the normal channels for providing capital that are available in the West. In addition, various sourcing, production and HRM issues has also received less attention than they merit, thus demonstrating that the study of foreign investors' behaviour in China lags well behind the practice of FDI. More effort is needed to expand the existing research to cover a more complete range of management issues in this important emerging market. Fortunately, there is evidence that many of these issues are now being tackled by international business scholars, as demonstrated by the contributions in this volume.

## AN OVERVIEW OF THIS VOLUME

These issues, related to the difficulties and opportunities facing foreign investors in China, are addressed by the contributors to this volume. The first two essays examine the impact of the enterprise reforms. The following three contributions consider various stages in the process of adding value: sourcing, distribution, and advertising. The final two authors address the issue of what China can learn from the success story of Japan. The cultural roots of the Chinese and Japanese are discussed, and the transferability of Japanese-style management to China is examined.

Athar Hussain and Juzhong Zhuang note four major changes in the economic environment during the reform period which have facilitated the transformation of the industrial structure. The first has been the growth of market transactions, which has taken captive markets away from the SOEs and forced them to compete through upgrading quality and cutting costs. The second has been the growing exposure of Chinese enterprises to international markets and foreign business practices, which has had an important impact on the organization and managerial structure of Chinese enterprises. The third has been the multiplication of the sources of funds for investment and working capital, which has helped to break the monopoly of enterprise governance by government agencies and facilitated the establishment of new enterprises. And the fourth has been the rapid growth of the economy which has both eased the process of restructuring and lowered the risks of failure for new enterprises.

Notwithstanding the considerable progress which has been made, Hussain and Zhuang then identify a number of interrelated areas to which future reforms should be addressed. The first problem area is enduring government interference in the day-to-day management not only in SOEs but also in the non-state sector (a problem highlighted in more detail by Pan and Parker's contribution). They suggest that the distancing of the government from the SOEs is contingent upon reforms in the tax and social security systems, and in banking and finance, but note that such reforms will take time. The second area relates to the structure of ownership of SOEs, which typically reflects the functional and territorial divisions of government. They recommend the displacement of monopoly ownership of large and medium-sized enterprises with more effective governance structures where ownership is diversified. Third, they point to the need for 'efficiency-enhancing' industrial restructuring, involving the closure of large numbers of enterprises, not just in the state sector but also in the non-state sector, and particularly in rural areas. And finally, they emphasize the importance of reform of employment relations and the social security system which is anchored in the SOEs, and which is a source of problems for employers and employees alike.

Weihwa Pan and David Parker attempt to find out whether management attitudes have changed in recent years as a result of the government's economic reforms and whether any notable differences in attitude and behaviour can be discerned between the managers in the various types of enterprises. To this end, they present the results of interviews with senior managers in a sample of corporatized and non-corporatized SOEs, collective enterprises (COEs) and joint ventures in Shanghai and Nanjing. Their results reveal that hardening budgetary constraints on firms in recent years has led to increased profit seeking and a decline in the influence of the government across all types of enterprises, except where the government remains a major customer (such as in the defence industry). However, the state still maintains control over a number of aspects of management including the appointment of senior management, investment decisions, restructuring and closure of firms. Only the managers of joint ventures feel that they exercise any real control over these decisions. In addition, the authors find that collective enterprises are restructuring on a much smaller scale than expected due to a lack of awareness of the relevant management techniques on the part of COEs managers.

In general, the attitudes of management in joint ventures may be more easily differentiated from attitudes in the other forms of enterprises. The attitudes of managers in COEs and SOEs are remarkably similar despite the different histories of the two types of enterprise. Also, COEs appear less interested in the introduction of new technology. In fact, one COE has changed its objective in recent years in favour of maintaining employment. The different attitudes adopted by joint ventures are to be expected given the likely transfer of knowledge from foreign partners to local joint ventures. The relative isolation of the SOEs and COEs force them to find other means of acquiring much needed knowledge such as technology, management skills and social knowledge.

International business theory suggests that, even though a firm may initially service a foreign market through exports, it will eventually move to local manufacture if justified by the size of the market and a significant reduction of transaction and other costs. However, the so far limited literature suggests a number of problems encountered by foreign firms with manufacturing affiliates in China, including the unreliable sourcing of locally produced components and materials. Stefan Kaiser reviews the extant literature on local sourcing in China and introduces a case study of Braun Electric (Shanghai) Co. Ltd. (BES). He documents a variety of problems encountered by BES, problems which may or may not be typical of those encountered by other MNEs manufacturing in China. Whereas BES have encountered difficulties such as the poor quality of components and unreliable deliveries, the company has not been adversely affected by poor delivery service of local suppliers or volume requirements not being met, as suggested in the reviewed literature. The case study of BES highlights the importance of local purchasing in China in ensuring just-in-time delivery, thereby reducing manufacturing costs while increasing cooperation between the foreign manufacturer and local suppliers. As a result of the study, the author is able to suggest a variety of potential strategies to exploit the advantages of local sourcing. Kaiser's study suggests that the quality of local sourcing will increase as more foreign manufacturers build relationships with local suppliers. Through building these relationships, local suppliers are able to acquire the necessary technology and knowledge in order to improve the quality of their products. This may be seen as an alternative method of knowledge transfer to a formal joint venture. However, it is highly likely that most local suppliers will be affiliates of foreign MNEs.

While Kaiser examines the inputs to the manufacturing process, Choo-Sin Tseng, Paula Kwan and Fanny Cheung examine choices concerning how best to distribute the output. Tseng, Kwan and Cheung trace the development of the distribution system in China from state-monopoly to the participation of foreign enterprises. With the existence of differences in linguistic, cultural and economic factors across China, as well as the increased power at the provincial level, the authors advise foreign investors to modify their distribution strategies according to local conditions, and not to treat China as one homogenous market. With more foreign retailers allowed to service the Chinese market, there have been marked improvements in China's distribution network. Hence foreign manufacturers are advised to make initial use of existing channels (that is, state, collective or foreign distributors or retailers). Only once they accumulate sufficient local market knowledge should they consider integrating distribution channels into their local market activities.

Once a foreign company has succeeded in getting its products to the market, there still remains the problem of persuading consumers to buy them. Nan Zhou and Linming Meng report the results of their study of human characters in advertising in China. Advertising had been banned under the Cultural Revolution, but was permitted under the reforms and has, since 1978, grown into a large industry in China. The authors describe the development of advertising in relation to economic and cultural changes in Chinese society since the reforms, and present the findings of a content analysis of Chinese consumer magazine advertising. They find that the Chinese advertising market is expected to follow a similar path to other developing countries – that is, the current seller-oriented market giving way to a buyer-oriented market. Advertisers will then increasingly segment the market while increasing the use of buyers' images in advertising. This is already happening to a certain degree with advertisers focusing on the younger population using sex-appeal and images of celebrities and foreigners enjoying an affluent lifestyle. However, advertisers are warned that there may be only a limited role for such imagery in selling products, since surveys have shown that consumers prefer images that more accurately reflect their simple and hardworking values. Though such views are to be expected in any emerging consumer society, advertisers need to be careful to avoid a consumer backlash by ensuring that any images employed take account of deeply-rooted Chinese cultural values and social and economic practices. Comparisons are drawn with Japan where, even though western models and language are found in advertisements, they are employed in a manner which appeals to Japanese sensibilities. The lesson for advertisers in China is that a complete westernization of local advertising would alienate consumers despite the changes in society.

The last two contributions continue the theme of comparison with practices in Japan. Zaixin Ma begins with the premise that, in general, Japanese-style management methods are easier to transfer to Asian host markets than to western countries. This is explained by the fact that many of the South East Asian countries belong to the Confucian cultural tradition which originated in China. Indeed, Ma asserts that many Japanese management practices draw upon material from ancient China. In order to examine the transfer of Japanese social knowledge, Ma presents an in-depth study of a Japanese-funded enterprise operating in the fashion industry in Beijing. The cultural communication between the Japanese and the Chinese company is analysed in the hope of understanding which management methods are difficult to transfer and why.

The study leads Ma to the belief that the continuing opening of the Chinese economy will reduce the obstacles standing in the way of learning from Japan as well as non-Asian developed countries. However, the Chinese also need to learn from their own history in order to develop appropriate ideas for Chinese-style management. This will enable Chinese managers to gain a new self-confidence and to contribute to the learning of foreign management methods, especially from the Japanese. Finally, the adoption of Japanese-style management methods is found to involve the learning of both management skills (external factors) and the essence of management (internal factors). The latter relates to the essence of the Japanese themselves. Therefore, when adopting Japanese management techniques, the Chinese need to be aware of Japanese internal factors and to adapt accordingly.

In contrast to Ma, John Ritchie sounds a cautionary note to those who believe that Japan's business success is assured due to the transferability of Japanese management techniques. He considers critically the idea that 'Global Japanization' will lead the Japanese to evolve grand strategies for China. While he agrees that the Japanese, along with the Americans and the overseas Chinese, are better placed than Western Europeans in developing state and corporate strategies for China, he finds the idea of Japanese management dominance in China premature. His contribution examines various historical Japanese approaches towards trade and business with China, and puts forward the following four-fold typology of modes: classic trader-merchanting, imperial-militarist, civil-nationalist, and strategic-managerial. He argues that the strategic-managerial mode is still emerging but that it presupposes rising Japanese intent and corresponding Chinese support for going beyond bilateral trade towards growing organization for, increasing direct investment to, and better management within China. The detail of this emerging mode remains provisional upon the realization of its full scope and potential, but he suggests that it may be differentiated from Western European approaches not just by the relative volumes of aid, trade and investment, but also through the extent of organizational coupling and managerial sustainability. Ritchie warns that, while the Japanese have not yet established a major presence in China, their approach of continuous and evolutionary learning will stand them in good stead should they decide to do so. For their part, Western European investors might particularly observe how, as well as what, Japanese firms learn from China, and thereby better prepare themselves for the major changes ahead.

## NOTES

1. A. Carver, 'Open and Secret Regulations and their Implication for Foreign Investment', in J. Child and Y. Lu (eds) *Management Issues in China, Volume 2: International Enterprises*, London, Routledge, 1996.
2. L. Yip. 'The Emergence of a Retail Market in China', in H. Davies (ed.) *China Business: Context and Issues*, Hong Kong, Longman Asia, 1995, pp.251–68.
3. K.K. Seo, 'Economic Reform and Foreign Direct Investment', in L. Kelley and O. Shenkar (eds) *International Business in China*, London, Routledge, 1993, pp.109–36.
4. See J. Frankenstein, 'Toward the Year 2000: Some Strategic Speculations about International

Business in China', in L. Kelley and O. Shenkar (eds) *International Business in China*, London, Routledge, 1993, pp.1–28; and S.R. Plasschaert, 'The Foreign-Exchange Balancing Rule in the People's Republic of China', in L. Kelley and O. Shenkar (eds) *International Business in China*, London, Routledge, 1993, pp.88–108.

5. On current account from December 1996.
6. A. Guo and R. Ackroyd, 'Overcoming Barriers to Technology Transfers into China', in J. Child and Y. Lu (eds) *Management Issues in China, Volume 2: International Enterprises*, London, Routledge, 1996.
7. See the similar comment made by Kaiser in this volume.
8. L. Yip, 'The Emergence of a Retail Market in China'.
9. J. Child and Y. Lu (eds) *Management Issues in China, Volume 2: International Enterprises*, London, Routledge, 1996 p.4.
10. H. Davies, 'Interpreting *Guanxi*: the Role of Personal Connections in a High Context Transitional Economy', in H. Davies (ed.) *China Business: Context & Issues*, Longman Asia, Hong Kong, 1995, pp.155–69.
11. I Björkman, 'Market Entry and Development in China', in J. Child and Y. Lu (eds) *Management Issues in China, Volume 2:International Enterprises*, London, Routledge, 1996.
12. M.F. Roehrig, *Foreign Joint Ventures in Contemporary China*, New York, St. Martin's Press, 1994, p.77.
13. H. Davies, 'Interpreting *Guanxi*', p.156.
14. M.F. Roehrig, *Foreign Joint Ventures in Contemporary China*, p.83.
15. I. Björkman, 'Market Entry and Development in China', p.70.
16. N. McGuiness, N. Campbell and J. Lenotiades, 'Selling Machinery to China: Chinese Perceptions of Strategies and Relationship', *Journal of International Business Studies*, Vol.21, No.2 (1991) pp.205–6.
17. See, for example, P.W. Beamish, 'Characteristics of Joint Ventures in the People's Republic of China', *Journal of International Marketing*, Vol.1, No.1 (1993) pp.29–48; J. Child, 'Managerial Adapatation in Reforming Economies: the Case of Joint Ventures'. Paper presented at the Annual Meeting of the Academy of Management, Miami Beach, 1991; J.D. Daniels, J. Krug, and D. Nigh, 'US Joint Ventures in China: Motivation and Management of Political Risk', *California Management Review*, Vol.27, No.4 (1985) pp.46–58; W.H. Davidson, 'Creating and Managing Joint Ventures in China', *California Management Review*, Vol.29, No.4 (1987) pp.77–94; M.M. Pearson, *Joint Ventures in the People's Republic of China: the Control of Foreign Direct Investment under Socialism*, Princeton NJ, Princeton University Press, 1991; R. Pomfret, *Investing in China: Ten Years of the Open Door Policy*, Ames, Iowa State University Press, 1991.
18. J. Zhang, 'Managing Sino–Foreign Joint Ventures: Lessons Learnt from Experience', in H. Davies (ed) *China Business: Context & Issues*, Longman Asia, Hong Kong, 1995, p.345.
19. A. Yan and B. Gray, 'Bargaining Power, Management Control, and Performance in United States–China Joint Ventures: a Comparative Case Study', *Academy of Management Journal*, Vol.37, No.6 (1994) pp.1479–80.20. See, for example, N. Campbell, *A Strategic Guide to Equity Joint Ventures in China*, New York, Pergamon, 1988; A.K. Ho, *Joint Ventures in the People's Republic of China*, New York, Praeger, 1990; L. Mathur and J.S. Chen, *Sttategies for Joint Ventures in the People's Republic of China*, New York, Praeger, 1987; W. Shan, 'Environmental Risks and Joint Venture Sharing Arrangements', *Journal of International Business Studies*, Vol.22, No.4 (1991) pp.555–78; R.L. Tung, 'US–China Trade Negotiations: Practices, Procedures and Outcomes', *Journal of International Business Studies*, Fall 1982, pp.25–38.
21. See, for example, N. Campbell, *A Strategic Guide to Equity Joint Ventures in China*, New York, Pergamon, 1988; D.K. Eiteman, 'American Executives' Perceptions of Negotiating Joint Ventures with the People's Republic of China: Lessons Learned', *Columbia Journal of World Business*, Vol.25, No.4 (1990) pp.59–67; S. Hendryx, 'Implememtaion of a Technology Transfer Joint Venture in the People's Republic of China: a Management Perspective', *Columbia Journal of Business*, 1996, pp.57–65; J. Mann, *Beijing Jeep*, New York, Simon & Schuster, 1989; A.J. O'Reilly, 'Establishing Successful Joint Ventures in Developing Countries: a CEO's Perspective', *Columbia Journal of World Business*, Vol.23, No.1 (1988) pp.65–71; O. Schnepp, M.A. Von Glinow, and A. Ghambri, *United States–China Technology Transfer*, Englewood Cliffs NJ, Prentice Hall, 1990.
22. But see H.M. Leung, J.T. Thoburn, E. Chau, and S.H. Tang, 'Contractual Relations, Foreign Direct Investment, and Technology Transfer: the Case of China', *Journal of International Development*, Vol.3, No.3 (June 1991) pp.277–91.

23. N. Campbell, 'The Patterns of Equity Joint Ventures in China'. Manchester Business School Working Paper No.156, p.6.
24. See, for example, P.W. Beamish, 'Characteristics of Joint Ventures in the People's Republic of China'; P.W. Beamish and L. Spiess, 'Foreign Direct Investment in China', in L. Kelley and O. Shenkar (eds) *International Business in China,* pp. 152–71, London, Routledge, 1993; J. Child, 'Managerial Adaptation in Reforming Economies'; J. Child and Y. Lu (eds) *Management Issues in China: Volume 2, International Enterprises,* London: Routledge, 1996; J.D. Daniels, J. Krug and D. Nigh, 'US Joint Ventures in China'; W.H. Davidson, 'Creating and Managing Joint Ventures in China'; D.K. Eiteman, 'American Exceutives' Persptions of Negotiating Joint Ventures'; A. Guo and R. Ackroyd, 'Overcoming Barriers to Technology Transfers in China'; S. Hendryx, 'Implementation of a Technology Transfer Joint Venture'; A.K. Ho, *Joint Ventures in the People's Republic of China*; J. Mann, *Beijing Jeep*; L. Mathur and J.S. Chen, *Strategies for Joint Ventures in the People's Republic of China*; W.H. Newman, 'Focused Joint Ventures in Transforming Economies', *Academy of Management Executive,* Vol. 6, No.1 (1992) pp.67–75; A.J. O'Reilly, 'Establishing Successful Joint Ventures in Developing Nations'; M.M. Pearson, *Joint Ventures in the People's Republic of China*; M.F. Roehrig, *Foreign Joint Ventures in Contemporary China*; K.K. Seo, 'Economic Reform and Foreign Direct Investment'; W. Shan, 'Environmental Risks and Joint Venture Sharing Arrangements'; C.L. Wagner, 'Perceived Correlates of Successful Joint Venture Negotiations in China: an Empirical Study', *International Journal of Management,* Vol.10, No.4 (1993) pp.413–21; A. Yan and B. Gary, 'Bargaining Power, Management Control, and Performance in United States–China Joint Ventures'; J. Zhang, 'Managing Sino–Foreign Joint Ventures'.
25. J. Zhang, 'Managing Sino–Foreign Joint Ventures', p.337.
26. J.D. Daniels, J. Krug, and D. Nigh, 'US Joint Ventures in China'.
27. K.W. Glaister and Y. Wang, 'UK Joint Ventures in China: Motivations and Partner Selection', *Marketing Intelligence & Planning,* Vol.11, No.2 (1993) pp.9–15.
28. J. Li and O. Shenkar, 'In Search of Complementary Assets: Co-operative Strategies and Knowledge Seeking by Prospective Chinese Partners', in J. Child and Y. Lu (eds) *Management Issues in China, Volume 2:International Enterprises,* London, Routledge, 1996, pp.54–5.
29. W.K. Awadzi, *Determinants of Joint Venture Performance: a Study of International Joint Ventures in the United States,* Unpublished doctoral dissertation, Louisiana State University, 1987.
30. W.A. Dymsza, 'Successes and Failures in Joint Ventures in Developing Countries: Lessons from Experience', in F. Contractor and P. Lorange (eds) *Co-operative Strategies in International Business,* Lexington, Lexington Books, 1988, p.406.
31. K.W. Glaister and Y. Wang, 'UK Joint Ventures in China'.
32. J. Li and O. Shenkar, 'In Search of Complementary Assets', p.53.
33. C. Wu, *A Research Report on Foreign Direct Investment in China,* Beijing, China Finance and Economics Press, 1991, pp.15–21.
34. J. Zhang, 'Managing Sino–Foreign Joint Ventures', p.338.
35. Ibid, p.339.
36. Ibid, p.340.
37. J.W. De Pauw, *US–Chinese Trade Negotiations,* New York, Praeger, 1981; L. Pye, *Chinese Commercial Negotiating Style,* Cambridge MA, Gunn & Hain, 1982; L. Pye, 'The China Trade: Making the Deal', *Harvard Business Review,* July–August 1986, pp.76–80; R.L. Tung, 'US–China Trade Negotiations'; R.L. Tung, *US–China Trade Negotiations,* New York, Pergamon, 1982.
38. See, for example, S. Hendryx, 'Implementation of a Technology Transfer Joint Venture'; K.H. Lee and W.C. Lo, 'American Business People's Perceptions of Marketing and Negotiating in the People's Republic of China', in L. Kelley and O. Shenkar (eds) *International Business in China,* London, Routledge, 1993, pp.208–224; O. Shenkar and S. Ronen, 'The Cultural Context of Negotiations: th Implications of Chinese Interpersonal Norms', in L. Kelley and O. Shenkar (eds) *International Business in China,* London, Routledge, 1993, pp.191–207; C.L. Wagner, 'Perceived Correlates of Successful Joint Venture Negotiations in China'; J. Zhang, 'Managing Sino–Foreign Joint Ventures'.
39. C.L. Wagner, 'Perceived Correlates of Successful Joint Venture Negotiations in China', p.421.
40. S. Hendryx, 'Implementation of a Technology Transfer Joint Venture'.
41. K.H. Lee and W.C. Lo, 'American Business People's Perceptions', pp.220–22.

42. O. Shenkar and S. Ronen, 'The Cultural Context of Negotiations'.
43. A. Cadbury, 'The Cadbury Report: the UK Perspective', Keynote address to the First Asian-Pacific Corporate Governance Conference, Sydney, May 1993.
44. B. Tricker, 'Dangers Focusing on Conformance rather than Performance', Keynote address to the First Asian-Pacific Corporate Governance Conference, Sydney, May 1993.
45. M.K. Nyaw, 'Managing International Joint Ventures in China', in L. Kelley and O. Shenkar (eds) *International Business in China*, London, Routledge, 1993, pp.172–90; M.F. Roehrig, *Foreign Joint Ventures in Contemporary China*; O.K. Tam, 'Corporate Governance in China's Listed Companies', *Corporate Governance Research Papers*, Vol.3, No.1, 1995.
46. As described in J. Child and Y. Lu (eds) *Management Issues in China*, p.3.
47. M.F. Roehrig, *Foreign Joint Ventures in Contemporary China*, p.39.
48. M.K. Nyaw, 'Managing International Joint Ventures in China', p.179.
49. Ibid, p.182.
50. The National Council for US–China Trade, *US Joint Ventures in China: a Progress Report*, Washington DC, US Department of Commerce, 1987.
51. J. Zhang, 'Managing Sino–Foreign Joint Ventures', p.344.
52. M.F. Roehrig, *Foreign Joint Ventures in Contemporary China*, p.42.
53. M.K. Nyaw, 'Managing International Joint Ventures in China',pp.182–185.
54. Ibid, pp.182–5.
55. Ibid, pp.182–5.
56. D.J. Teece, 'Multinational Enterprise: Market Failure and Market Power Considerations', *Sloan Management Review*, Vol.22, 1981, pp.3–17.
57. R. Rimington, 'The Management Process of Developing a Sino–British Joint Venture', in J. Child and Y. Lu (eds) *Management Issues in China, Volume 2: International Enterprises*, London, Routledge, 1996, p.129.
58. A. Guo and R. Ackroyd, 'Overcoming Barriers to Technology Transfers into China', p.32.
59. J. Li and O. Shenkar, 'In Search of Complementary Assets', p.53.
60. S.J. Chang and P.M. Rosenzweig, 'A Process Model of MNC Evolution: the Case of Sony Corporation in the United States', Carnegie Bosch Institute Working Paper 95–9, Carnegie Mellon University, p.15.
61. R. Rimington, 'The Management Process of Developing a Sino–British Joint Venture', p.129.
62. J. Li and O. Shenkar, 'In Search of Complementary Assets', p.53.
63. I. Björkman, 'Market Entry and Development in China', p.66; L. Yip, 'The Emergence of a Retail Market in China', p.260.
64. I. Björkman, 'Market Entry and Development in China', p.71.
65. E.J. de Brujn and X. Jia, 'Managing Sino–Western Joint Ventures: Product Selection Strategy', *Management International Review*, Vol.33, 1993–94, pp.335–60.
66. N. McGuiness, N. Campbell and J. Lenotiades, 'Selling Machinery to China'; I. Björkman, 'Market Entry and Development in China'.
67. I. Björkman, 'Market Entry and Development in China', p.69.
68. N. McGuiness, N. Campbell and J. Lenotiades, 'Selling Machinery to China', p.206.
69. M. Lockett, 'Culture and the Problems of Chinese Management', Paper presented at the Conference on the China Enterprise, Manchester Business School, June 1987; R. Sheng, 'Outsiders' Perceptions of the Chinese', *Columbia Journal of World Business*, Summer 1979, pp.16–22; J. Walls, 'China: Cross-cultural Business Skills', *Issues*, Spring 1986, pp.1–8; L. Pye, 'Chinese Commercial Negotiaitng Style'.
70. J. Wong, 'The Concept of 'Face' in Asian Culture: its Implications for Marketing', in Chin Tiong Tan, William Lazer and V.H. Kirpilani (eds) *Emerging International Frontiers*, Chicago, American Marketing Association, pp.183–186.
71. L. Pye, 'Chinese Commercial Negotiating Style', p.32.

# Chinese State Enterprises and Their Reform

## ATHAR HUSSAIN and JUZHONG ZHUANG

SURVEY OF DEVELOPMENTS AND PROBLEMS

In terms of progress towards a market economy, Chinese industry presents a mixed picture with both bleak and bright elements. On the bleak side, despite 17 years of reform, the state industrial sector continues to display many of the ills which afflict state firms all over the world, such as lack of managerial autonomy, poor financial performance, and featherbedding. Serious problems have mounted, rather than diminished. Government interference in enterprise management remains pervasive. Not only do a substantial proportion of State-Owned Enterprises (SOEs) run at a loss, but the percentage has been rising, from 26.4 per cent in 1992 to 44 per cent in 1995 (World Bank, 1996). Loss-making SOEs are subsidized either through the government budget increasing further the pressure on strained public finances or, increasingly in recent years, through government-directed loans from the state banking system. These loans do no more than transform the problem of SOE losses into another problem of non-performing loans in banks' portfolios. Facing neither the threat of bankruptcy nor demanding owners, SOEs exhibit an insatiable hunger for investment which has to be periodically curbed through administrative controls. About 15–20 per cent of the 44 million employees in state industrial enterprises are reckoned be redundant. Recent years have also seen improper and/or illicit appropriations of state assets.

On the bright side, there has been an emergence of a diverse industrial structure since 1978. The enterprise population currently stands at 7.3m, of which a mere 118,000 are SOEs (1.6 per cent of the total). A total of 5.7m small, privately-owned units dominate the population. In addition, the non-state sector also includes urban and rural collectively-owned, and increasingly privately-owned, enterprises under various guises together with Sino–foreign joint ventures. The emergence of this large and diverse enterprise population marks a clear break from the pre-reform economy, and has three implications conducive to enterprise reform and the development of the market economy:

- barriers to setting up non-state enterprises are low;

- the capacity for industrial organization is widespread;

Athar Hussain and Juzhong Zhuang, London School of Economics and Political Science.

• the Chinese economy has an industrial structure that is consistent with a highly competitive internal market.

Although the share of the SOEs in industrial production is much larger than their share of the enterprise population, the percentage has dropped sharply from 78 per cent in 1978 to 34 per cent in 1995 (see Table 1). This drop of 44-percentage points over 17 years compares favourably with the record of any economy in recent years regarding the withdrawal of the state from industry. Moreover, this reduction in the importance of the state sector has been accompanied by an increase in domestic competition and a wider exposure to the international market, developments which we discuss later. A further remarkable feature of China's present-day industrial structure is the growing weight of rural industrial enterprises: their share of gross industrial output has risen from a mere 9 per cent in 1978 to almost 56 per cent in 1995.

TABLE 1

CHINESE INDUSTRIAL STRUCTURE, 1978–95

| Year | State-Owned Enterprises | Township and Village-run Enterprises | Urban Collectively-owned Enterprises and Others |
|------|-------------------------|--------------------------------------|-------------------------------------------------|
| 1978 | 77.6 | 9.1 | 13.3 |
| 1979 | 78.5 | n.a | n.a |
| 1980 | 76.0 | 9.9 | 14.1 |
| 1981 | 74.8 | n.a | n.a |
| 1982 | 74.4 | n.a | n.a |
| 1983 | 73.4 | n.a | n.a |
| 1984 | 69.1 | 16.3 | 14.6 |
| 1985 | 64.9 | 18.8 | 16.3 |
| 1986 | 62.3 | 21.6 | 16.1 |
| 1987 | 59.7 | 23.5 | 16.8 |
| 1988 | 56.8 | 24.9 | 18.3 |
| 1989 | 56.1 | 23.8 | 20.1 |
| 1990 | 54.6 | 25.3 | 20.1 |
| 1991 | 56.2 | 30.8 | 13.0 |
| 1992 | 51.5 | 36.8 | 11.7 |
| 1993 | 47.0 | 44.5 | 8.5 |
| 1994 | 37.3 | 42.0 | 20.7 |
| 1995 | 34.0 | 55.8 | 10.2 |

*Notes:*  The data for the Township and Village-run Enterprises include all rural enterprises, whether collectively-owned, privately-owned, or self-employed. The data for Urban Collectively-owned enterprises and others covers all non-state industrial enterprises in urban areas.
All figures are expressed as percentages of total industrial output.

*Sources:* China Industrial Statistics Yearbook 1988 p.7; 1989 p.3; 1993 pp.7, 23 and 26: *China Statistical Yearbook* 1981 p.192; 1984 p.183; 1985 p.297; 1986 pp.255–65; 1993 p.414; 1995 pp.19, 25 and 401–3; 1996 pp.389 and 403.

Rural enterprises are different from urban enterprises – state as well as collectively-owned – in several essential respects. They have to find a niche in the product market, rather than having one assigned, and they have to compete for inputs. They face a comparatively high risk of closure. They lay off their employees during downturns, and pay wages according to the conditions in the local labour market. They vary greatly in entrepreneurship and efficiency: a proportion are second to none in East and South-East Asia. Many have deep roots in the local community, and their ownership structure is vague: the rural enterprise does not lend itself to an easy classification of being private or public. Their growth and dynamism act a a salutary antidote to the usual presumption in post-communist economies that well-defined ownership is a pre-condition for the transition from a command to a market economy (Weitzman and Xu, 1994). Nor are all rural enterprises of post-1978 origin: a percentage of them date from the pre-reform period. Although their proliferation has altered the structure of the Chinese economy, it would be a mistake to regard rural enterprises as the organizations of the emerging market economy which in time would engulf and displace the old command economy represented by state enterprises. They are transitional phenomena, and many are already undergoing important changes. Some have outgrown their local confines: for example, there are now 5000 large and medium-size rural township enterprises and 736 conglomerates.[1]

Thus whilst the bleak elements of the picture focus on the pathological symptoms of the state industrial sector, the bright elements concentrate on two developments in the industrial structure: the sharp reduction in the output share of the SOEs, and the growing diversity of enterprises. These two perspectives are not mutually exclusive, and we would argue that the problems of SOEs have to be seen in the wider context of developments in the industrial structure. Many of these problems, such as large percentage of SOEs running at a loss, are not carryovers from the command economy, but have arisen because of the change in the environment within which the SOEs operate, a point to which we shall return later.

Turning to the question of the strategy of enterprise reform, an influential view outside China is that a wide-ranging privatization is the necessary first step. A variant of this view would be that if privatization is ruled out for political and ideological reasons, as it is in China, the next best reform strategy would be to keep SOEs under tight control and to focus on removing the disadvantages from which the non-state sector suffers, thus allowing it to flourish. The argument is that such a strategy would not only progressively reduce the deadweight of the state industrial sector on the economy, but would also force it further to adapt to a market economy. We would argue that this perspective, although neat, is mistaken as it is based on a gross oversimplification of the reality. It overlooks the synergy between state and non-state enterprises. SOEs are indeed beset with many ills, but they are not all members of a moribund species. Nor are all non-state enterprises fit for survival in a market economy.

The distinction between the state and the non-state sector is sometimes treated as equivalent to the distinction between, on the one hand, the remnants of the pre-reform economy and, on the other hand, market-oriented organizations. This dualism is misplaced and does not square with the reality. The distinction does not indicate much about the actual or potential efficiency of enterprises, and is thus a poor basis for discriminating between enterprises. Both sectors are heterogeneous. Many non-state (in particular collective) enterprises resemble SOEs, except in name, and depend on local governments for their survival. Several SOEs are as dynamic as any in the non-state sector. Rather than being separated by a 'great wall', they are inter-linked. Many collective enterprises and Sino–foreign joint ventures are subsidiaries of SOEs. Increasingly SOEs contract out production to non-state enterprises, and the relationship is similar to that between large and small firms in Japan. Most of the large and medium size enterprises, which are crucial for exploiting economies of scale and scope, are state-owned; and SOEs dominate key sectors such as the capital goods industry. They are crucial for the upgrading of technology, and also set norms for the non-state sector in the fields of the management structure and employment contracts. The implication is that SOEs remain central to enterprise reform in China. What is needed is the progressive elimination of the status distinction between the state and the non-state industrial sector in terms of government control, access to credit, and social security: that is, the creation of a level playing field regardless of ownership structure.

## CHANGES IN THE ECONOMIC ENVIRONMENT

As noted above, the shifting balance between the state and the non-state sectors over the reform period has been accompanied by far-reaching changes in the economic environment which have directly affected enterprise behaviour and which have important implications for enterprise reform. We would single out the following four as being crucial:
- the development of internal product markets and increased competition;
- the growing exposure of Chinese enterprises to international markets and foreign business practices;
- the multiplication of the sources of external funds for investment and working capital;
- the high growth rate of the economy.

### Internal Product Markets and Competition

Internal product markets are now well developed and most prices are no longer determined by the government, though significant internal trade barriers still remain and the government is prone to fall back on price controls to rein in inflation. The displacement of state-administered commerce by market transactions has been due both to the expansion of the non-state sector and to the introduction of a two-track system allowing SOEs to sell output in excess of the plan quota. Indeed the two-track system, introduced in 1984, has now almost disappeared and been replaced by the market. Furthermore, the growth of market transactions has been accompanied by an increase in competition in the economy. In a wide range of industries, SOEs no longer have a captive market, and the increased competition has forced them to cut costs and upgrade product quality. A concerted policy to enhance competition is needed, and is as important for enterprise reform as organizational changes.

*Exposure to International Markets and Foreign Business Practices*

The Chinese economy is now as open to international trade and foreign investment as any large developing economy. The ratio of exports to GDP has risen from around 5 per cent in 1978, to around 20 per cent in 1995 (see Table 2), and broadly the same holds for the ratio of imports to GDP. These ratios are higher than those for the United States and Japan, but such comparisons are rather dubious because China's GDP would appear to be underestimated.[2] Furthermore because foreign trade consists mostly of industrial goods, it has a major direct impact both upon the allocation of resources in industry and upon the behaviour of Chinese enterprises. This impact is also particularly widespread as the Chinese economy exhibits one of the world's highest shares of industrial output in GDP (World Bank, 1996).

TABLE 2

CHINESE EXPORTS AND IMPORTS, 1978 1995

|  | Exports/ GDP | Manufacturing exports/ manufacturing output | Imports/ GDP | Manufacturing imports/ manufacturing output |
|---|---|---|---|---|
| 1978 | 4.62 | 5.42 | 5.16 | n.a. |
| 1979 | 5.10 | n.a. | 6.01 | n.a. |
| 1980 | 6.00 | 5.22 | 6.62 | 7.57 |
| 1981 | 7.20 | n.a. | 7.61 | n.a. |
| 1982 | 7.58 | n.a. | 6.82 | n.a. |
| 1983 | 7.37 | n.a. | 7.23 | n.a. |
| 1984 | 8.10 | n.a. | 8.65 | n.a. |
| 1985 | 9.02 | 8.18 | 14.03 | 22.37 |
| 1986 | 10.61 | 11.57 | 14.69 | 21.90 |
| 1987 | 12.29 | 13.06 | 13.49 | 18.09 |
| 1988 | 11.83 | 13.44 | 13.77 | 18.35 |
| 1989 | 11.57 | 12.92 | 13.01 | 16.34 |
| 1990 | 16.10 | 19.89 | 13.89 | 18.72 |
| 1991 | 17.70 | 22.55 | 15.72 | 21.44 |
| 1992 | 17.55 | 24.15 | 16.68 | 23.94 |
| 1993 | 15.32 | 19.76 | 17.35 | 23.62 |
| 1994 | 22.34 | 27.59 | 21.46 | 26.97 |
| 1995 | 21.32 | 28.21 | 18.96 | 23.86 |

*Notes*:   The figures for manufacturing output in 1993–95 were calculated on the assumption that the proportion of manufacturing output in total industrial output in these years remained at the 1992 level: these figures are likely to under-estimate the true value of manufacturing output.
All ratios are expressed as percentages.

*Sources*: *China Statistical Yearbook* 1993 pp.31 & 633; 1996 pp.42, 403 and 579–83: *China Industrial Economic Statistical Yearbook* 1988 p.18; 1990 pp.7 and 17; 1992 pp.7 and 17; 1993 pp.7 and 17.

One index of the increased exposure of the industrial sector to international markets is the dramatic rise in the share of the output of manufactures destined for exports. The share rose from a mere 5 per cent in 1978, to around 28 per cent in 1995. The share of imports in the domestic supply of manufacturing industry shows a similar strong upward trend. The general implication is that the expansion of foreign trade has provided Chinese enterprises with competition from foreign firms both in the domestic market and in the international market. *Prima facie*, this will have the same beneficial effects on costs, the product range, and technical change as those noted for the eight 'high-performing Asian economies' (World Bank, 1993). China's admission to the World Trade Organization (WTO) would probably do more to transform Chinese enterprises than many reform packages.

Foreign investment currently accounts for around 8 per cent of total investment in the state sector (see Table 3), and about 11 per cent of total investment (when both the state and non-state sectors are considered), according to published data. However, the actual proportions are likely to be rather lower because a part of reported foreign investment is in fact domestic capital recycled through Hong Kong. Foreign investment is now permitted in most industries and in most regions of China, and a substantial proportion is in joint ventures with SOEs. Its contribution to the upgrading of technology, product ranges, and management methods, and to the increase in exports has probably been far more important than its addition to domestic savings which are exceptionally high by international standards. Foreign investment has also made an important contribution to an upgrading of the organization and managerial structure of Chinese enterprises, and it is likely to assume a important role in the reform of SOEs. The Chinese government is now favourable to the takeover of SOEs by foreign investors, in a radical departure from the previous policy of preserving their ownership structure.

*Sources of External Funds*

The third change is the multiplication of sources of investment funds for Chinese enterprises, especially over the last few years (see again Table 3). In the state sector (including industry, agriculture, transport and communication, and commerce), fixed investment financed by the state budget has declined dramatically, amounting to only 5 per cent in 1995. Bank loans and self-raised funds have become principal sources of investment capital in the state sector, together accounting for over 72 per cent in 1995. These sources include funds from investment banks, the main commercial banks, secondary banks, retained profits, the bond and equity markets (including the Hong Kong, New York and, lately, the London markets), and the informal credit network. Borrowing through the issue of bonds and equities is much more widespread than is indicated by the figures of primary issues on the Shenzhen and the Shanghai stock markets. There is a huge informal financial market, especially in rural areas where the sale of

TABLE 3

STATE SECTOR FIXED INVESTMENT BY SOURCES OF FUNDING, 1978–95

| Year | State Budget | Bank Loans | Foreign Capital | Self-raised | Other |
|------|------|------|------|------|------|
| 1978 | 41737 | n.a. | n.a | n.a | |
| 1979 | 41857 | n.a. | n.a | n.a | |
| 1980 | 34927 | n.a. | n.a | n.a | |
| 1981 | 25750 | 9062 | 3609 | 28330 | |
| 1982 | 26543 | 13690 | 6013 | 38285 | |
| 1983 | 33680 | 13572 | 6583 | 41361 | |
| 1984 | 41795 | 18249 | 6982 | 51492 | |
| 1985 | 40300 | 38713 | 8856 | 67935 | 12247 |
| 1986 | 43849 | 44995 | 12829 | 76029 | 20147 |
| 1987 | 47215 | 56436 | 16835 | 87787 | 21527 |
| 1988 | 40520 | 66851 | 24766 | 144139 | 32264 |
| 1989 | 33871 | 52866 | 25741 | 108527 | 32543 |
| 1990 | 38542 | 68947 | 26600 | 123011 | 34763 |
| 1991 | 37098 | 101807 | 30261 | 156421 | 37225 |
| 1992 | 33244 | 160141 | 42116 | 245758 | 46106 |
| 1993 | 44772 | 201653 | 48724 | 380534 | 115022 |
| 1994 | 47819 | 247097 | 68988 | 490493 | 111756 |
| 1995 | 54498 | 257819 | 85938 | 530715 | 173182 |

*Notes*: The data cover new and replacement investments, productive and non-productive investments, urban and rural investments, and industrial and non-industrial investments. Figures are expressed in million yuan

*Sources*: *China Statistical Yearbook* 1984 p.301; 1993 p.150; 1994 p.139; 1996 pp.139 and 143: *China Fixed Assets Investment Statistics* 1950–85 pp.5 and 14; 1986–87 pp.18 and 20.

bonds to the enterprise labour force is widespread. The dramatic growth of non-state enterprises would seem to suggest that they have plenty of ways and means, fair and foul, of acquiring investment funds.

The diversification of the sources of finance is relevant to enterprise reform in two respects. On the one hand, it facilitates the establishment of new enterprises, and provides enterprises with wider opportunities for diversifying risks, potential if not actual. On the other hand, it helps to break the monopoly of enterprise governance by government agencies, given the maxim 'he who pays the piper calls the tune'. However, recent developments in the financial sector have tended to race ahead of prudent control and rest on fragile foundations: they have contributed to the inflationary pressures of 1993–95. The development of a sound regulatory structure would seem to be an urgent priority.

*Rapid Growth of the Economy*

The fourth and the final component of the economic environment which has facilitated the transformation of the industrial structure is the rapid growth of the economy (see Table 4). The dramatic decline in the share of the state sector in industrial output by 44 percentage points since 1978 has proceeded remarkably smoothly, and without any major resistance either from management or from the labour force in the state sector. The rapid growth

TABLE 4

OUTPUT, EMPLOYMENT AND CAPITAL IN THE CHINESE INDUSTRIAL SECTOR, 1978–1995

| | Real output | | Employment | | Capital | |
|------|---------|---------|---------|---------|---------|---------|
| | Total | SOEs | Total | SOEs | Total | SOES |
| 1978 | 100.00 | 100.00 | 100.00 | 100.00 | 100.00 | 100.00 |
| 1979 | 108.81 | 108.88 | 103.40 | 102.20 | 109.38 | 108.56 |
| 1980 | 118.90 | 114.99 | 110.23 | 106.21 | 119.45 | 118.46 |
| 1981 | 124.00 | 117.90 | 114.51 | 111.12 | 129.59 | 126.27 |
| 1982 | 133.69 | 126.21 | 118.27 | 114.11 | 141.67 | 137.00 |
| 1983 | 148.65 | 138.06 | 121.44 | 115.71 | 155.26 | 149.30 |
| 1984 | 172.86 | 150.38 | 130.19 | 116.88 | 170.12 | 161.90 |
| 1985 | 209.83 | 169.83 | 137.07 | 121.54 | 199.15 | 187.39 |
| 1986 | 234.32 | 180.33 | 147.43 | 126.00 | 227.78 | 211.21 |
| 1987 | 275.77 | 200.71 | 153.39 | 130.17 | 263.35 | 240.43 |
| 1988 | 333.10 | 226.02 | 158.61 | 134.72 | 305.99 | 275.42 |
| 1989 | 361.54 | 234.74 | 157.08 | 136.13 | 358.69 | 318.18 |
| 1990 | 389.60 | 241.69 | 159.20 | 139.03 | 413.79 | 363.57 |
| 1991 | 447.14 | 262.52 | 163.31 | 142.47 | 493.34 | 424.52 |
| 1992 | 570.20 | 295.07 | 167.77 | 144.03 | 574.05 | 490.69 |
| 1993 | 725.86 | 311.89 | 171.84 | 143.29 | 742.42 | 597.06 |
| 1994 | 901.52 | 332.16 | 176.88 | 139.25 | 961.63 | 723.43 |
| 1995 | 1084.53 | 359.40 | 180.48 | 140.01 | n.a | 968.74 |

*Notes*: The output and employment figures cover the entire industrial sector, including SOEs, urban COEs, TVEs, privately owned enterprises, self-employed, and others such as Sino-foreign joint ventures. The capital figures only cover enterprises which are independent accounting units at or above township levels.

Output is measured at constant prices. Employment is measured in numbers of workers. Capital is measured at the original installation prices, and not adjusted for inflation. All figures are expressed as index numbers (1978=100)

*Sources*: *China Statistical Yearbook* 1993 pp.98, 107, 413 and 430; 1996 pp.94, 102, 403, and 415: *China Industrial Economic Statistical Yearbook* 1993 pp.65–6; 1995 pp.53–4.

has provided enough room for the non-state sector to expand, without imposing significant costs in terms of jobs or output on the state sector. It has also provided for quick correction of any initial misallocation of resources and lowered the risk of failure for new enterprises. However, the rapid growth remains a major source of macro-economic problems.

## MICROECONOMIC ASPECTS OF THE TRANSFORMATION

Having outlined the changes in the industrial structure and the economic environment and their implications for enterprise reform, we turn now to some organizational aspects of enterprise reform and, begin with some general observations. The ultimate objective of enterprise reform is to transform existing enterprises into organizations which, in structure and in operation, are akin to firms in well-functioning market economies. However, this only provides broad guidelines, rather than a detailed blueprint, for reform because the industrial structures and the organization of firms in well-functioning market economies vary very widely. Whilst we may be able to point to the aspects of industrial structure which are inimical to a well-functioning market economy, it does not seem possible to establish an unambiguous relationship between economic performance, on the one hand, and the industrial structure and the organization of firms on the other. A wide variety of organizational forms would seem to be compatible with a well-functioning market economy. An important lesson from the East Asian experience is that industrial organizations and practices which appear to be at variance with economic logic may be important contributors to high growth and economic performance (World Bank, 1993). Moreover, the industrial structure and the organization of firms are not static, but change over time and these changes are calibrated in decades rather than years.

These observations suggest two related considerations in assessing enterprise reforms not only in China, but also in other countries in transition from command to market economies. First, factors which facilitate organizational changes and adaptation to changes in the future are as important as the current structure. Thus diversity in organization, size and ownership of enterprises or firms is desirable in this respect because it increases the capacity of the economy to adapt to changes. Second, institutional changes take time, and attempts to force the pace through a shock therapy or – more apt in the Chinese context, a 'Great Leap Forward' – do not necessarily lead to a faster transformation over time. The upheavals these create can become a major barrier to change in the future.

Enterprises inherited from the command economy were not created with regard to their financial viability, either immediate or distant, and they are in certain key respects not compatible with a well-functioning market economy. Enterprise reform consists of a number of different strands and we will restrict ourselves to the following four interrelated aspects:

- government interference in day-by-day management;
- the structure of state ownership;
- the industrial structure;
- the employment contract and the social welfare role of enterprises.

We shall take these in turn, discussing the changes that have taken place and the problems which still remain with respect to SOEs in China.

*Government Interference in Day-by-Day Management*

A central and commonly-recognized problem with SOEs is that their operation and performance depend upon the decisions not only of their managers but also of supervisory government agencies (industrial ministries or bureaus). This problem, however, is not exclusive to the SOEs but also extends to the non-state sector, which suggests that government interference is not due simply to ownership but also to other factors. The experience of planning in ex-command economies, and of public-sector enterprises in market economies, demonstrates that such split decision-making gives rise to a structure of constraints and incentives for enterprises which is inimical to the efficient utilization of resources and innovation. The devolution of decision-making to the enterprise management and the correlated withdrawal of the government from day-by-day management is generally regarded as a priority. The Chinese enterprise reforms, like those in pre- and post-communist economies, have transferred a great deal of discretion to the enterprise management. With the expansion of markets in products, most decisions about inputs and output are now made by the enterprise management. However, managers of SOEs in China still do not have the same decision-making power as their counterparts in market economies, in particular in matters concerning investment and labour management.

Notwithstanding the major changes that have taken place, government interference shows a remarkable capacity to persist, albeit in a different form. We would like to argue that this is not due simply to the fact that bureaucratic practices die hard, but also to a series of factors which create mutual dependence between the government and enterprises. The implication is that government interference in enterprises cannot be banished just by a formal devolution of decision-making to enterprise managers, but that it depends crucially on a series of reforms addressing particular factors which underlie the mutual dependence. In the Chinese context, the important considerations would seem to be:

- that state enterprises are by far the most important tax handle;
- that enterprises are the centrepiece of social welfare;
- that enterprises, in turn, depend heavily on the government for access to bank credit and still some crucial inputs.

This suggests that the distancing of the government from SOEs is contingent upon reforms in the tax and the social security systems, and in banking and finance. All these are at the top of the current reform agenda in China, but will take some time to implement. The implications are that the process of the government's withdrawal from enterprises, in an economy such as that of China, must inevitably be a piecemeal process, and that government intervention will remain a fact of life for some time to come. This would suggest that the focus of attention should be not just on government intervention, but also on the particular form it takes.

The ownership status matters for the relationship between the government and enterprises. As we discuss later, the particular form which state ownership takes in China creates a relationship of dependence between SOEs and their supervisory agencies. But it is also important to emphasize that the effect of a change in ownership on enterprise–government relations depends crucially on the type of economy in which it takes place. The success of privatization in distancing the government from ex-public firms in developed market economies, such as the United Kingdom, is due to factors such as developed financial markets and well-established governance structures where ownership and management are separated. The UK experience is a poor guide to the outcome of privatization in transitional economies. The fact that economies with similar ownership structures perform very differently should also suggest care in considering the transformation of ownership a panacea to problems of inefficiency.

Finally, it is important to emphasize that the transfer of decision-making to managers does not guarantee an efficient utilization of resources. In the absence of an effective mechanism to monitor their performance, the transfer may simply provide them with licence to pursue their personal objectives, a drawback which is well-recognized in market economies under the heading of 'agency problem' but which is often overlooked in transitional economies. In China, enterprise managers, and officials in industrial ministries or bureaus, are not different species. They tend to have the same career paths, and are in most cases interchangeable.

*The Structure of State Ownership*

In the case of the SOEs, the government is both the owner and the tax authority: the distinction between proceeds from the ownership of capital (dividends) and from taxes does not exist. Beginning from 1983, the government has collected revenue from state enterprises in the form of taxes which have been generally higher than those for non-state enterprises, though that is now changing.[3] The supplementary tax notionally represents the proceeds from ownership. Separate tax regimes for state and non-state enterprises have over the period become increasingly untenable because it is possible for state enterprises to establish subsidiary collective enterprises or joint ventures with foreign partners. The profit tax rates for state and non-state enterprises have recently been equalized, but Sino–foreign joint ventures continue to be taxed more lightly than domestic enterprises. This provides an incentive to state and non-state enterprises to hive off their profitable activities to Sino–foreign joint ventures.

In China, as in the ex-command economies of Eastern Europe, state-ownership is not a unified but a segmented category. It reflects the territorial and functional divisions of the government. Aside from a relatively few SOEs entirely owned by the central government, the ownership of SOEs is divided amongst lower government tiers, provinces, municipalities and counties. Almost all SOEs, even very large ones, are confined to one location. Multi-plant enterprises straddling the boundaries of sub-national governments are rare, though they have been rising in numbers as a result of government-arranged mergers and takeovers. Thus the general pattern is that various territorial tiers of the government not only own SOEs in their domain (in the sense of having a claim to revenue or enterprise taxes), but also administer trade, prices, investment and the allocation of credit. The result is a coincidence of the boundaries of ownership and general economic administration or regulation. This coincidence gives government tiers powerful leverage over enterprises in their domain and in turn also provides enterprises (especially larger ones) with the ability to get their supervisory government tiers to exercise regulation to their advantage – what is commonly known as 'regulatory capture'. To break out of this circle of dependence, reforms are needed so as to drive a wedge between the boundaries of ownership and regulation. These reforms will need to be applied to the structure of both regulation and ownership.

Focusing on ownership, what is required is the displacement of the monopoly ownership of large and medium-size SOEs with a diversified ownership, whereby owners include several government tiers and public agencies such as pension and mutual funds, banks and other financial institutions. Diversified ownership is not unknown in China: there are cases (almost all in the coal or electricity industries) where several provinces have jointly invested in an enterprise. Diversified ownership will bring a number of benefits but will also create new problems. On the benefit side, not only would it loosen the monopolistic hold of one government tier on enterprises but it would also facilitate industrial restructuring in particular mergers and capital flows across government boundaries. However, it would also give rise to the problem of designing a governance structure with multiple owners. But China has to face this problem because diversified ownership is the norm for medium and large enterprises all over the world.

The last two years have seen the conversion of selected SOEs into joint-stock companies with a part of their equity traded on the two domestic stock markets (Shanghai and Shenzhen) and, in some cases, also on the Hong Kong and New York markets. The sale of shares to individuals is highly desirable from the point of view of widening the range of financial assets available to households, given that bank deposits remain the main form of wealth for urban households. But it does not change the structure of effective ownership, because a large number of small owners do not alter the relationship between the enterprise manager and the dominant owner. In case of large or medium-size SOEs, what is needed is a number of owners with similar or countervailing equity stakes. Aside from tiers of the territorial government, there are as yet no institutions in China which are capable of holding significant equity stakes in joint-stock enterprises. The creation of such institutions would be an important step towards developing alternative structures of governance.

The Chinese government has recently decided to promote the corporatization of medium and large SOEs, but only some of them will be listed on the stock market. As the stock market is likely to remain marginal to the governance of enterprises for some time to come, listing is not currently an important issue. Rather the important aspects of corporatization – which is commonly equated with privatization – will be the transformation of enterprises into legal persons, together with the formalization of the rights and duties of managers and, equally important, a stocktaking and valuation of their assets. However, it is not a miracle cure for the ills of the state sector, but rather it is simply a step towards developing an alternative governance structure for state enterprises. It will raise the issue of the agency which would be responsible for appointing managers and monitoring their performance. Developing effective governance structures where ownership is diversified and separated from management will, in coming years, be the crucial issue with respect to large and medium-size enterprises. The institutional form of the separation of the government as regulator, from its role as owner, is still under discussion and has not taken a definite shape.

## The Industrial Structure

As indicated above, China has a large number of small enterprises and its industrial structure is very different from those of other post-communist economies. The preponderance of small enterprises is tied up with internal trade barriers and local protectionism. Thus small enterprises, although a source of flexibility and dynamism, have a number of negative consequences such as the non-exploitation of economies of scale, and variations in quality without the attendant advantages of product differentiation. These disadvantages are very similar to those associated with industries operating behind international trade barriers, which is not surprising given that the segmentation within the Chinese economy resembles the division of the world economy into semi-insulated national economies.

A general implication is that the current industrial structure is incompatible with an integrated market economy, and a transition towards such an economy is likely to lead to a radical change in the industrial structure and the disappearance of a large number of enterprises, not only in the state sector but also in the non-state sector, especially in rural areas. There is a need for 'efficiency-enhancing' industrial restructuring in the Chinese economy, and the central task is not so much the breaking-up of monopolies and giant enterprises as in some post-communist economies, but the merger and closure of enterprises. Who will perform this task and how? Bankruptcy is a blunt weapon and questionable on the grounds of efficiency. Given widespread price and trade distortions, it is highly doubtful that bankruptcy would select inefficient enterprises leaving the efficient ones to survive. Moreover, bankruptcy has a high economic cost and its benefits in furthering efficiency are far from incontrovertible. Bankruptcy on the lines used in market economies is also not sensible for the Chinese economy because, in the case of insolvent SOEs, the government is both the owner and the debtor. In the Chinese context, bankruptcy would mean no more than the government closing down an enterprise. The Stock Market can not perform any role in industrial restructuring, such as through mergers, because only a small number of enterprises are listed and most of them are profitable. There is thus no other option than that the government has to take the lead on industrial restructuring, and such restructuring has to proceed together with other enterprise reforms rather than being left until later.

## The Employment Contract and the Social Welfare Role of Enterprises

Traditionally employment in the state industrial sector was usually for life, and the right to permanent employment was taken to mean the right to occupy the same job for life. The reforms have introduced some important changes in labour recruitment and the terms of employment. Labour assignment by government agencies still exists, but both employers and prospective employees have the option of bypassing it. Since 1986 all new recruits to blue collar jobs are recruited on fixed-term renewable contracts ranging from one to seven years. Their numbers have risen steadily, and they currently account for around 40 per cent of the labour force in the state sector (see Table 5). Plans to convert all permanent employment into contract employment are under way in a number of industrial centres. Layoffs, once rare, have become more common: total employment in SOEs fell by 1.2 million between 1992 and 1995. It has become much easier for employees to change jobs, though the fact that most of the urban labour force lives in housing provided by employers hinders job mobility.

TABLE 5

PERCENTAGE OF CONTRACT EMPLOYEES IN CHINESE URBAN SECTOR, 1983–95

| | Total urban sector contract employees (Total urban employees=100) | State sector contract employees (Total state employees=100) | Urban collective sector contract (Total urban collective employees=100) | Other urban sector contract employees (Total other urban employees=100) |
|------|------|------|------|------|
| 1983 | 0.6 | 0.6 | 0.3 | n.a. |
| 1984 | 1.8 | 2.0 | 1.0 | 8.1 |
| 1985 | 3.3 | 3.7 | 2.2 | 11.4 |
| 1986 | 4.9 | 5.6 | 2.7 | 14.5 |
| 1987 | 6.6 | 7.6 | 3.6 | 18.1 |
| 1988 | 9.1 | 10.1 | 5.8 | 20.7 |
| 1989 | 10.7 | 11.8 | 7.0 | 25.1 |
| 1990 | 12.1 | 13.3 | 8.1 | 26.3 |
| 1991 | 13.6 | 14.9 | 8.9 | 28.0 |
| 1992 | 17.2 | 18.9 | 11.0 | 29.8 |
| 1993 | 21.0 | 21.9 | 15.5 | 37.4 |
| 1994 | 25.9 | 26.2 | 20.1 | 45.6 |
| 1995 | 40.9 | 40.1 | 37.4 | 62.8 |

Source: *China Statistical Yearbook* 1993 p.117; 1996 p.107.

The terms of employment inherited from the pre-reform economy are not conducive to efficiency. But it is important to emphasize that efficiency requires neither instantly revocable employment contracts, nor a market-clearing wage rate. Long-term attachment, and the payment of wage rates higher than the market-clearing rate, are common in market economies and can be justified in terms of efficiency (Krueger and Summers, 1988). We should thus not use the casual labour market as the yardstick for assessing the success of labour market reforms.

Turning briefly to the urban social security system, it is largely anchored in the SOEs. The SOEs house their employees, and administer and finance old-age pensions and health insurance. The current social welfare role of enterprises is an anachronism, and is a source of problems both for employees and employers. It is a problem for employees because it ties them to a particular enterprise, and because benefits vary when they are meant to be uniform. It is a problem for employers because it makes social security cover dependent on the enterprise, eroding its uniformity and reliability. A number of steps have been taken to divest enterprises of their social welfare obligations (Hussain, 1994). Unemployment insurance, which was introduced in 1986 together with contract employment, is managed by government agencies. The cost of pensions is pooled across enterprises, and a number of provinces have province-wide pools. Some cities have taken preliminary steps to pool large medical costs across enterprises. In principle, the housing reforms foresee enterprises being freed from their obligation to provide housing. But there is still a long way to go. A number of cities are already pressing ahead with their own social security reforms, and a national framework for the social security system is under discussion.

## LOSS-MAKING STATE-OWNED ENTERPRISES

The substantial number of enterprises running at a loss is the most visible problem in the state sector, and one which has attracted a great deal of attention. As noted above, profit is a highly ambiguous index of efficiency in the present-day Chinese economy. It is paradoxical to treat it otherwise in a transitional economy. Such an economy has, by definition, markets which are more imperfect and incomplete than a well-functioning market economy, otherwise it would not be a transitional economy. Thus the simple fact that loss-making enterprises continue operating is not compelling evidence of the failure of enterprise reforms.

Loss-making on a significant scale in the state sector was not a pre-reform phenomenon. The pre-reform state sector was highly profitable, and loss-making only emerged in the second half of the 1980s after the generalization of the pilot enterprise reforms – see Table 6. Loss-making on a large scale would seem to be due to two factors: increased competition in product markets (McMillan and Naughton, 1993),[4] and a rise in the share of value-added accruing to labour due to a loosening of administrative wage controls.[5] Loss-making is a serious problem, but one which concerns the public finances more than efficiency. This does not make it any less serious, but does have an effect on possible solutions to the problem. If an enterprise is inefficient, the best solution is to close it down. If, however, it is loss-making but not inefficient, then the solution lies in finding an appropriate way of subsidizing the enterprise. It is important to qualify this recommendation by noting that the subsidization of loss-making enterprises is not simply a financial issue: it also has implications for incentives because subsidization is likely to alter the behaviour pattern of enterprises. Enterprises are more likely to undertake risky investments if they know that they will be subsidized when they make a loss. This observation does not

TABLE 6
SCALE OF LOSS-MAKING IN INDEPENDENT ACCOUNTING INDUSTRIAL UNITS AT OR ABOVE TOWNSHIP LEVELS, 1978–95

| | Numbers and percentages of loss-making enterprises | | | | Total losses (in 100 million yuan) and percentage of losses in value added | | | |
|---|---|---|---|---|---|---|---|---|
| | Total | | SOEs | | Total | | SOEs | |
| | No. | % | No. | % | Losses | % | Losses | % |
| 1978 | n.a. | n.a. | n.a. | n.a. | 45.1 | 3.2 | 42.06 | 3.8 |
| 1979 | n.a. | n.a. | n.a. | n.a. | 40.2 | 2.6 | 36.38 | 2.8 |
| 1980 | n.a. | n.a. | n.a. | n.a. | 38.8 | 2.4 | 34.30 | 2.6 |
| 1981 | n.a. | n.a. | n.a. | n.a. | 53.5 | 3.1 | 45.96 | 3.3 |
| 1982 | n.a. | n.a. | n.a. | n.a. | 55.8 | 3.1 | 47.57 | 3.3 |
| 1983 | n.a. | n.a. | n.a. | n.a. | 37.6 | 1.9 | 32.11 | 2.0 |
| 1984 | n.a. | n.a. | n.a. | n.a. | 34.2 | 1.5 | 26.61 | 1.5 |
| 1985 | n.a. | n.a. | 6749 | 9.6 | 40.5 | 1.5 | 32.44 | 1.6 |
| 1986 | 55537 | 13.2 | 9221 | 13.1 | 72.42 | 2.4 | 54.49 | 2.5 |
| 1987 | 60085 | 14.4 | 9459 | 13.0 | 84.68 | 2.4 | 61.06 | 2.4 |
| 1988 | 49082 | 11.7 | 7912 | 10.9 | 106.57 | 2.5 | 81.92 | 2.7 |
| 1989 | 66723 | 15.9 | 11785 | 16.0 | 234.05 | 4.8 | 180.19 | 5.2 |
| 1990 | 87886 | 21.1 | 20603 | 27.6 | 453.68 | 8.9 | 348.76 | 9.8 |
| 1991 | 78453 | 18.7 | 19443 | 25.8 | 475.49 | 8.0 | 367.00 | 9.1 |
| 1992 | 64900 | 15.9 | 17299 | 23.4 | 469.06 | 6.3 | 369.27 | 7.6 |
| 1993 | | | | | | | 452.64 | 6.2 |
| 1994 | | | | | | | 482.59 | 6.1 |

Source: China Statistical Yearbook 1993 p.430; 1995 pp.392 and 403;
China Industrial Economic Statistics 1949–84, pp.41–2;
China Industrial Economic Statistical Yearbook 1992 pp.90 and 129; 1993 pp.35, 64, 90, 129 and 142.

rule out subsidies, but suggests that they should be designed taking into account their effects on incentives. Moreover, the issue of incentives is not restricted to loss-making enterprises but also applies to enterprises which make a positive profit. Hardening the budget constraint, in the sense of forcing a loss-making enterprise to show a positive profit, is a crude incentive scheme.

## CONCLUDING REMARKS

The above discussion of recent developments related to progress towards a more market-oriented economy in China has generated a number of conclusions and/or recommendations for the future reform of Chinese SOEs. These may be summarized as follows:

- The SOEs are beset with many serious problems, but it would be wrong to conclude that they have not changed much. They face enhanced competition in the internal market and have been increasingly exposed to international markets;
- It is simplistic to regard the state sector as the remnant of the pre-reform economy, and the non-state sector as the mainstay of the nascent market economy. The distinction between them is blurred. Many non-state

enterprises resemble SOEs, and a proportion of SOEs is as dynamic as any in the non-state sector. Rather than being separated by a 'great wall', the two groups of enterprises are closely inter-linked;

- The current distinction between state and non-state enterprises is administrative, and a legacy from the pre-reform period. What is needed is the progressive elimination of the status distinction between them and the creation of a level playing field regardless of their ownership structure;

- There are two general considerations which seem to be important in assessing enterprise reforms. First, diversity in the organization, size and ownership of enterprises is desirable because it increases the capacity of the economy to adapt to changes. Second, institutional changes take time, and attempts to force the pace do not necessarily lead to a faster transformation;

- Government intervention in enterprises, which remains pervasive, is due to a whole host of factors, creating mutual dependence between enterprises and the government. This intervention should be recognized as a fact of life, and attention focused on the particular forms it takes;

- The transfer of decision-making to managers does not guarantee an efficient utilization of resources. In the absence of effective mechanisms to monitor their performance, the transfer may simply provide them with licence to pursue their personal objectives. Developing effective governance structures when ownership and management are separated is the central problem in reforming large and medium-size enterprises;

- The current pattern of the assignment of the ownership of SOEs to territorial governments creates a nexus of mutual dependence with adverse implications for incentives. What is required is the displacement of the monopoly ownership of large and medium-size SOEs with diversified ownership;

- The current industrial structure is, in some respects, incompatible with an integrated market economy. Industrial restructuring should be a central component of enterprise reform and has to be undertaken by the government;

- The fact that a large proportion of SOEs make a loss and continue to survive is not compelling evidence of the failure of the enterprise reforms. Measured profit is a highly ambiguous index of efficiency. Forcing loss-making enterprises to close is a blunt instrument for dealing with the problems of inefficiency, and hardening the budget constraint is a crude incentive scheme;

- Enterprise reform cannot be reduced to the question of ownership. Privatization, now officially accepted as an option for reforming small state enterprises, is not quick. The lessons from the experience of privatization in market economies are of limited applicability to the transformation of enterprises in transitional economies. The experience of post-communist economies shows that privatization, contrary to what was initially imagined, is not a speedy but a long drawn-out process. The decision of the Chinese leadership not to go for wide-ranging privatization makes economic sense and should not be fully attributed to ideology and politics;

- Corporatization and the diversification of ownership are two important steps towards developing an alternative governance structure for SOEs. Apart from government agencies, there are currently no organizations which have the task of monitoring the performance of managers: the development of such organizations is crucial for the institution of an alternative governance structure for enterprises. There are considerable doubts about the ability of 'state asset management companies' to perform this task effectively. Banks, investment companies, mutual and pension funds may have an important role to play in this regard.

## NOTES

1. See the report in the *Beijing Review*, 1977, No.5, p.4.
2. This is because the output of many service sectors (such as health, education and housing) is under-valued.
3. A. Hussain and J. Zhuang, 1993, 'Functional Distribution, Enterprise Taxation and Profitability in Chinese Industry, 1986–1991', mimeo, STICERD, London School of Economics.
4. See also G. Jefferson and T.G. Rawski, 1994, 'A Model of Endogenous Innovation, Competition and Property Rights Reform in Chinese Industry', Paper prepared for the annual World Bank Conference on Development, April.
5. L. Putterman, 'Contradictions and Progress: the State, Agriculture, and "Third" Sectors in China's Economic Reforms' in Yang Gan and Zhiyuan Cui (eds), 1993, *China: a Reformable Socialism?* (Oxford: Oxford University Press, forthcoming); T.W. Woo, W. Hai, Y. Jin and G. Fan, 'How Successful has Chinese Enterprise Reform Been?', mimeo, Institute of Government Affairs, University of California Davis.

## REFERENCES

Hussain, A. (1994), 'Social Security in Present-day China and its Reform', *American Economic Review*, Vol.84, No.2, May, pp.276–80.

Krueger, A.B. and L.H. Summers, 1988), 'Efficiency Wages and Inter-industry Wage Structure', *Econometrica*, Vol.61, pp.259–94.

McMillan, J. and Naughton, B. (1993), 'How to Reform a Planned Economy: Lessons from China', *Oxford Review of Economic Policy*, Vol.8, No.1, pp.130–42.

Weitzman, M. and C. Xu (1994) ,'Chinese Township and Village Enterprises as Vaguely Defined Cooperatives', *Journal of Comparative Economics*, Vol.18, pp.121–45.

World Bank (1993), *The East Asian Miracle: Economic Growth and Public Policy*, Washington DC.

World Bank (1996), *World Development Report*, Washington DC.

# A Study of Management Attitudes in Chinese State-Owned Enterprises, Collectives and Joint Ventures

WEIHWA PAN and DAVID PARKER

Since 1978, the Chinese economy has moved away from a reliance on centralized planning and state ownership to more localized decision making, a greater emphasis on market signals and more private ownership (Hay, 1994; Naughton, 1994; Nolan, 1995). Nevertheless, there are still today around 100,000 State-Owned Enterprises (SOEs), accounting for about 41 per cent of output, of which about one-third is loss making. More than 70 per cent of all investment in China still flows into the SOEs. Alongside the state-owned firms, collectively-owned enterprises (COEs) account for 38 per cent of output, and the remainder is accounted for by other ownership forms that are mainly town and village enterprises, private enterprises and joint ventures with firms based outside China (Parker and Pan, 1996). In the past, the COEs, being collectives, had more ambiguous property rights than SOEs, and traditionally pursued objectives involving the maximization of workers' welfare. In the early 1990s, the government launched the programme 'Redefining the Property Right' to put property rights in China on a firmer foundation. The capital of the COEs was deemed to belong to the state, except if the assets were financed by borrowing or self-funding. By these reforms, the assets of the collectives seem to have been brought more closely under the control of the authorities, at a time when, officially, the SOEs were granted more managerial autonomy. It is possible therefore that attitudes and behaviour have converged in the SOEs and COEs since the early 1990s.

Foreign investment began slowly after the passage of the Law on Joint Ventures in July 1979, and the establishment of Special Economic Zones in 1980. During the 1980s the restrictions on the terms of joint ventures (JVs) were eased. After 1986, wholly foreign-owned enterprises were encouraged. In general, the Chinese government is expected to refrain from interfering in joint ventures to avoid creating a disincentive for FDI. However, most foreign joint ventures in China are with SOEs and therefore it is possible that the characteristics of the SOEs may be apparent in at least some JVs.

In this study we attempt to shed light on management attitudes in China today. The discussion is based upon a study, undertaken between October and December 1995, of 16 enterprises in Shanghai and Nanjing. The study

Weihwa Pan, University of Birmingham and David Parker, Aston University consisted of structured interviews with senior officials in each of the enterprises based upon an extensive questionnaire designed to reveal managerial attitudes and behaviour. The objectives were twofold: to find whether management attitudes had moved appreciably away from those to be expected under state planning, notably a reluctance to take responsibility, hierarchical and formalized reporting and a reverential attitude to political control; and to discover whether managerial attitudes differed between the SOEs and other forms of ownership. We might expect a more commercialized or 'western' approach to management in firms with some private ownership and particularly in those with foreign capital. The study was limited to 16 firms because of the labour-intensive nature of the research method adopted. This may limit the applicability of the conclusions, though we have no reason to believe that the firms that took part in our study are atypical in any obvious way.

## THE PROGRAMME OF ENTERPRISE REFORM

After 1949, the new Communist government transformed China into a socialist, planned economy. By the end of the 1950s, private ownership had been largely eliminated in favour of SOEs, and collective firms and farms. The central government set targets for production, allocated labour, appointed management, arranged raw material supplies and managed sales. In 1978, 97 per cent of retail commodities, 94 per cent of agricultural produce, and 100 per cent of capital goods were sold at planned prices.

Prior to the 1980s, the government owned, funded and managed the SOEs through the planning system and unified control of income and expenditure (*tongshou tongzhi*) (Chen, 1995: 114). Central and local bureaus in close consultation with party officials allocated labour, appointed managers, decided the levels of output and investment, and fixed prices. Recruitment was based on assignments from the State Labour Bureau, perhaps influenced by family and political connections. Wages and salaries were unrelated to individual performance, and workers benefited from welfare services, notably housing, health and education, provided at the workplace. Funds for both fixed investment and working capital came largely from government, which owned the factory buildings and plant and machinery, and were determined by the central Plan.

In December 1978, the first tentative economic reforms of the communist system were agreed at the Third Plenum of the Central Committee of the Communist party. Over the next decade or so, more management autonomy was encouraged. In particular, management was permitted to produce output above planned levels and thereby generate surplus revenue. Whereas all profits were previously paid over to the state, some profit could be retained within the SOEs. Also, prices were gradually freed from central control, and profit incentives and market prices for inputs and outputs became more firmly established. By 1987, around 65 per cent of agricultural goods, 55 per cent of consumer goods and 40 per cent of capital goods had prices that were either freely set in the market or floated around an officially determined price. Further price liberalization occurred in the early 1990s. By 1993 only 10 per cent of agricultural goods, 5 per cent of consumer commodities and 15 per cent of capital goods were still sold at planned prices (Lardy, 1994: 11).

Paralleling the price and output reforms, a limited amount of labour market restructuring was introduced. In 1986, payments over and above the basic state wage were permitted to reward performance. Also contract working, instead of jobs for life, began as an experiment in some industries in 1980, and was gradually extended across the economy for new workers. Other important reforms related to greater autonomy for firms to export and import; the introduction of land transfers through leasing; and encouragement to SOE managements to take more individual responsibility for outputs and investments through the 'enterprise responsibility system'. By the early 1990s, most investment in the SOEs was financed from retained earnings and bank loans rather than, as formerly, from direct state grants.

The 'enterprise responsibility system' was designed to create some distance between the management of SOEs and political control. The intention was to decentralize responsibility for the operation and performance of the enterprise down from administrative bureaus to the firms. In July 1992, further reforms were promulgated under the name of 'the Regulations for Transforming Managerial Mechanisms of the State-Owned Enterprises'. These changes were intended to build upon the 'responsibilities system' by clarifying the role of management over production, pricing, trade, labour, organization and assets. Detailed rules were set out to restrict interference by government departments and bureaus.

In addition to these reforms, during the late 1980s the SOEs became more reliant on banks than on government for finance. From 1988, some SOEs were permitted to restructure into shareholding companies and, following the establishment of stock exchanges in Shanghai and Shenzhen in 1990 and 1991, a few state-owned firms sought stock market listings. By 1994, more than a hundred Chinese companies had acquired foreign shareholdings and over thirty had been permitted to issue shares in overseas Stock Exchanges.[1]

Alongside the changes in the SOEs in the 1980s and early 1990s, there was a marked expansion in other forms of enterprise, notably collectives (including so-called town and village enterprises[2]), and 'other' ownership forms. Figures for the percentage shares of gross output and net fixed assets accounted for by firms in each of the three broad ownership groups in 1983 and 1993 are provided in Table 1. The table also provides figures on the percentage of enterprises falling in each category. It is evident that while the SOEs have broadly retained their share in terms of the number of enterprises in China, their share of net fixed assets and more especially output has declined sharply. The collectives have benefited from this trend, but the major gainers have been firms in the 'other' category. This category consists

TABLE 1

STATISTICS ON CHINESE ENTERPRISES, 1983 AND 1993

| Ownership form | as % of all enterprises | | as % of gross output | | as % of net fixed assets | |
|---|---|---|---|---|---|---|
| | 1983 | 1993 | 1983 | 1993 | 1983 | 1993 |
| State-Owned | 18.3 | 18.2 | 76.7 | 56.7 | 87.6 | 72.9 |
| Collectives | 81.5 | 76.7 | 22.2 | 30.4 | 12.4 | 16.4 |
| Other | 0.2 | 5.1 | 1.1 | 12.9 | negligible | 10.7 |

Source: China Statistical Yearbooks, 1983-94.

of private firms, state joint stock companies, and foreign and domestic equity joint ventures. By 1993, the SOE share of output had fallen to 57 per cent and the 'other' category firms had increased their share to almost 13 per cent. In other words, the traditional (unincorporated) SOE continued to dominate industrial production in China in 1993, but the collective and 'other' enterprises had made significant advances.

In November 1993 the party announced a further stage of the reform programme involving further corporatization of state firms, more autonomy for SOEs to control their assets, and more financial autonomy for the SOEs. Under the proposals, enterprises that were identified as perennial loss makers were to be considered for closure or bankruptcy. Bank lending to state firms was to be placed under three 'policy banks', leaving other banks to pursue commercial lending (Parker and Pan, 1996). The possibility of further sales of shares in corporatized SOEs was sanctioned, including the possibility of a majority transfer of some state firms to the private sector. However, the government has since refrained from an unambiguous sanctioning of privatization.

The major changes in policy towards the SOEs during the 1980s and early 1990s might be expected to have led to a change in managerial attitudes and behaviour. The expectation is that management will have become more concerned with financial and economic objectives, and less with political and social goals. In particular, capitalist investment from outside China might be expected to have led to a more entrepreneurial and less rule-bound form of management. Today, in principle, managers of SOEs have more freedom to make decisions and may even, in some cases, own shares in their enterprise. At the same time, the SOE sector continues to record high levels of losses. Although a Bankruptcy Law was passed in 1988, so far few loss-making SOEs have been made bankrupt.

It is claimed that the SOEs still face a 'soft budget constraint' (IMF 1993: 19; Perkins, 1995: 4). The banks have remained state-owned, and they have faced political and economic pressures to dispense loans liberally. This has led to growing bad debts in the banking system alongside rising inter-firm debts, as firms have postponed payments for supplies. At the end of 1994, indebtedness amongst Chinese SOEs had risen to RMB400 bn (approx. US$50 bn). Notwithstanding the Bankruptcy Law which came into effect in November 1988, only 52 SOEs had been declared bankrupt by 1994. In consequence of the continuing 'soft budget constraint', perhaps there remains a distinct difference in management attitudes and behaviour between managers in SOEs and in other types of Chinese enterprises. Also, other forms of enterprise in China are often highly dependent upon SOEs either as customers or suppliers. The failure to reform successfully the finances of the SOEs may be having repercussions for management attitudes and behaviour in other enterprises, including collectives and joint ventures. Our study is intended to shed some light on the extent to which management attitudes do differ in the various main types of Chinese firms.

## PREVIOUS STUDIES OF MANAGEMENT BEHAVIOUR IN CHINA

There have already been a number of studies that have looked at managerial attitudes and behaviour in China. Some studies have suggested that, while managers may have felt themselves to have more freedom of manoeuvre during the 1980s, '... when their managerial discretion was placed alongside that of western managers of equivalent official rank, it became quickly apparent that they had little more scope than the first-line supervisor in a western manufacturing plant and that the threads that tied them to their supervisory bureaucracy were as tight as ever' (Boisot, 1994: 30; Child and Lu, 1989; Boisot and Child, 1988; Boisot and Xing, 1992). Lu (1991) found that in the late 1980s enterprise managers had more freedom over pricing and procurement but not necessarily investment. Investment was still mainly integrated into the planning system.

A study by Warner (1995), based on ten large SOEs in the north-east of China, investigated the effect of labour market reforms. Western-style human resource policies were found not to exist and labour turnover remained low, suggesting continued rigidity in the labour market. Chow (1992), from a questionnaire survey of 97 middle managers in Henan province in May 1989, commented that on average they attached high importance to party contacts within the organization and to ensuring that employees had the proper political attitude.

In a further study, Chen (1995) argued that, following the reforms of the 1980s, there was 'rapidly rising interest' amongst SOE managers in western management concepts. At the same time, the possibility of a significant difference in attitudes, where a foreign partner owned more than 50 per cent of the equity and imposed foreign managers on the enterprise, was suggested by Child.[3] In a study of Coca Cola's joint venture in China, Nolan (1995) reported that there were major efficiency gains and 'a massive change in work attitude incorporating both positive and negative incentives conducive to harder and more effective work'.

In a study of other foreign JVs in China, Roehrig (1994: 12–13) found that bargaining with the authorities did not end after the terms of the investment were agreed. He puts the continued stress on bargaining down to 'a traditional preference in China for the "rule of man" (*renzhi*) over the "rule of law" (*fazhi*)', which leads to the conducting of business through personal contacts (Roehrig, 1994: 108). In turn, this process was encouraged by the unreliability of bureaucratic and administrative channels. He also found that decentralization had vested more powers in the hands of local officials.

Other studies have argued that the authorities continue to intervene in the management of JVs in the choice of technology, personnel, the setting of salaries and in foreign exchange matters. Field research in 1988 and 1989 by the China–EC Management Institute in Beijing, involving thirty joint ventures (23 in Beijing, and seven outside) found that democratic centralism had led Chinese managers to 'a passive, responsibility-shy, participative style. ... They tended to be punished for committing errors rather than rewarded for taking initiatives' (Boisot, 1994: 34).[4]

A further study, reported in Child (1994), involved six SOEs in Beijing between 1985 and 1988–1990. The SOEs were headed by reform-minded managers, and Child accepts that the results may not be typical. The study found that state control of SOEs still existed, though it differed in nature from that of pre-reform. Management autonomy had increased but the state remained a powerful part of enterprise decision-making, especially in the appointment and dismissal of managers, and influence over the granting of bank loans. There was considerable evidence that the 1980s reforms had shifted power from the centre to local politicians, rather than wholly to SOE management: 'Local economic areas are thus continuing to operate in many respects as fiefs with relations of hierarchical dependence in which informal contact and personal association count for a great deal.' (Child, 1994: 104). Such continued political control helps to explain findings of lower productivity growth, reported in a number of statistical studies (such as Perkins, 1995), in the SOEs in comparison to the non-SOEs in China

In general, these earlier studies suggest a change in attitudes amongst Chinese management resulting from the economic reforms during the 1980s. But they also suggest that the degree of managerial autonomy remained partial and heavily constrained with management continuing to attach great importance to political contact and the planning process. In addition, management remained defensive, fearing the consequences of crossing party officials, though where foreign capital was involved this could be associated with a greater degree of independence of action. We now turn to our questionnaire study, which was intended to advance some of the issues covered in the earlier studies.

## THE CURRENT STUDY

A number of the earlier studies of management attitudes were limited in terms of comparative material. Moreover, most of the studies are rather dated, relating to the late 1980s or very early 1990s. The pace of economic change in China is such that evidence from this period may paint a distorted picture of the position today.

Our study consisted of structured interviews based around a questionnaire which included 50 questions aimed at assessing the attitudes and behaviour of senior management in a range of Chinese enterprises.[5] All the firms were based in Shanghai and Nanjing, a major city in the coastal province of Jiangsu. Jiangsu Province is the second most prosperous region in China. The results from the study should therefore not be generalized to the whole of China, especially the West which has been relatively unaffected by foreign investment. Nevertheless, the results give an indication of the attitudes of senior management in industries operating in a region of economic transformation.[6]

Sixteen enterprises were visited where at least one member of the senior management agreed to be interviewed. In almost all cases the person interviewed was the Director, Vice-Director or Assistant Director of the enterprise. These personnel represent the top three layers of enterprise management in China. The exceptions involved one firm that had its 'head office' elsewhere and where the Director of the Shanghai branch of the business agreed to be interviewed, and another firm where the party Secretary represented the firm. In each enterprise, between one and three members of the senior management took part in the interviews. Some of the firms agreed to participate in the study on the understanding that their individual responses would not be identified. For this reason, in the reporting of the results each firm is given a letter, A, B, C etc., in place of its name.

The enterprises were selected from a list of SOEs, collective and JV enterprises prepared from information supplied by the City Administration of Nanjing and the Banking Association of Shanghai. A few of the enterprises initially selected refused to become involved in the study. At least some of these were known to be in serious financial difficulty. It is possible therefore that the sample includes a disproportionate number of relatively good performers amongst Shanghai and Nanjing enterprises (though a number are currently loss-makers). This should be borne in mind when interpreting the results.

Of the 16 firms, three were JVs, two were COEs, and eleven were SOEs.[7] The JVs were Firm A, which produces stationery; Firm B, a producer of optical fibre and other cables for telecommunications; and Firm C, which is involved in motor repairs. Two – Firms A and C – have majority Chinese ownership, and one – Firm B – has 51 per cent Taiwanese ownership. Firm C's foreign investor is a Hong Kong-based company. Firm A has a number of foreign investors but still classifies itself as a joint venture. Its shares were floated in the 'B-share' stock market to attract foreign capital. The foreign investors do not have any representatives on the board and this leaves the Chinese management with entire control over decision-making. This makes Firm A a different type of JV to the other two, and the differences are evident in the following discussion. In all cases, the Chinese investors in the JV were SOEs and, especially in the case of Firm A, we might therefore expect the venture to operate much like a SOE.

The COEs were Firm D, which produces clocks, watches, timers and meters; and Firm E, which manufactures textiles. Firm D was founded and initially financed by a SOE, whilst Firm E was set up by local residents and was self-financed or had to borrow from the banks. Hence, though only two COEs are included in our study, they do reflect the wide differences in this sector in terms of origins.[8]

The SOEs came from a wide range of industries, as is evident from the details in Table 2 below. Some of the SOEs were of the traditional, unincorporated form, while some had already corporatized (obtained joint stock status but with shares held by government). Corporatization of an SOE is regarded in China as a means of introducing more commercial operation. Rather than the industries being directly owned and controlled by a government department, the intention is that each SOE should be headed by its own board of directors. The expected result is less day-to-day intervention by industrial bureaus. However, so far only two of the SOEs, Firms N and P, have boards of directors, even though many more had been transformed into limited companies during 1995. Firm P is a recently established business belonging to a state university. The absence of boards and the evidence of the continuing importance of 'upper bureaus' in management decision-making in SOEs, revealed in the answers reported below, means that there must be some doubt as to whether corporatization has so far really changed the SOE sector, though it is still early days.

In stark contrast, the three JVs investigated have boards that do help to keep the state at arm's length. Turning to the two COEs, Firm D has been changed into a limited company, while Firm E remains a traditional form of collective. Table 3 provides some background information on the board composition of the JVs, COEs and the two SOEs with boards of directors.

Table 2 above also provides details of the firms' current financial standing and details of the budget constraint facing management revealed in the interviews.[9] Since the 1980s, the 'soft budget constraint' found under Communism (Kornai, 1979) should have hardened because of the 'responsibilities system' aimed at more enterprise autonomy, and more recent banking reforms. But, as we have seen, the reforms were insufficient to impose the kind of 'hard' budget constraint typically found in the private sector outside China.

At the collective Firm E and at SOEs G, H, I and J, the management revealed that they were finding difficulty raising further bank finance because of tight credit control or existing outstanding loans. The final column of Table 2 summarizes whether management felt that the budget constraint had changed significantly in recent years. It is evident that, for managers in the JVs studied, the budget constraint does not seem to have changed. This is probably because they faced more commercially-oriented financing from the outset. There is, however, strong evidence of a tightening of the budget constraint for the two COEs and for some (though not all) of the SOEs. The SOEs generally reported that they still had to get approval from upper bureaus for investment funds though not loans for working

TABLE 2

THE ENTERPRISES STUDIED, THEIR LEGAL STATUS,
AND THEIR FINANCIAL POSITION

| Name of Enterprise | Ownership Type | Financial Status | Budget Constraint | Has the Budget Constraint Changed in Recent Years |
|---|---|---|---|---|
| **JVs** | | | | |
| A | Listed JV | Good | 1 | no change |
| B | JV | Excellent | 1 | no change |
| C | JV | Good | 2 | no change |
| **COEs** | | | | |
| D | COE | In long-term loss | 2 | stronger |
| E | COE | In long-term loss | 1, 2, 3 Comment: increasingly difficult to borrow from the bank because of tight credit control | stronger |
| **SOEs** | | | | |
| F: panels factory | traditional SOE | In loss in the past 3 years | 1, 3 Comment: collateral needed | stronger |
| G: metallurgical equipment | traditional SOE | In loss in 1995 | 2, 3 Comment: not enough loan finance available. Need to repay existing loans before further borrowing occurs | stronger |
| H: yarn-dying fabric mill | traditional SOE | Good | 2 3 Comment: repay first before further borrowing/ collateral needed | stronger |
| I: colour printing factory | traditional SOE | In loss | 1, 2 Comment: it is still possible to borrow but is much more difficult to do so nowadays | stronger |
| J: analytical instrument factory | Corporatized SOE | Fair | 1, 2 Comment: very difficult to borrow so borrowing reduced | stronger |
| K: machinery cutting and measuring tools producer | Corporatized SOE | Fair | 1, 2 | no change |
| L: metallurgical company | Corporatized SOE | In loss | 1, 2 | no change |
| M: textile group | Corporatized SOE | In loss | 1 | no change |
| N: electronics group | Corporatized SOE | Good | 1, 2 | no change |
| O: automobile company | Corporatized | Good | 1, 2 | no change |
| P: biotechnology industry | New company with state ownership through a university | Good | 1, 2 | new company |

*Note:* Budget constraint key –   1 if the main form of financing is to extend the loan duration
2 if the main form of financing is to provide new loans with which to repay old loans
3 for other main forms of financing.

TABLE 3
BOARD COMPOSITION

| JVs | State representatives | Institutional representatives (i.e. from a Chinese bank or holding company) | Foreign representatives |
|---|---|---|---|
| A | 8 | 1 | |
| B | 6 | | 7 |
| C | 3 | | 2 |

| COEs | SOE holding company representatives | Representatives from the collective | |
|---|---|---|---|
| D | 4 | 3 | |
| E | not applicable (traditional collective) | | |

| SOEs | State representatives | Company representatives | Others |
|---|---|---|---|
| N | | 7 | |
| P | 1 | 2 | 2 (university representatives) |

capital. Once approval was obtained, then loans from the banks would be forthcoming. Clearly 'policy lending' within China continues. The JVs and COEs did not need to obtain government approval for loans.

Overall, the budget constraint facing Chinese enterprises still seems to be softer than that faced by firms in market economies and there is still a high degree of political control of borrowing in the state sector. However, in a number of the firms we studied, the financial constraints have been tightened compared with the past. Interestingly, it is mainly the relatively unreformed SOEs that registered a strengthening of the budget constraint recently. This may reflect the fact that financing has been on a more commercial basis in the reformed SOEs for a much longer period. Of course, the existing financial position of the enterprise can also be expected to affect the ability to access further loans, and both of the COEs were making losses. The results suggest that the budget constraint is sometimes tighter when the enterprises are loss making.

In addition to questions aimed at revealing the enterprise's current financial state and access to finance, a series of questions was asked on the following subjects:

- Enterprise objectives. Managers were asked to name what they considered to be their three primary objectives, in descending order.

- Management appointments. A series of questions were asked about the method of appointment and background of senior management.
- Internal structure and restructuring. Management were asked questions about the extent to which their firms had undergone internal restructuring in recent years and the form this restructuring had taken.
- The technology in use. Questions were asked with a view to ascertaining to what extent the different firms had introduced or were introducing new forms of technology.
- Relationships with upper bureaus. The extent to which management considers itself independent of government departments and the Communist party was of special interest in the light of the reform process outlined earlier and the uncertainty on this matter evident in earlier studies of Chinese management. Questions were directed at ascertaining the source from which management primarily got information for managerial decision-making, and the degree to which management felt they had the power to make key decisions relating to inputs, outputs and the organization of production.
- Attitudes to privatization.[10] Finally, management were asked about their attitude to privatization and more specifically their views on whether it would be possible to privatize their enterprise. The answers reflect the continuing uncertainty in China about the official line on privatization.

*Enterprise Objectives*

Fifteen enterprises answered questions on objectives and how objectives had changed in recent years, including ten of the eleven SOEs, both COEs, and the three JVs. The results for the SOEs are summarized in Table 4. All of the SOEs, irrespective of whether or not they were corporatized, placed increasing output, followed by profit, as the two main objectives. None, for instance, selected objectives such as increasing or maintaining employment, increasing salaries, or fulfilling the goals of the upper bureaus. The answers seem to testify to the degree to which China has moved away from the pursuit of socialist goals. This was underlined when, for purposes of comparison, the managers were asked about their goals in 1990. At the same time, however, objectives such as increasing salaries and employment, and fulfilling upper bureaus goals featured as 'second' or 'third' level objectives, suggesting that the shift in attitude may not be so profound.

Table 5 provides similar information on the objectives of management in the JVs and COEs, though because they are fewer in number the table can be set out more simply. Firm C is a new company with profitability as a clear objective. Firm B is a joint venture between a Taiwanese cable company and a state-owned cable supplier. The Taiwanese investor has majority control on the board and the JV has just gained a big contract to supply cable for a major telecommunications construction project in China. As Firm B is only a medium-sized company in terms of its capital assets, and a small enterprise in terms of its employment, the contract is straining the company's productive capacity. This helps to explain the emphasis on

TABLE 4

OBJECTIVES OF MANAGEMENT IN THE STATE-OWNED ENTERPRISES

| | The First Objective of SOEs | Present | | In 1990 | |
|---|---|---|---|---|---|
| 1 | Increase output volume | 6 | 60% | 5 | 55% |
| 2 | Increase profits | 4 | 40% | 1 | 11% |
| 3 | Increase or maintain the employment of workers, | | | | |
| | their relations and local people | 0 | 0% | 0 | 0% |
| 4 | Increase employment salaries | 0 | 0% | 0 | 0% |
| 5 | Accomplish contracted missions or goals set by | | | | |
| | upper bureaus | 0 | 0% | 3 | 33% |
| 6 | Promote the firm | 0 | 0% | 0 | 0% |

| | The Second Objective of SOEs | Present | | In 1990 | |
|---|---|---|---|---|---|
| 1 | Increase profits | 6 | 60% | 4 | 44% |
| 2 | Increase output volume | 3 | 30% | 0 | 0% |
| 3 | Accomplish contracted missions or goals set by | | | | |
| | upper bureaus | 1 | 10% | 2 | 22% |
| 4 | Increase or maintain the employment of workers, | | | | |
| | their relations and local people | 0 | 0% | 0 | 0% |
| 5 | Increase employment salaries | 0 | 0% | 2 | 22% |
| 6 | Promote the firm | 0 | 0% | 1 | 11% |

| | The Third Objective of SOEs | Present | | In 1990 | |
|---|---|---|---|---|---|
| 1 | Increase employment salaries | 6 | 60% | 2 | 22% |
| 2 | Increase or maintain the employment of workers, | | | | |
| | their relations and local people | 2 | 20% | 1 | 11% |
| 3 | Accomplish contracted missions or goals set by | | | | |
| | upper bureaus | 2* | 20% | 2 | 22% |
| 4 | Promote the firm | 1* | 10% | 2 | 22% |
| 5 | Increase output volume | 0 | 0% | 1 | 11% |
| 6 | Increase profits | 0 | 0% | 1 | 11% |

*Notes:* 'Promote the firm' means promoting the firm's hierarchical status
      * one enterprise answered 3 and 4 as joint third objective
      One of the 10 firms was established after 1990 and therefore only nine firms feature in the
      1990 column.

expanding production. It is also noticeable how the company has moved away from increasing salaries as a prime objective in recent years. A similar movement towards more commercial goals is evident at firm A.

In summary, there is *slight* evidence in the results summarized in Tables 4 and 5 of a bias towards the pursuit of an output objective amongst the SOEs; *slight* evidence that the COEs stressed employment benefits more highly; and *some* evidence of a more prominent profit objective in the JVs (except at Firm B for reasons already explained). But also apparent is the *similarity* in goals across the ownership types. A sharp difference between SOEs, COEs and JVs was not found. Equally, although for reasons of space separate results for corporatized and non-corporatized SOEs cannot be presented here, the objectives did not seem to differ significantly between the two types of organization.

TABLE 5

OBJECTIVES OF MANAGEMENT IN THE JOINT VENTURES AND THE COLLECTIVES

**(a) Joint Ventures**

| Firm | Most important | 2nd most important | 3rd most important |
| --- | --- | --- | --- |
| A: Present | Increase the profits | Increase output volume | Maintain employment |
| In 1990 | Accomplish contracted mission set by upper bureaus | Promote the firm | Maintain employment |
| B: Present | Increase output volume | Increase profits | Maintain employment, fulfil goals of upper bureaus |
| In 1990 | Increase salaries | Accomplish contracted mission set by upper bureaus | Maintain employment |
| C: Present | Increase profits | Maintain employment | Increase output volume, accomplish contracted mission of upper bureaus |
| In 1990 | Not applicable* | | |

*Note*: * firm C was not established until early in 1995.

**(b) Collectives**

| Firm | Most important | 2nd most important | 3rd most important |
| --- | --- | --- | --- |
| D: Present | Maintain employment | Increase profits | Utilize local non-labour resources |
| In 1990 | Accomplish contracted mission of upper bureaus | No information provided | No information provided |
| E: Present | Increase output volume | Increase profits | Maintain employment |
| In 1990 | Increase output volume | Increase profits | Maintain employment |

When asked whether the objectives of management and 'owners' differed, the managers of SOEs and COEs answered that since all objectives had to be negotiated first with owners there were no differences. This suggests that managers in these enterprises still see themselves as being in an intense negotiating process with upper bureaus, something revealed by earlier studies. The prior agreement of objectives may help to explain why, even in SOEs, 'filling goals set by upper bureaus' did not feature as the most important first, second or third level objective. In effect, the objectives such as output and profit that were singled out had already been agreed with the bureaus.

Some differences between management goals and those of investors were evident in the answers from the JVs – see Table 6. It is to be expected that foreign investors will differ from local Chinese management on priorities. Also, in principle, JVs should be less constrained by accountability to upper bureaus and this may mean that enterprise management are freer to set their own goals.

TABLE 6

RELATIONS WITH INVESTORS IN THE JOINT VENTURES

| Firm | Comments from answers provided regarding differences in attitudes between management and investors |
|------|------|
| A | Shareholders pursue and favour short-term rewards, especially a rise in the share price. |
| B | Taiwanese investor prefers reinvesting profits to expand production capacity, while Chinese counterparts favour profit distribution to employees. |
| C | Hong Kong investor prefers expanding production capacity, but Chinese management prefer accomplishing 'indicators' from upper bureaus. |

## Management Appointments

Questions were asked about the appointment of directors and general managers. Research has found that good management is an important factor in the successful adaptation of business to changes in the external environment (Torbert, 1989). Certainly, existing management can disrupt change; in the Chinese context existing directors may be reluctant to impose the radical changes that the new environment of market-directed reform requires.

From our study, it is clear that the power of appointing and dismissing directors (or general managers) in the SOEs and COEs is still retained by the political authorities in the shape of industrial bureaus. This applies irrespective of whether or not the enterprise has been corporatized. Table 7 provides details of the background and appointment process of the chief director for each of the enterprises studied.

In the case of the Firm A (a joint venture) the General Manager is still appointed by the upper bureau. In the case of the other two JVs, greater autonomy in management appointments is in evidence with the board being responsible in both cases. The likely reason for the lack of independence at Firm A lies in the nature of the shareholding of its foreign investors. Firm A's foreign investors are simply equity holders and numerous in number. There are no foreign representatives at board level to protect the enterprise from political interference. In a few cases the general managers of the SOEs and COEs were appointed by their holding companies. However, the so-called 'holding company' is often essentially the former industrial bureau and hence political control still continues.[11]

TABLE 7

THE BACKGROUND OF THE CHIEF DIRECTOR/GENERAL MANAGER

| Firm | Background/Appointment Process |
|------|-------------------------------|
| **JVs** | |
| A | Former director of a state-owned camera factory |
| | University background |
| | Appointed by upper bureau |
| B | Former director of a state-owned wires factory |
| | Appointed by the Board |
| C | Former official of Nanjing Economic Planning Committee |
| | Appointed by the Board |
| **COEs** | |
| D | Former director from the enterprise's subsidiary factory |
| | Appointed by the parent holding company |
| E | Philosophy background |
| | Appointed by upper bureau |
| **SOEs** | |
| F | Wood processing background |
| | Appointed by upper bureau |
| G | Appointed by upper bureau |
| H | Worked way up in the factory starting at the age of 17 |
| | Appointed by upper bureau |
| I | Appointed by upper bureau |
| J | Appointed by upper bureau |
| K | Former Party Secretary and vice director of the firm |
| | Appointed by upper bureau |
| L | Appointed by upper bureau |
| M | Former director of the industrial bureau, became general manager when the industrial bureau became a holding company. Appointed by upper bureau |
| N. | Appointed directly by Premier Li Peng |
| O | Former director of the second engine factory |
| | Appointed by upper bureau |
| P | Biochemistry professor from a Jiangsu university |
| | Appointed jointly by upper bureau and the board |

*Note*:   Not all SOEs provided information on the background of the Chief Director/General Manager.

Some further questions were asked to ascertain the knowledge of the senior management of modern western management techniques, for example just-in-time (JIT) production. The management of the JVs and SOEs demonstrated a higher level of knowledge, and therefore perhaps better management training, than managers in the COEs. Some of the managers, especially in the JVs, were young and newly promoted.

*Internal Structure and Restructuring*

State enterprises in China are notorious for their hierarchical structures and systems for 'reporting up', ultimately to upper bureaus. The organizations also typically include non-productive departments, such as departments in charge of political education and welfare services. The expectation is that the reform process will have led to significant internal restructuring within Chinese enterprises. The 'responsibilities system' implies more local

TABLE 8

RECENT RESTRUCTURING IN THE CHINESE FIRMS

| | Organizational Changes | | Employment Firm |
|---|---|---|---|
| | Vertical | Horizontal | Effects |
| **JVs** | | | |
| A | N | Y: reduced some service departments. | Y: 5% of employees were affected |
| B | N | Y: merged some administrative departments | N |
| **COEs** | | | |
| D | N | Y: closed the propaganda and education departments | N |
| E | N | Y: merged some service departments | N |
| **SOEs** | | | |
| F | N | Y: number of departments reduced from 19 to 8 during 1995 | Y: 10% of staff were transferred to service companies |
| G | N | Y: number of departments reduced from 29 to 8 | Y: 15% of staff were reallocated to service companies; some left voluntarily |
| H | N | Y: security department was merged | N |
| I | N | Y: education and construction departments reduced | Y: 10% of staff were made redundant |
| J | N | Y: party and political departments were reduced | Y: over 200 staff retired early or left the firm |
| K | N | Y: reduced some political and administrative departments | Y: 700 staff were either transferred to new service companies, retired early or became self-employed |
| L | N | Y: political and propaganda departments were reduced | Y: encouraged staff to retired or they were transferred to new positions |
| M | N | Y: merger of some production and management departments | Y: transferred some workers to new service companies and encouraged early retirement |
| N | Y: but have increased the number of vertical levels | Y: increased investment and sales departments | Y: 500 staff were retired in 1995 |
| O | N | Y: merged some offices | Y: many employees transferred to newly founded service companies; more than 1,000 staff retired early |

*Note*:  Y = if important organizational changes have been introduced.
        N = if important organizational changes have not been introduced.

management accountability and decision making and therefore less 'referring up'. Perhaps departments will have been merged and 'unproductive departments' closed.

Table 8 summarizes recent changes at the enterprises studied. A 'Y' entry signifies change, whilst a 'N' entry signifies no change. Vertical organization refers to changes in hierarchy levels and accountability within the firm. Horizontal organization refers to the number of departments and cross-department functions within the firm. The final column indicates whether there were important changes affecting employment. Firm C (a joint venture) was founded only in March 1995, and Firm P (a SOE) is also a new company. Both are therefore excluded from the table.

The majority of SOEs have carried out organizational changes at the horizontal level and this has often involved the merger or closure of political departments. There have been some, though fewer, changes involving departments involved in the provision of welfare services, which suggests that the welfare of staff remains a high priority in the SOEs in the absence of a comprehensive national welfare system. The exception is perhaps education departments where there is evidence of some closures. These departments usually had close ties with the political office. Balanced against this, however, there is evidence of staff redundancies and early retirements aimed at reducing staff numbers. With one exception, none of the enterprises (irrespective of ownership form) claimed important changes in vertical organization. The exception was Firm N (a SOE), which recorded an *increase* in hierarchy. This is explained by the fact that this SOE is a fast-growing enterprise, which has incorporated some two hundred smaller SOEs in recent years. This has necessitated additional bureaucratic levels to ensure an effective span of control.

Turning to the two COEs, they have also been involved in some horizontal mergers of departments. However, it is worth noticing that in neither case had there been a laying-off of staff in spite of the changing economic environment the firms faced. This is probably explained by the fact that the COEs have the strong characteristics of self-managed firms. It is perhaps to be expected that where workers are involved in management, job preservation will feature highly and this was reflected in the earlier discussion of objectives, especially at Firm D (see Table 5(b) above).

Of the two JVs studied, there is evidence of some horizontal reorganization though with only a minor effect on employees. These findings may be explained by the fact that JVs are likely to be nearer to having optimal manpower and an organizational structure appropriate to current needs.

*The Technology In Use*

Questions were asked about the technology used. When an enterprise faces a more challenging economic environment not only might we expect the internal organizational structure to change, but there may well be an impact on the technology-in-use with a view to reducing costs, speeding up

TABLE 9

HAS NEW TECHNOLOGY BEEN INTRODUCED?

| Firm | Y/N | Description |
|------|-----|-------------|
| **JVs** | | |
| A | Y | In 1992, introduced CAD, CAM moulds. |
| B | Y | In 1995, introduced new optical fibres. |
| C | Y | New JV, new equipment. |
| **COEs** | | |
| D | N | '... we cannot introduce new equipment, ..... the workers' passion for technology is declining'. |
| E | N | Last major introduction of equipment in 1980. |
| **SOEs** | | |
| F | Y | In 1988 introduced Swedish MDF machine. |
| G | Y | Since 1992 been building new factory and installing new productive equipment. Old equipment will soon be totally replaced. |
| H | Y | In 1990 introduced Italian textile machines. |
| I | Y | In 1995 introduced German Rolan R704 printing equipment. |
| J | Y | During 1986-90 introduced seven new products requiring more advanced technology. |
| K | Y | In 1992 introduced a new PCV machine. |
| L | Y | Key technological restructuring projects are underway at the rate of one or two per year. |
| M | Y | In 1992-93 introduced new woollen manufacturing machines. |
| N | Y | Introduced new video technology. |
| O | Y | Since 1985, co-operating with the Italian company IVECO (part of the FIAT group). |
| P | Y | In 1993 introduced a new patented nutrition product requiring advanced technology. |

*Note*:     Y = if new technology has been introduced
            N = if new technology has not been introduced.

delivery or improving product quality. Answers to this series of questions are summarized in Table 9. All of the SOEs recorded current new investment or investment in the recent past, which suggests a degree of dynamic change in the state sector: the same, less surprisingly, was true of the JVs studied. Interestingly, however, the two COEs reported no major changes in technology used. The senior manager at Firm D commented that '... we cannot introduce new equipment, ... the workers' passion for technology is declining'. The last time Firm E had introduced significant new technology was in 1980. Once again, it seems that the degree of worker involvement in the management of the enterprise may be slowing down the pace of change in the collectives compared both with the JVs and the SOE sector. Another factor could be access to funds for investment. The JVs are supported by foreign capital and the SOEs are backed by the government, which permits more favourable access to loans from the state-owned banks. The COEs have neither of these advantages.

## Relationships with Upper Bureaus

The Chinese reform programme since 1979 has attempted to distance enterprises from the state to provide more managerial autonomy and accountability. Therefore, it is interesting to examine the relationship between enterprises and upper bureaus today. Previous studies, reviewed earlier, have suggested a continuing important role for the state, including provincial government, in the operations of the SOEs. In his study of enterprises in Beijing in 1990, Child (1994) found that higher authorities remained the most frequent provider of information for enterprise decision-making. The reason for the continued reliance on bureaucratic information sources lay in the industrial bureaus having better information about sources of supply of scarce materials and other inputs. They also had advance knowledge of impending policy changes at government level that might impact on the enterprises.

Our study suggests that since 1990 government has become much less important as a source of information for managerial decision-making. Table 10 summarizes the results. From the table it is evident that the government's role as an information provider varies and is heavily dependent on the products and industries. Those companies which rely on government information sources are mainly the central government-controlled ones and

TABLE 10

WHAT ARE THE MAIN INFORMATION SOURCES?

| Firm | Government | Own Channels (self-generated information e.g. from sales teams or own market research) | Other sources |
|------|-----------|----------------------------------------------------------------------------------------|---------------|
| **JVs** | | | |
| A | | Y | Y: other enterprises |
| B | Y | | |
| **COEs** | | | |
| D | | Y | Y: market information; |
| E | | Y | newspapers |
| **SOEs** | | | |
| F | | Y | Y: Industrial association |
| G | Y: but very limited | Y | Y: other enterprises |
| H | | Y | Y: other enterprises |
| I | Y: but very limited | Y | |
| J | | Y | Y: Industrial association |
| K | | Y | Y: other enterprises |
| L | Y | Y | |
| M | | Y | Y: other enterprises |
| N | Y | Y | |
| O | Y | Y | |
| P | | Y | Y: other enterprises |

*Note*: Y= if a main source of information. No answer to this question was given by Firm C.

have strategic or military importance, notably Firm N which is in electronics, and Firm O which is involved in motor vehicle production. Both of these SOEs produce some military equipment. Similarly, Firm B (a joint venture) is dependent on government bodies for information because its product, cables for telecommunications, are sold to a government department.

In contrast, the enterprises in the other industries seem to rely more on their own channels of information and other enterprises in the same industry. The industrial associations, which are usually encouraged and organized by the government, also seem to be playing an important role.

Turning to the subject of bureaucratic intervention, Child (1994) describes the autonomous rights or complete discretion of management as a 'precarious autonomy' in Chinese enterprises. The autonomous rights were investigated through a series of questions centred on:

- the appointment of directors and deputy directors
- the recruiting and dismissing staff
- the investment and expansion of capacity
- the sale of assets
- the freedom to join a business grouping eg. trading consortium
- the freedom to enter into mergers and acquisitions
- the powers over changes in ownership, and
- bankruptcy, stopping production and closing the firm down.

The results are given in Table 11. Clearly some managerial discretion has been delegated to the enterprise level in the SOEs, but many powers still remain at the central or local government levels. In the cases of the JVs, the state still has a majority stake in Firms A and C, and hence the state retains more powers, especially in the case of Firm A compared with Firm B, the JV with majority Taiwanese investment. The autonomous rights in the COEs can be differentiated into personnel issues, investment and sales of spare assets and equipment. The answers to further questions indicated that if investments and assets were financed from self-raised funds then there was substantially greater enterprise autonomy.

There is clear evidence of much more referring-up in the SOEs. Indeed, our study reveals the extent to which, despite all of the past reforms, senior management in the SOEs (both corporatized and non-corporatized firms) feel they have limited autonomy. At the present time, the sale of assets and equipment by managers is a particularly sensitive issue in the light of some well-publicized cases of local corruption and malpractice. A number of the enterprise directors or managers commented that, while spare assets could be sold much more easily than in the past, they preferred to avoid possible political 'incorrectness' and danger. Hence, they chose to continue to 'refer up' for approval before embarking on sales. A seemingly in-built predilection to refer up, cultivated by years of central planning, is now reinforced by the current government drive against corruption.

TABLE 11

ARE THE FOLLOWING POWERS HELD BY THE ENTERPRISE?

(Y=Yes; N=No. Numbers refer to notes below)

| Firm | Appointment of Director/deputy | Recruiting/dismiss staff | Investment and expansion of capacity | Sales of assets | Enter into a consortium | Merger with other enterprises | Ownership change | Bankruptcy, stop production, closure |
|---|---|---|---|---|---|---|---|---|
| **JVs** | | | | | | | | |
| A | N | Y2 | Y | Y | Y | N | N | N |
| B | Y | Y | Y | Y | Y | Y | Y | Y |
| C | Y | Y | Y | Y | Y | Y | N | Y |
| **COEs** | | | | | | | | |
| D | N | Y | Y3 | Y3 | N | N | N | N |
| E | N | Y | Y3 | Y3 | Y | N | N | N |
| **SOEs** | | | | | | | | |
| F | N | Y | N | Y | N | N | N | N |
| G | N | Y | N | N | N | N | N | N |
| H | N | Y2 | N | N | N | N | N | N |
| I | N | N | N | N | N | N | N | N |
| J | N | Y | N | N | N | N | N | N |
| K | N | Y | N | Y | N | N | N | N |
| L | N | Y2 | Y2 | Y | Y | N | N | N |
| M | N | Y2 | N | Y1 | Y | N | N | N |
| N | N | Y2 | N | Y1 | N | N | N | N |
| O | N | Y | N | Y1 | N | N | N | N |
| P | N | N | Y2 | Y2 | N | N | N | N |

*Notes:*  Y = if power is held by the enterprise;  N = if the power is not held by the enterprise.
The numbers should be interpreted as follows:

1  but the proceeds are restricted to certain purposes, eg. reinvestment.
2  but must refer-up for agreement first.
3  applies provided the enterprise remains self-funding.

TABLE 12

DO YOU THINK IT WOULD BE POSSIBLE TO PRIVATIZE YOUR ENTERPRISE?

| JVs | Yes/No | Manager's Comment |
|---|---|---|
| A | N | Smaller enterprises have been privatized and allowed in some coastal cities, but large and medium sized enterprises will not be privatized. |
| B | Not applicable | Taiwanese investors have a 51% stake therefore the firm is already privatized. |
| C | N | Ownership is restricted by state policy. |
| **COEs** | | |
| D | N | Not an issue since current state policy does not permit privatization. |
| E | N | 1. State policy will not allow privatization. 2. Staff are not capable of operating in an environment of private enterprise. |
| **SOE** | | |
| F | N | 1. The firm's assets are too big for any individual person to own. 2. If privatization occurs it would be preferable if it took the form of a 'share co-operative scheme'. |
| G | N | 1. The firm is of too large a scale to be privatized. 2. Private individuals have insufficient money to buy it. 3. The business risk is too large for private individuals. |
| H | N | 1. The factory should belong to the state. 2. If privatized, half of the workforce would have to be sacked. |
| I | N | Not an issue since current state policy does not permit privatization. |
| J | N | As above. |
| K | N | As above. |
| L | N | 1. The total asset value of the firm makes it too large to be privatized. 2. No one would be interested in buying the firm as it makes losses. |
| M | N | Not an issue since current state policy does not permit privatization. |
| N | N | As above. |
| O | N | As above. |
| P | N | As above. |

## Attitudes to Privatization

Wide-scale privatization is not official policy in China, but it could become so in the future. The opinions of Chinese managers on the possible privatization of their enterprises were therefore investigated. Table 12 presents the views of the managers interviewed. In summary, most of the managers interviewed thought that privatization was not possible because state policy was still not favourable to the idea. There was no discernible difference of views between managers in the COEs, the JVs, and the corporatized and uncorporatized SOEs. In three firms, managers also dismissed the notion of privatization on the grounds that their enterprises were too large to be sold to the private sector, and one manager was dismissive because his firm was making losses and therefore would be unattractive to buyers. There was also evidence that at least some managers recognized that privatization would inevitably bring large-scale rationalization, including redundancies. More generally, there was a distinct (and understandable) reluctance to discuss the subject of privatization in any real detail given uncertainty about future government policy on ownership. This did not prevent, however, four of the managers (including three SOE managers) commenting 'off-the-record' that they favoured privatization.

## CONCLUSIONS

This study has been concerned with management attitudes in eleven corporatized or non-corporatized SOEs, three JVs, and two COEs, based in Shanghai or Nanjing. The objective has been to see whether management attitudes have changed in recent years and whether there are noticeable differences in attitude and behaviour between the managements in the various types of enterprises. The study was conducted in late 1995 using structured interviews based on an extensive questionnaire.

The results show that the budget constraint on firms has become stronger in recent years, implying both a reduction in managerial discretionary behaviour and the scope for political intervention in decision making. The SOEs studied were noticeably more output- and profit- conscious than five years earlier, and this was also true of the two JVs that had been operating in 1990. There was much less emphasis on pursuing the goals of upper bureaus, which may imply a decline in the influence of government departments in these enterprises. One of the two COEs had also changed its objectives, but this time more in favour of maintaining employment. It is perhaps to be expected that a COE will show the most interest in the welfare of its employees. However, the other COE showed no change in objectives in recent years.

In spite of these results, the authorities still continue to have a significant influence on the management of Chinese enterprises, though less so where private investors are prominent at board level. Previous studies pointed to continuing high levels of political contact between enterprise management and upper bureaus. Our research suggests that the government is becoming less important as a source of information for managerial decision-making, and this applies across all types of enterprises. The exception, understandably, is where the government remains the prime purchaser as, for example, in defence supplies. Nevertheless, the state still retains wide powers in areas such as the appointment of senior managers, recruiting and dismissing staff, investment and the expansion of capacity, sales of assets, business restructuring, ownership change and bankruptcy and closure of the firm. Only the managers in the JVs believed that they had real power over such decisions.

Also, there is no evidence of recent vertical restructuring in the enterprises, which could have been a sign of a move away from 'referring up'. There has been restructuring at the horizontal level with a view to reducing the role of political and, to a lesser extent, welfare departments. One common result of restructuring has been a reduction in employment. But, interestingly, the scale of change seems smaller in the COEs, and the COE management seemed less aware of capitalist management techniques. Another finding is that the drive towards corporatization of the SOEs seems thus far to have had little effect on management attitudes.

In general, the attitude of management in the JVs could be more clearly differentiated from attitudes in the other types of enterprise studied. There seemed to be few discernible differences in attitudes in the COEs and SOEs. In spite of their different histories, the COEs and SOEs appear to have senior management that are very similar in attitude. At the same time, COE management seemed the least interested in the introduction of new technology. Without new capital injections the COEs may fall further behind the other firms in terms of their technological capability.

The last questions related to privatization. Interestingly, none of the enterprise managers believed that privatization was imminent. In any case, a number believed either that their enterprises would be unattractive to private investors because of losses being made, or that they were too large to be sold, or that the consequences would be too dire for their staff. There will need to be considerable 're-educating' of management should official policy change in favour of widespread privatization.

Since the beginning of the marketization reforms, the central-planning mechanism has become much less important and, in principle, the SOEs have been granted considerably more managerial autonomy. The research results reported in this study add to those of earlier studies in the late 1980s and early 1990s that questioned the extent to which powers have actually been devolved to enterprise management and the extent to which management attitudes have changed. Of course, our sample of Chinese firms, especially of COEs and JVs, is very small and ideally the study would be replicated in more enterprises and in other parts of China. In addition, it is possible that the managers interviewed may not have been entirely candid in their answers and the study may have omitted the worst financial performers. Some managers in large loss-making enterprises refused to be interviewed. Nevertheless, despite the shortcomings of such a small survey, the study makes a useful contribution to the knowledge of management in Chinese firms and therefore to our understanding of the Chinese economy at a time of considerable economic change.

### NOTES

1. 'China Stirs its Sleeping Giants', *The Economist*, 27 August 1994, p.55.
2. The Town and Village Enterprises are heterogeneous in nature. Some are collectives while others are privately owned.
3. J. Child, 'Exercising Strong Direction', *Financial Times*, 6 November 1995, p.14.
4. For further discussion of this and related studies see J. Child, 'The Character of Chinese Enterprise Management', in J. Child and M. Lockett (eds), *Reform Policy and the Chinese Enterprise*, Advances in Chinese Industrial Studies, Greenwich CN, JAI Press, 1990; J.

Child and T. Lu, 'Industrial Decision Making under China's Reform 1985–1988', *Organization Studies*, Vol.11, 1990, pp.321–51; J. Child and X. Xu, 'The Communist Party's Role in Enterprise Leadership at the High-Water of China's Economic Reform', in N. Campbell, S.R.F. Plasschaert, and D.H. Brown (eds) *The Changing Nature of Management in China*, Advances in Chinese Industrial Studies 2, Greenwich CN, JAI Press, 1991; J. Child and L. Markoczy, 'Host Country Managerial Behaviour and Learning in Chinese and Hungarian Joint Ventures', *Journal of Management Studies*, Vol.30, No.4, 1993, pp.631–51; J. Child and L. Markoczy, 'Host Country Managerial Behaviour in Chinese and Hungarian Joint Ventures: Assessment of Competing Explanations', in M. Boisot (ed) *East–West Business Collaboration:the Challenge of Governance in Post-Socialist Enterprises*, London, Routledge, 1994; and J. Child, *Management in China During the Age of Reform*.

5. The interviews were conducted in Chinese and the answers were then translated by Weihwa Pan.

6. Central planning continued for longer and was more pervasive in Shanghai than in certain other coastal areas of China. This held back Shanghai's economic growth in the 1980s. In the last few years, however, Shanghai has undergone an economic boom.

7. For reasons of time and resources, our study omitted wholly privately-owned firms.

8. The original COEs were created in the waves of collectivization after 1955. Later some COEs became locally-managed SOEs. COEs were governed by local industrial bureaus and adopted the same accounting systems as SOEs. After 1979, a series of programmes were introduced to revitalize the COEs and more autonomy was granted to the enterprises, including accountability for profits and losses. The COEs have expanded since the early 1980s filling the gap in the economy left by the SOEs which are mainly concerned with heavy industry. They have become particularly prominent in the service sector and small-scale industry. In addition to COEs which originated from the efforts of a SOE or the efforts of local residents, a third main type of COE is the private enterprise. This type is found mainly in the southern provinces where private economies are flourishing. However, because of the political uncertainty about the future of private enterprise in China, many prefer to disguise themselves as COEs. According to the Guangdong provincial government, around 60 per cent of its 2000 private manufacturing enterprises are registered as collectives.

9. Unfortunately, it is not possible to be more precise about each firm's financial position because none of the enterprises was willing to supply financial accounts. Some managers said there was no point in seeing them since their firm's accounts were not accurate (!), while others said that they were not permitted to provide accounts to outsiders without permission from above. The financial position, as summarized in Table 2, is based on answers to questions asked about recent profits and unprofitable output.

10. Questions were also asked on other subjects, such as industrial relations and wage and bonus payments. The answers to these questions will appear in a separate article.

11. At the time of the fieldwork, for example, nine Shanghai industrial bureaus had been transformed into holding companies.

## REFERENCES

Boisot, M. (1994), 'The Lessons from China' in M. Boisot (ed.), *East-West Business Collaboration: the Challenge of Governance in Post-Socialist Enterprises*. London: Routledge.

Boisot, M. and J. Child (1988), 'The Iron Law of Fiefs: Bureaucratic Failure and the Problem of Governance in the Chinese Economic Reforms', *Administrative Science Quarterly*, Vol.33, No.4, pp.508–28.

Boisot, M. and G. Xing (1992), 'The Nature of Managerial Work in the Chinese Enterprise Reforms: A Study of Six Directors', *Organizdtion Studies*, Vol.13, No.2, pp.161–84.

Chen, M. (1995), *Asian Management Systems: Chinese, Japanese and Korean Styles of Business*. London: Routledge.

Child, J. (1990), 'The Character of Chinese Enterprise Management' in J. Child and M. Lockett (eds), *Reform Policy and the Chinese Enterprise*. Greenwich CN: JAI Press.

Child, J. (1994), *Management in China in the Age of Reform*. Cambridge: Cambridge University Press.

Child, J. and T. Lu (1989), 'Changes in the Level of Decision Making in Chinese Industry: a Window on the Progress of Economic Reform, 1985–88', Aston Business School Working Paper.

Child, J. and L. Markoczy, (1993), 'Host Country Managerial Behaviour and Learning in Chinese and Hungarian Joint Ventures', *Journal of Management Studies*, Vol.30, No.4, pp.631–651.

Child, J. and Markoczy, L. (1994), 'Host Country Managerial Behaviour and Learning in Chinese and Hungarian Joint Ventures: Assessment of Competing Institutions' in M. Boisot (ed.), *East–West Business Collaboration: the Challenge of Governance in Post-Socialist Enterprises*. London: Routledge.

Child, J. and X. Xu (1991), 'The Communist Party's Role in Enterprise Leadership at the High Water of China's Economic Reform' in N. Campbell, S.R.F. Plasschaert, and D.H. Brown (eds), *The Changing Nature of Management in China*. Greenwich CN: St Martin's Press.

Chow, I.H. (1992), 'Chinese Managerial Work', *Journal of General Management*, Vol.17, pp.53–67.

Hay, D.A. (1994), *Economic Reform and the State-Owned Enterprises in China, 1979–1987*. Oxford: Clarendon.

IMF (1993), *China at the Treshold of a Market Economy*. IMF Occasional Paper, No.107. Washington, DC: IMF.

Kornai, J. (1979), 'Resource-constrained versus Demand-constrained Systems', *Econometrica*, Vol.47, No.4, pp.801–19.

Lardy, N.R. (1994), *China in the World Economy*. Washington, DC: Institute for International Economics.

Lu, T. (1991), 'A Longitudinal Study of Chinese Managerial Behaviour: an Inside View of Decision Making under the Economic Reform'. Unpublished PhD, Aston University.

Naughton, B. (1994), *Growing Out of the Plan: Chinese Economic Reform, 1978–1993*. Cambridge: Cambridge University Press, 1994.

Nolan, P. (1995), *China's Rise, Russia's Fall: Politics, Economics and Planning in the Transition from Stalinism*. Houndsmills: Macmillan.

Nolan, P. (1995), 'Joint Ventures and Economic Reform in China: a Case Study of the Coca-Cola Business System, with particular reference on the Tianjin Coca-Cola Plant, ESRC Centre for Business Research Working Paper Series WP24. University of Cambridge.

Parker, D. and W. Pan (1996), 'Reform of the State-Owned Enterprises in China', *Communist Economies and Economic Transformation*, Vol.8, No.1, pp.109–27.

Perkins, F. (1995), 'Productivity, Performance and Priorities for the Reform of China's State-Owned Enterprises', Economics Division Working Paper 95/1. Research School of Pacific and Asian Studies, Australian National University, Canberra.

Roehrig, M.F. (1994), *Foreign Joint Ventures in Contemporary China*. New York: St Martin's Press.

Torbert, W.R. (1989), 'Leading Organizational Transformation' in R.W.Woodman and W.A.Pasmore (eds), *Research in Organizational Change and Development*, Vol.3. Greenwich CN: JAI Press.

Warner, M. (1995), *The Management of Human Resources in Chinese Industry*. Basingstoke, Hampshire: Macmillan.

# Local Sourcing in China: The Case of Braun Electric (Shanghai) Co. Ltd

## STEFAN H. KAISER

Due to high competitive pressures in domestic and world markets, companies are increasingly forced to improve their cost position. Reducing manufacturing costs through foreign production is one possibility. Some governments require local production from manufacturers intended to service their domestic markets. Since the importing of components and materials is expensive due to high import tariffs and transportation costs, and also restricts the enterprise in flexible planning, many companies seek the possibility of local sourcing in these markets. However, in China, as in many developing countries, local sourcing is accompanied by various problems.

This article examines the case of Braun, the German manufacturer of small electronic appliances, and its problems with and strategies of using local suppliers for its production of electric foil shavers in the People's Republic of China. After evaluating the literature on local sourcing in China, the study introduces Braun Electric (Shanghai) Co. Ltd, describes the methodology used for writing the case, and discusses the company's problems of local sourcing and its strategies of overcoming them. The case study is based on a two-week research visit to the company in January 1996. It was written in March 1996.

### PROBLEMS OF LOCAL SOURCING IN CHINA

Scholars have written extensively about foreign direct investment in China. However, relatively few writers have addressed the problems of managing direct foreign investments in China.[1] Trommsdorff *et al.* (1994), in their investigation of Sino–German joint ventures (JVs) in China, suggest that the sourcing of raw materials, semi-finished goods and services in the quantity and quality required, and at the right time, is a critical aspect for many JVs. Campbell (1989) argues that, apart from quantity and quality, the time component of keeping dates is a critical area. Schuchardt (1994), referring to the Trommsdorff sample, proposes that the securing of agreed deliveries is frequently not possible, with typical problems being delivery bottlenecks and quantity shortages. In some cases, quality is so poor that it causes damage to the production facilities or causes production failures (Schuchardt, 1994: 160).

Stefan H. Kaiser, Durham University

Most of the JVs in the Trommsdorff sample complained about low delivery reliability, particularly the poor keeping of agreed dates and poor delivery service. Thus, the contractually agreed local content for production was frequently not met, the main problem being the securing of the quality required and loyalty of delivering when working with local suppliers (Schuchardt, 1994: 161). In a second survey, Schuchardt (1994) found that the local content of production was relatively stable. According to Trommsdorff *et al.* (1994), the factors causing difficulties for local sourcing are:

- dark bureaucracy without defined contact partners,
- unclear Chinese priorities of distribution,
- potential conflicts of interest, and
- a missing network of markets.

Article 58 of the 'Regulations for the Implementation of the Law of the People's Republic of China on Joint Ventures Using Chinese and Foreign Investment'[2] clearly suggests the channels through which JVs can purchase materials in China.[3] Also, Article 9 of the 'Law of the People's Republic of China on Joint Ventures Using Chinese and Foreign Investment'[4] says that '... in its purchase of required raw and semi-processed materials, fuels, auxiliary equipment, etc., a joint venture should give first priority to Chinese sources, but may also acquire them directly from the world market with its own foreign exchange funds'. However, as Lu (1989) argues, in reality it is difficult to follow these procedures when interacting with the hierarchical distribution system.

Certainly, one strategy for bypassing these problems is overseas sourcing. However, sourcing outside China has to be approved by officials and a plan for securing foreign exchange has to be presented (Cohen, 1988; Schneider *et al.*, 1986; Duscha, 1987). The above-mentioned Article 9 says that a JV may purchase its needed materials 'with its own foreign exchange funds.' In Article 57 of the Implementing Regulations, the requirement of giving priority to purchases in China is qualified with the additional remark 'where conditions are the same'. For Co-operative Joint Ventures, the 'Law of the People's Republic of China on Sino–Foreign Co-operative Enterprises'[5] has similar provisions, stating that 'within its approved business scope, it may purchase the raw materials, fuels and other materials either in the domestic market or in the world market.'

Chinese law extends the right to Wholly Foreign-owned Enterprises (WFOEs) to manage their affairs entirely on their own (Chu and Dong, 1987). Article 15 of the 'Law of the People's Republic of China on Enterprises Operated Exclusively with Foreign Capital'[6] suggests that 'within the scope of operations approved, the WFOE may purchase, either in China or from the world market, raw and semi-finished materials, fuels and other materials it needs.' The decision rests within the foreign firm itself. But again, preference should be given to purchases in the domestic Chinese market, when equal conditions prevail. Article 44 of the 'Detailed

Rules for Implementing the Law of the People's Republic of China on Enterprises Operated Exclusively with Foreign Capital' further states that 'in purchasing goods and materials in China, a Wholly Foreign-Owned Enterprise shall receive the same treatment as a Chinese enterprise under like conditions.'

Notwithstanding the above, the securing of the foreign exchange balance has to be made sure. According to the 'Law of the People's Republic of China on Enterprises Operated Exclusively with Foreign Capital', the WFOE shall handle its foreign exchange matters in accordance with relevant state regulations and shall take care to balance its foreign exchange receipts and payments. However, when the products made by the WFOE are needed urgently and may substitute for imports, they can be sold in China with permission, and foreign exchange may be collected upon the approval of the authority for exchange control of China.[7]

In recent years, however, increasing economic development and the growing need for materials, has led not only to a liberalization of sourcing and delivery structures, but also to an increase in the price of local components above the Asian and, in some cases even, world market levels. Some suppliers with good quality parts and materials started exporting and, within a short time, increased their prices several-fold. Thus, in some cases, raw materials in the required quantities have had to be re-imported (Schuchardt, 1994: 161).

As outlined above, the literature frequently suggests four main problem areas with local sourcing:

- poor quality components,
- delays in component delivery,
- quantity requirements not met by the supplier and
- poor delivery service by the local supplier.

The following case study reveals to what extent Braun Electric (Shanghai) Co. Ltd is confronted with these problems.

## BRAUN ELECTRIC (SHANGHAI) CO. LTD

### The Braun Group

Braun Electric (Shanghai) Co. Ltd (BES) is a 100 per cent wholly-owned subsidiary of Braun AG of Germany. Braun, the German manufacturer of small electronic appliances, was founded in 1921 in Frankfurt.[8] It manufactures a range of some 200 products, including electric shavers, household appliances, oral hygiene appliances, hair care products, clocks, calculators and female hair removers. In its industry it is a global leader.[9]

Braun AG sells its products all over the world with its own marketing and production subsidiaries in Europe (Austria, Belgium, Czech Republic, Denmark, Finland, France, Germany, Hungary, Italy, Ireland, The Netherlands, Norway, Portugal, Spain, Sweden and UK), North America

(Canada, Mexico and USA), Australia and Asia (Japan). Since July 1994, it has also had a subsidiary in China. In addition, its network of distributors covers virtually every country in the world.[10] Eighty per cent of the company's sales originate outside Germany.[11] The company's most important markets outside Germany are Japan, USA, Italy, UK and Spain.[12]

The electric shaver is Braun's most important core business, contributing some 40 per cent[13] of total sales and a vital share of the company's profit.[14] In foil shavers, Braun is the number one manufacturer world-wide. For its shaver business, Braun's most important national markets are Japan, Germany, USA and Italy.[15] According to Braun's product catalogue of 1993/94,[16] the electric shaver's product line covers a range of 24 individual types which are available as rechargeable cordless, cord and battery versions, in colours black and grey, and as single or double cutter block versions.

To date Braun's production is distributed among eight plants located in Germany (3), Ireland, France, Spain, Mexico and China.[17] According to the managing director of BES, the reason why Braun is present in China is its need for geographic growth, since 'nobody can bypass the Asian market'. For years, Braun has enjoyed prosperous business in Japan with its electric shavers. 'The Japanese customers are running for "Made in Germany",' the managing director says, while in Korea the company is experiencing growth rates of 15–20 per cent per annum.

BES is Braun AG's fifth manufacturing plant outside Germany, but its first production facility manufacturing electric shavers outside of Germany. It is also Braun's first investment project in the People's Republic of China. To date, the total investment of BES accounts for some US$10.6 m. BES is based in Minhang Economic and Technology Development Zone, approximately 30 kilometres southwest of central Shanghai on China's east coast. At the end of December 1995, BES employed some 206 staff, including its marketing and sales force. By the end of 1997, it intends to increase its workforce to 350.

BES specializes in the manufacturing of electric shavers. Currently, the company produces three different types of shavers, in more than 20 different sub-types with a daily output of approximately 5,000 items. The main types of shavers are:

- Type *Pocket* (in 14 sub-types)
- Type *Plug-In* (in six sub-types)
- Type *Entry* (in four sub-types)

While the *Pocket* type is a simple battery shaver with a non-rechargeable battery, the *Plug-In* and *Entry* types have a rechargeable battery. They are available either as the one hour recharge-duration version or the eight hours recharge-duration version. Braun's electric shavers are available in black, light-grey and dark-grey. From May 1996, it was planned to manufacture a fourth category of electric shaver, *Flex 200,* which was already established in markets outside of China. Pre-production of this type of shaver, which has a loose cutter block and is available either as a battery or rechargeable version, commenced at the end of January 1996. In addition to the wide range of shavers, BES produces shaver service parts for the Chinese and overseas markets.

Currently, the company sells 30 per cent of its manufactured shavers in the Chinese market, and the remaining 70 per cent are exported. It is intended to change these proportions in the future to approximately 48 per cent and 52 per cent respectively. This would reduce the company's foreign exchange earnings. Some sub-types of the *Plug-In* and *Pocket* shavers are designed specifically for the Chinese domestic market. A new product sub-type of the *Plug-In* has been developed for the Asian market due to different requirements, and a special version of the *Pocket* type is manufactured exclusively for the Japanese market. Other sub-types have been designed for the remaining export markets. For the sub-types of the *Entry* type no orders have yet been received.

BES's Chinese customers (approximately 20 wholesalers) are distributed strategically along China's east coastal regions. The three main centres are Guangzhou for south China, Shanghai for the east, and Beijing for the north of China. Customer service, as one of Braun's marketing tools, is provided by authorized dealers. Spare parts for all Braun shavers sold in the Chinese market are supplied from the plant in Shanghai. According to Article 46 of the 'Detailed Rules for Implementing Law of the People's Republic of China on Enterprises Operated Exclusively with Foreign Capital',[18] BES has the right to sell its products by itself in the domestic Chinese market in line with its approved sales ratio. If BES intends to sell more of its products in the Chinese market than the approved sales ratio it would need approval from the examination and approval authority.

All shavers destined for markets in America and Europe are first shipped to Germany. BES exports these products by itself without the use of a Chinese intermediary, taking advantage of its right under Article 46 of the 'Detailed Rules'. Braun's headquarters in Kronberg, Germany is in charge of the further distribution of these products and the servicing of these markets. Japan, Hong Kong, Singapore and other Asian markets are served directly from Shanghai.

From 1996 onwards, BES's second pillar would be the manufacture of conductor plate components. BES aimed to produce these electronic components in the form of SMD-equipping (automatic component equipping), both for its own production and for export to other European Braun plants. In addition, starting in September 1996, BES planned to manufacture electronic hair dryers.

*The Case Study Methodology*

After a first interview with the managing director of BES in June 1995, a two-week research visit to the company was undertaken in January 1996 in order to gain insight into the case and to collect information. The research visit to BES involved desk research, in-depth interviews with several functional managers, observation and participation. Various BES documents were made available to support the writing of the case. These documents came from various departments including materials, engineering and manufacturing, and provided organization and process charts, parts lists, direct cost calculations, production forecasts and local production plans. For reasons of confidentiality, absolute figures cannot be presented in this analysis, and the information has been converted into ratios. Internal communication was in English, and useful information in Chinese was translated into English.

In-depth unstructured and semi-structured interviews were carried out with all department heads and function managers in the area of materials sourcing, quality control, engineering and manufacturing. The average duration of the interviews was approximately two hours. Interviews were carried out in English. In studying the manufacturing (moulding) process of BES, the author joined the moulding manager on his inspection tour through the factory covering the variety of automated or semi-automated working stations. The author shadowed the purchasing manager in his meetings with potential local suppliers of components. These meetings were mainly conducted in Chinese and – for the benefit of the researcher – in English. In cases where the supplier's representative did not speak English, the purchasing manager interpreted in summary. Since most of the purchasing meetings were introductory meetings, the duration of the sessions, on average, did not exceed one hour.

*Production*

BES assembles its shaver products from a wide range of individual components, including plastic parts, electronic parts, metal parts, display and packaging material. BES shavers use a minimum of 50 and a maximum of 141 individual components and materials. These figures, however, exclude the sub-assemblies imported from Braun AG in Germany. While the company purchases most of the electronic and all metal and miscellaneous parts from its headquarters in Germany,[19] all plastic components are produced within BES. On average, 60 per cent of all components are produced in the company. This percentage is typical for Braun AG which, in a recent company and product presentation,[20] stressed its high degree of vertical integration.

*Moulding*

BES produces its own moulding parts, such as the shaver housings, both upper and lower, frame chassis, and switchboards. The plastic components are produced in a range of three colours: black, light-grey and dark-grey. Twenty moulding parts are sandblasted to get a uniform, even and matted surface for the individual shaver housings and visible parts. The sand for the blasting process has to be imported from Germany. To date, no substitute products are available in China. After sandblasting, the individual parts are washed and, after departmental inspection, are ready for assembly.

Currently, the moulding department is working around the clock (three shifts) in order to produce sufficient quantities of moulding parts for the two-shift operation of the assembly department. Even in times of capacity bottlenecks, out-sourcing or subcontracting of moulding parts is not considered. As the moulding manager suggests, out-sourcing or subcontracting would require a local Chinese company to be supplied with both the moulding equipment and the moulding technology. This would give rise to the possibility that the Chinese company might someday produce its own shavers (or at least the moulding parts).

Further, purchasing plastic parts from outside means losing control of plastic raw material sourcing and in-factory handling. BES's moulding department uses three different plastic types: polycarbonate (PC), polyoximethylene (POM) and acrylonitrile-butadiene-styrene resin (ABS). Two plastic material types, PC and ABS, have to be dried prior to usage and handled very carefully, since only careful handling guarantees moulding parts meeting the quality requirements of Braun. In addition to new material, BES also uses re-generated polycarbonate. However, the moulding manager has to make sure that certain fixed proportions of re-generated to new polycarbonate are maintained in order to guarantee the consistency of the finished parts. Also, re-generated polycarbonate is only used for the moulding of parts which do not have to be moved or are not under pressure.[21] The sourcing of these parts from outside would imply losing control of all these essential quality factors. Therefore, due to BES's need to mould high quality parts and its fear of know-how dissemination, it refrains from out-sourcing any moulding activities.

*Assembly*

Currently, BES assembles all delivered and manufactured parts in three production lines. In its printed circuit board (PCB) workshop, BES completes PCBs purchased in Malaysia for its rechargeable shavers, fixing between 25 and 100 electronic components on the PCB. After a 100 per cent function test, the PCBs are assembled with the other parts from moulding and the other components. After a final function and high voltage test, the shavers are ready for sale. From May 1996, two more production lines will would be producing electric shavers.

### BES's REASONS FOR LOCAL SOURCING

To date, BES sources indirectly in Germany through Braun AG and directly in Asia. From Malaysia, the company purchases printed circuit boards (PCB), rechargeable cells[22] and motors from Japan, and the majority of its plastic materials from German and American chemical manufacturers in Hong Kong and Japan. Some electronic components – some resistors, capacitors and diodes – are sourced locally in China from Sino–foreign JVs and Chinese state-owned enterprises (SOEs). However, the majority of electronic parts and important metal parts are purchased in Germany.

Currently, only 30 per cent of the quantity of parts and materials used for production in China are sourced in China. This is far too small, as the purchasing manager acknowledges.

BES wants to increase the local content of its production on a step-by-step basis. 'Of course, in the beginning, almost everything is purchased from Germany,' according to the purchasing manager: 'Local sourcing should be implemented gradually'. For the *Flex* shaver, for instance, which is now in the process of pre-production, nearly all assembly components are purchased in Germany. Currently, the moulding department has only five moulds available for this product type, and the rest are purchased from Germany. Only later can the substitution of parts from Germany be introduced. In sum, BES wanted to save RMB2m through local sourcing in 1996. Apart from potential cost savings, the managing director also stresses the current inability to be flexible. Since deliveries from Germany, for instance, take up to three months, he is very inflexible in planning. 'A factory is like an oil tanker,' he says, meaning that the planning system is very sluggish and cannot react to orders with only short notice.

According to the purchasing manager of BES, local sourcing would be of value for a variety of reasons, such as:

- Just-in-time delivery (lower inventory costs)
- Decrease in direct product costs
- Improved delivery service
- Easier communication.

### Just-In-Time Delivery

BES uses a variety of moulding parts, of which 84 different items are produced in Shanghai. Of the total moulding parts, 32 are washed parts, 75 are electronic and metal components, and 60 are different display and packaging materials, including display box, instructions for use, and shipping boxes. Plastic raw material is currently purchased from international chemical giants, which ship their deliveries from Hong Kong and Japan over to Shanghai. However, including customs clearance, shipments from Hong Kong have a lead time of approximately one month. In order to avoid production stoppages caused by a shortage of plastic raw material, BES has to keep a security stock of raw plastic in its warehouse. This, however, gives rise to overhead costs that increase the total production costs. Similarly, the majority of electronic components are currently purchased overseas. Only a small number of electronic parts are sourced locally from Sino–foreign JVs or Chinese state-owned companies. Display material is only partly purchased locally (maximum 30 per cent). The majority of display boxes are shipped to Shanghai from Germany by sea. Lead time, including customs clearance, is approximately three months. For this material, large stocks have to be kept in the warehouse in Shanghai.

The following figures relate to a sub-type of the *Plug-In* shaver. Plastic components account for more than 7 per cent, electronic components for almost 27 per cent, and display materials for over 5 per cent of the total material costs.[23] Local sourcing of these items would certainly reduce overall costs by a considerable amount. Resistors, capacitors, power cord coiled, plastic and display material, therefore, are to be purchased locally. The remaining material costs may be attributed to parts, such as shaver foils and liquids for printing processes.

The implementation of just-in-time operations with parts and materials could be supported by local sourcing. The current warehouse policy of keeping a security stock of parts and materials would not be necessary any longer. However, the purchasing manager also recognizes that local sourcing would not be possible with key parts. The headquarters in Kronberg has very high investment in new technology development and testing, and produces precision parts for supply to other Braun plants world-wide. Local sourcing of these parts seems very unlikely. They would still have to be imported from Germany.

### Decrease in Direct Product Costs

For the components purchased overseas, BES has to pay import duties. Using the example of a sub-type of the *Pocket* shaver, the share of import duties in total direct costs of the product is 27.9 per cent. The average rate of import duties of this product type is 57.4 per cent. However, it has to be noted that BES has to pay import duties for only 30 per cent of the goods imported, since the company exports as much as 70 per cent of its local production.

In addition to import duties, the purchasing manager believes that parts purchased overseas are more expensive than locally sourced components. Thus, local sourcing could reduce the direct costs of the products manufactured in China, since parts and materials would be cheaper, transportation costs would decrease and import duties would be avoided. An analysis of a selected number of product types underlines this.[24] The number of imported items ranged from 29 to 96 parts per product type, with the share of import duties in the total standard costs ranging from 25.4 to 31.2 per cent. From a cost perspective, pursuing a strategy of local sourcing would undoubtedly pay off, since the direct material costs of the shaver products manufactured at BES account for more than three quarters of the total direct costs.

### Improved Delivery Service

It is in the nature of transportation that materials and goods sometimes get damaged and quality standards are not met satisfactorily. In such cases, there may be considerable benefits if the supplier of materials is near the location of manufacture. Currently, for its export and import handling, BES co-operates with Braun AG's German forwarding companies, major operators in the global forwarding business. 'We are only a small customer for them,' suggests the materials manager who is not totally satisfied with the service BES gets from the international forwarder. Thus, recently he accepted a meeting with a smaller western forwarding company based in China, Triple X,[25] and asked them to provide a price quotation. If this small forwarder can meet the price expectations of BES, the materials manager will seriously consider the company's offer, since he believes that the smaller company would provide a better service, supported by personal communication and relationships. However, since Triple X is only a small forwarding company, it might have difficulties in ordering freight capacity for urgent deliveries at times when available freight capacity is a scarce resource.

Local sourcing can increase the efficiency of delivery and customer service. In addition, large global suppliers of materials and parts often do not appreciate the needs of their customers. Local suppliers, sometimes often serving the needs of their local client solely, can develop a closer, more personal relationship with their customer.

### Easier Communication

BES sources its parts from Germany from the company's headquarters. The headquarters, in turn, sources its parts from suppliers in Germany (and possibly on a world-wide basis). Thus, the sourcing of BES is indirect. This provides potential for hampering the efficiency of communication between final user and producer of parts and materials. Also, if BES has need to complain about certain component deliveries, this can only take place through the medium of Braun AG, Germany.

Local sourcing thus provides an opportunity for direct sourcing. Communication between the Chinese purchasing manager of the manufacturer and the engineer at the supplier can take place efficiently on a direct basis. Additionally, language barriers do not exist thus reducing the potential for misunderstandings.

### Foreign Exchange Savings

An issue that was not of primary interest to the purchasing manager, but would be to the finance department, is that local sourcing helps save foreign exchange. This is particularly important for BES, since the company wants to increase its sales to the domestic Chinese market from 30 per cent to about 48 per cent. This will be difficult as long as a balance has to be achieved on its foreign exchange transactions.

### BES AND LOCAL SOURCING PROBLEMS

BES has encountered two main problems in its attempts to increase its local sourcing of parts and components:

- poor quality of components; and
- delays in the delivery of components.

*Quality*

Braun sets very high quality standards and its products have a well-deserved reputation for quality.[26] The company is convinced that a truly superior product fully meeting customer expectations can be created only through high standards of quality. Thus, the company invests in a comprehensive total quality system (TQS) of testing and monitoring – from R&D, through production, all the way to customer service.[27] In order to guarantee consistent quality, the products are subjected to numerous tests and inspections at every stage of production, ranging from simple visual and measurement checks, to complex functional tests involving computer analysis as well as simulated application testing.[28]

Every local supplier of BES must meet certain quality requirements. However, both the materials manager and the purchasing manager of BES report that the local Chinese supplies frequently do not meet these high quality requirements of the company. Apparently, two different concepts of quality exist and restrict the local sourcing efforts of BES.

For its electric shaver products, BES uses a display box. The display box has a different form for each type but basically all are rectangular, show the product and its main features, and exhibit the company logo, the product name and a short product description. All display boxes are printed in four colours. The company once tried to purchase the display box locally from a state-owned company based in Shanghai. However, this company could not maintain the quality of the product on a permanent basis. 'One lot was OK, the next was not,' says the materials manager. However, the overseas markets would not accept a low standard of display boxes. As the materials manager puts it: 'Good products must be in a good package'. Chinese customers on the other hand accept the lower quality of the locally-sourced display material, relative to the German display product, paying more attention to product features like price. For all shaver products destined for overseas markets (70 per cent of total output of Braun's Shanghai plant), therefore, the display box is sourced in Germany and shipped to China. Only for the remaining 30 per cent of the products distributed in the Chinese market are locally sourced display boxes sometimes used[29] – if the lot is acceptable.

Components and materials purchased locally from a Chinese supplier (or a Sino–foreign joint venture) are rigorously tested before being approved for manufacturing. The successful sourcing of local parts and materials is not easy for the company. The use of certain locally sourced parts is subject to a range of different steps:

1. If the purchasing manager is successful in finding a potential local supplier of parts or material, a sample of the component is sent to Braun's R&D Department at its headquarters in Germany. R&D carefully investigate the component's specification and test whether the part meets the quality requirements of Braun.

2. If R&D give approval for the locally purchased part for potential use in the production line, the purchasing manager will send at least one small lot (2,000–5,000) of the components to Germany. There, it will be used for production and if it meets the quality required, manufacturing will provide a second approval.

3. If the purchasing manager of BES gets both approvals, from R&D and from the manufacturing departments of Braun AG in Germany, he can start to source the component locally.

Furthermore, BES operates a rigorous Quality Assurance (QA) system for its materials sourcing. All parts used in the assembly process of the shavers are tested for their quality. Apart from the components produced at BES (such as moulding parts), this applies also, and in particular, to components purchased locally and from other markets outside of Braun AG, Germany.

For its products, BES purchases the motor and rechargeable cells from suppliers in Japan. From every lot (2,000 – 3,000 pieces), the Quality Assurance department checks 50 parts randomly, testing the number of rounds per minute (rpm) and the electric current (ampere) for each of the selected items. 'Until now, we did not find bad parts,' remarks the QA manager of BES. In-house quality assurance also covers resistors, capacitors, transistors and diodes, purchased locally in Shanghai. Rechargeable cells, used for *Plug-In* and *Entry* type shavers are sent for testing to Braun AG in Germany. The Quality Assurance department of BES also tests incoming mechanical parts which are, or are to be, purchased in China or other overseas markets apart from Germany. Currently, QA also tests display and packaging material, assessing dimensions such as size, material, surface and colour. Figure 1 presents the quality assurance procedure within the local sourcing process of Braun Electric (Shanghai) Co. Ltd.

*Delayed Delivery*

Local sourcing can improve the efficiency of delivery and customer service. In practice, the reliability of deliveries to BES has been inadequate. According to the managing director, local Chinese suppliers lack the necessary discipline to deliver on time, with the worst offenders being the State-Owned Enterprises (SOEs). Mu (1995) notes that the SOEs operate in accordance with a comprehensive State Plan, and that supervising government agencies dictate every detail of their operations, such as the range of products, the quantity and quality, and the prices of raw materials and products. The managers have no say and their primary duty is not to make a direct profit, but to ensure maximum growth. Thus, the managing director of BES demands that Chinese suppliers have to be educated in terms of delivery discipline as well as quality. However, parts purchased from Frankfurt are often delayed also. This makes precise planning difficult.

FIGURE 1

THE QA PROCEDURE WITHIN THE LOCAL SOURCING PROCESS OF BES

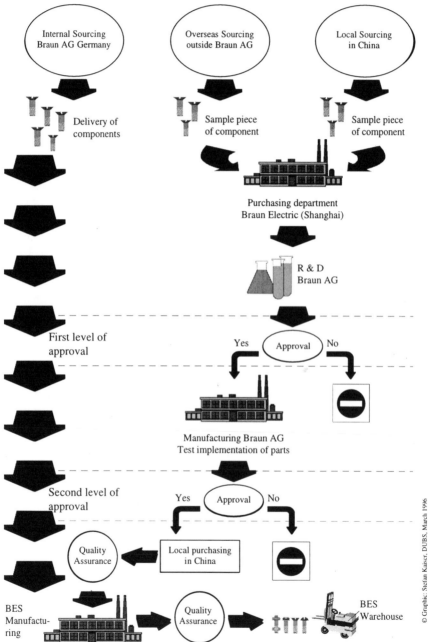

*Summary*

The interviews held with the purchasing manager of BES show clearly that the company is confronted mainly, and to a great extent, with poor quality standards of local Chinese suppliers. This complaint is voiced also by the materials manager of BES. Further, as the interview with the managing director of BES revealed, the company also faces the problem of unreliable deliveries. However, the other problems of local sourcing in China, as suggested in the literature, are not experienced by BES. On the contrary, the purchasing manager of BES hopes, through the extended use of local suppliers, to be able to improve the delivery service. He stresses the sometimes weak delivery service when purchasing from overseas and, implicitly, emphasizes that he is satisfied with the delivery service of Chinese local suppliers. With regard to the limited availability of components from local suppliers, the purchasing manager argues that BES is not at all confronted with this kind of problem. 'Sometimes it is difficult to get small quantities,' he suggests. This was also found in an earlier interview, carried out with the production manager of a major Sino–German JV company near Shanghai, KMP.[30] Schuchardt (1994) stresses the importance of personal relationships with officials in order to get raw materials and components of sufficient quality and quantity. Both the purchasing manager and the material manager of BES lack these, but do not have problems of this kind.

## BES AND LOCAL SOURCING STRATEGIES

In order to overcome the problems associated with local sourcing, BES has adopted a variety of strategies to improve the quality/reliability of components and materials purchased in China and to identify possible alternative sources of supply. These strategies are discussed below under the following five headings:

- mental and personal directories
- active consumption of information
- exhibitions
- component quality development
- supplier development.

*Mental and Personal Directories*

Usually, purchasing staff of manufacturers consult directories and catalogues when seeking component suppliers. BES's purchasing manager suggests that these kinds of directories are available in Taiwan, for instance, but not in the PRC. 'Maybe in the future', he believes. To date, only 'mental' directories exist in the heads of experienced purchasers. Although Shanghai does have Yellow Pages, 'Shanghai is only one part of China,' says an industry observer. 'There might be a very good supplier somewhere in the northwest of China, but how can we know this?' The purchasing manager of BES has been working in the electronic component sourcing business for ten years. He brought an extended mental data base and a variety of personal contacts to BES and is able to draw upon his experience in this field.

Rechargeable cells for the *Plug-In* and *Pocket* shavers are currently sourced in Japan. Import duties for the battery are set at 24 per cent and contribute significantly to the direct cost balance of the product. Using the example of a sub-type of the *Plug-In* shaver, import duties for the rechargeable cell account for 1.9 per cent of the direct costs. In his search for a potential local supplier of batteries, the purchasing manager recently contacted a producer of batteries and asked for a sample and quotation. The sample is already in Germany for testing. If the component gets approval from Germany, the local purchase of the batteries could decrease the direct costs of the product by an average of two per cent. The strategy derived from this case could be to engage only experienced local purchasers who have worked in the area (industry and function) for a considerable time.

*Active Consumption of Information*

Good management and decision-making needs a considerable input of information. Word-of-mouth communication and consumption of information from the printed media is still one of the most efficient and effective sources of relevant information. The purchasing manager of BES came across an advertisement in a local newspaper of MFG Co.,[31] a printing company from Hong Kong, in which they announced their wish to recruit people for their US$10m Shanghai plant to be opened in October 1996. Inspired by the idea that where people are needed for production there will also be products for sale, he approached the company and invited its sales staff to BES. MFG Co. Ltd has 30 years printing experience, and since 1993, they have been focusing increasingly on the Chinese market and pursuing an aggressive business development strategy. MFG is particularly aiming at the needs of many multinational companies moving into this huge and promising market.

After inspecting the display material which the purchasing manager would like to source locally in China, the assistant business development manager of MFG for the Asia Pacific Region was confident that he would be able to meet BES's high expectations. Apart from sophisticated printing technology, MFG sources its raw materials in Europe (Sweden, Finland, England) and USA where, especially in Europe, they can get the finest paper. From Korea and Taiwan, MFG sources its recycled paper. Chinese paper is not used by the printing company at all since the quality is too poor. The company would provide a quotation and, if BES was impressed by the price, further negotiations would take place. Price satisfaction, however, would be difficult to reach, since MFG tries to persuade with product quality and not a low price, and the materials manager of BES expects comparable quality with the deliveries from Germany, but for less money.

The case shows clearly that active acquisition of information can be supportive in finding potential suppliers of components and thus enhance the local sourcing of the company. Apart from general newspapers, specific commercial and engineering magazines could be scanned for acquisition of further information.

### Exhibitions

Every year, a variety of fairs and exhibitions take place all over China, with the biggest and most important being in Shanghai, Beijing, Guangzhou and Shenzhen. Some of these exhibitions are very specific and only relevant and interesting for a certain group of people.

For certain tools in its production lines, BES uses and needs a variety of springs which have to be replaced from time to time. Currently, springs are imported from Germany, but they are much more expensive than they would be if purchased locally. Recently the purchasing manager has attended an exhibition in Shanghai, actively seeking potential suppliers for particular components and spare parts for manufacture. At the exhibition, the purchasing manager approached several potential suppliers. Shortly after this, he was asked for a meeting by one of the exhibiting suppliers. Although BES currently has no need for Chinese springs, the purchasing manager asked the supplier (an SOE) representative to provide a quotation and so extended his base of information should the need arise in the future.

The strategy derived from this example could be the need to seek continuously for information about potential suppliers. Attendance at exhibitions not only in the location of production, but also on a national basis, is thus recommended. Actively presenting at an exhibition is another strategy. Suppliers are also in search of potential customers and will actively approach a manufacturer and offer their products and services.

### Component Quality Development

Components purchased locally in China often lack the quality required by the manufacturer. BES's materials manager confirms this. 'Sometimes Chinese local suppliers do not have the appropriate equipment.' Sometimes the poor quality is based on a simpler reason (from the western perspective), namely different concepts of quality of the foreign manufacturer and the local supplier of components. To date, BES has no formal collaboration with a local Chinese supplier. However, collaboration on an informal, more encouraging level exists. When material supplies, for instance, are not good enough they will be rejected and the supplier is told the reasons in detail. This process is iterative, meaning that BES gives the supplier more than just one attempt to satisfy its requirements and improve the quality of the component. However, the materials manager of BES can see the potential benefits and also possibilities of future, closer collaboration with a supplier. 'We have to grow with our supplier,' he urges. Pursuing this 'win–win strategy' generates, he believes, profits for both partners in the collaboration.

For its rechargeable Plug-In and Entry shavers,[32] BES needs seven different types of printed circuit boards (PCB), one for each shaver. The different versions of PCBs have varying recharge durations. The PCBs are completed in BES's PCB workshop by fixing, that is welding, a minimum of approximately 25 and a maximum of 100 electric components on the printed circuit board. All PCBs are sourced from Malaysia. 'Once,' the materials manager says, 'Braun had problems with the quality of the PCBs and, thus, sent an expert to Malaysia to help improve the quality. We have to educate them how to improve their system of manufacturing and quality.' Sending experts to the supplier's production sites is common if it can help improve the quality and also the manufacturing process.

*Supplier Development*

Local Chinese suppliers frequently do not meet the quality requirements of foreign manufacturers producing in the PRC. Thus, frequently, manufacturers seek sourcing of certain components from foreign suppliers with production facilities in China. These foreign component suppliers are able to provide parts and materials that meet the quality requirements the manufacturer is used to from its production base in the home country.

As outlined earlier, for its electric shaver products, BES uses a display box. The company once tried to purchase the display box locally from an SOE based in Shanghai. However, this company could not maintain the quality of the product on a permanent basis, as required by the overseas markets and increasingly also by the Chinese market. With the increasing sophistication of the Chinese consumer, the poor quality Chinese display box may not even be sufficient any longer. Thus, the materials manager at BES believes that the Chinese product packaging material market holds considerable potential for investing foreign companies. He refers to the recent efforts of a western packaging material manufacturer inquiring about the possibility of setting up a production facility in China, and approaching BES to identify potential customers and forecast potential material or parts needs.

This should be shown by using another example: BES uses roughly 75 different electronic components for its shavers, including resistors, diodes, and capacitors. Currently, the company uses three different products of GP,[33] two standard rectifiers and a single phase bridge rectifier. To date, these rectifiers have been purchased through Braun AG in Germany and shipped to Shanghai. Recently, BES has considered the possibility of purchasing these three types of rectifiers in China directly. Thus, the company has encouraged GLM Ltd[34] to provide a quotation for the above semiconductors. Since April 1995, GLM has been the exclusive sales representative of GP's power semiconductor division for Hong Kong and China with an office in Hong Kong. Since May 1995, GLM Ltd. has also had an office in Shanghai. The application engineer of GLM Ltd. suggested that his company could supply BES with rectifiers produced by the Taiwan-based GP subsidiary GPT.[35] Later (at the end of 1996), GLM Ltd will produce its own rectifiers in Tianjin, in a factory which was established in October 1995.

Although the potential local sourcing of rectifiers, first through GLM Ltd from GPT in Taiwan, and later directly from GLM's Tianjin plant, would reduce transportation and import duties and increase the ability of just-in-time manufacture, several questions arise, namely:

- Can the rectifiers produced by GPT Taiwan and subsequently by GLM in Tianjin meet the quality standard of the rectifiers currently purchased by Braun AG in Germany?
- Will the subsequent decrease in purchasing orders placed by Braun AG with GP in Germany affect the fixed price conditions Braun AG is currently receiving from GP? The purchasing manager believes that, due to the fact that BES only acquires small quantities, the price conditions of Braun AG Germany will not be affected. This, however, raises the question of whether the quantities ordered by BES are large enough to get good price conditions from GLM Ltd. The materials manager of BES suggests that, in cases like this, global contracts should be signed, involving all production sites and the headquarters of the customer company. Then, the material or parts could be purchased from any subsidiary of the supplier on a world-wide basis.
- Moreover, too small order quantities are frequently a problem with local sourcing, especially if the product has specifications or characteristics for one particular customer (especially developed plastic materials). In such cases, the quantities have to have a certain lower limit. However, this often means that customers purchase materials needed for a whole production year, for instance. As will be appreciated, this increases the costs of warehousing and requires careful consideration of local sourcing.

As noted above, raw plastic material accounts for 7.3 per cent of the total material costs of one sub-type of the *Plug-In* shaver. This plastic material is currently sourced from the American Three Y's[36] plants in Japan and Hong Kong, and from other international chemical manufacturers with warehouses in Hong Kong. Recently, a major American chemical company, one of BES's current suppliers, is said to be setting up a production joint venture in Shanghai. This implies that, in the future, the raw plastic material could be purchased locally, bypassing long shipment and customs procedures. Another of BES's current plastic suppliers is also said to be setting up a production venture in Guangzhou. BES could then purchase directly from China. 'If the quality requirements are met,' remarks the purchasing manager, while the materials manager does not doubt the quality standard of those producers setting up ventures in China. 'They have certain quality standards and will control quality in every plant,' he says. A problem, however could be that 'they do not produce in the plant in China what we need.'

These examples show that it is increasingly necessary for the suppliers of components to follow their customers. Otherwise they could lose their present customers (at least its foreign production facility) to competitors. By setting up business in China, GP, for instance, tries to avoid this.

## DISCUSSION

In the previous section, a number of strategies were identified that BES has adopted in an effort to improve the quality and delivery of its locally-sourced components and materials. Other companies too have used similar strategies, and it is wise to consider the limitations of these strategies.

It was suggested first that it might be advantageous to recruit only experienced local purchasing managers who have worked in the area (industry and function) for a considerable time, and who have thus built up extensive mental and personal directories. Finding a skilled and experienced purchaser, however, is costly. Almost invariably, head-hunters have to be involved and the personnel recruitment companies charge the equivalent of between one month's salary plus 20 per cent service charge, up to the equivalent of one year's salary of the hired person.[37] According to a recent survey among German foreign direct investors in Shanghai (Delegation of German Industry and Commerce, 1996), the monthly salary for a materials manager[38] is between 830 and 9,081 RMB.[39]

The strategy also has other drawbacks. Employing purchasing managers who have been working in the function *and* in the industry for a certain time has potential dangers. As an industry observer expressed, 'they have established their pool of suppliers with whom they are friends and then try to purchase as much as possible from them, regardless of whether better quality and price are available elsewhere.' Employing purchasing managers with long-time relationships with actual or potential suppliers involves an additional danger in the case of low-quality deliveries and non-acceptance through the foreign company. The Chinese manager might feel that his good, long-time relationship with the supplier is endangered if he has to insist on the high-quality requirements of 'the foreigner' and possibly make the supplier lose face. Thus, it is suggested that employers should engage experienced purchasers 'who know their business', but who have not worked in the same industry previously.

In order to improve the quality of its printed circuit boards (PCBs), Braun AG once sent an expert to Malaysia to help improve the quality of the component. Schuchardt (1994) also found that component quality development as a strategy of local sourcing was undertaken by several Sino-German JVs. These JVs dispatched German experts to the supplier for training and the transfer of know-how. Pursuing such a 'win–win strategy' was suggested as the best solution by the materials manager of BES in order to improve quality. This is supported by a recent McKinsey study where it is proposed, in detail, that 'often, though, close co-operation with a good supplier turns out better than going it alone' (Brück, 1995).

According to Trommsdorff *et al.* (1994), however, the direct training of local suppliers is, due to its high time consumption, frequently only possible in a very limited way. In order to reduce deficits on a long-term basis, Trommsdorff *et al.* suggest the strategy of supplier development and argue that the integration of technology-oriented JVs in the supply sector has the following advantages:

• technology and know-how for production of the required quality is available,
• products of those JVs can be purchased on the open market, and
• other foreign ventures purchasing from those JVs can meet their local content requirement.

Brück (1995) explicitly argues that the approach of global sourcing and, thus, local sourcing in, for instance, China, can only be successful if manufacturers provide funds and management resources to bring development and production know-how up to western standards, or if they can induce their traditional western suppliers to provide such 'development aid' through JVs or long-term purchasing guarantees. In late 1993, for instance, BMW, the German car manufacturer, initiated the joint support of the establishment of an automotive components industry in collaboration with two other German automotive companies, Volkswagen-Audi and Mercedes-Benz (Kaiser, 1995).

Another example is the case of Technoplast GmbH, a medium-sized enterprise based in Germany. This company, operating in the plastics-processing industry, joined its main customer, Siemens AG, in Malacca, Malaysia, when the multinational company shifted its manufacture of semiconductors there from Regensburg, Germany. In July 1992, Technoplast founded Deutsche Technoplast (M) Sdn. Bhd. to manufacture components for Siemens Malacca – and possibly for Siemens sister companies in Penang and Singapore, since Siemens Components (Advanced Technology) Sdn. Bhd. could not find a qualified supplier.[40] Supplier development through the initiation of supply JVs or co-operation with German and Chinese suppliers was also found by Schuchardt (1994) in several cases.

BES has encouraged a company in the product packaging material industry to consider the possibility of investing and producing in the country. GP's decision to produce rectifiers in a plant in Tianjin and then provide BES with parts produced in China is just another example of supplier development. However, if a company decides to develop a supplier (such as a Sino–foreign JV) it should concentrate, in order to reduce factor costs, on one supplier for a certain family of parts. Brück (1995) found that the successful companies in his study in over 50 per cent of cases buy parts of a similar type from a sole supplier.

## CONCLUSIONS

The case of Braun Electric (Shanghai) Co. Ltd clearly documents the variety of problems faced by multinational companies manufacturing in China. Whereas the purchasing manager, the materials manager and the managing director of BES have all suggested that BES is confronted with problems such as poor quality and unreliable deliveries of components, the company is not troubled by poor delivery service of local suppliers and unmet quantity requirements, as frequently suggested in the literature.

The case has also shown the importance of local purchasing. This enables the company to produce on a just-in-time delivery basis, to decrease direct product costs, to improve delivery service, to ease communication between supplier and manufacturer, and to save foreign exchange. Finally the case has suggested a variety of potential strategies to achieve the advantages of sourcing locally as much as possible. Strategies such as keeping (employing) mental and personal directories, active consumption of information, attendance at exhibitions, and component quality and supplier development have all been highlighted.

Western multinational companies with manufacturing bases in China can, as the case of Braun Electric (Shanghai) Co. Ltd. has shown, increasingly source their components locally. Chinese suppliers, in co-operation with their western customers, will gradually improve the quality of their products and delivery reliability. Equally, the number of western suppliers following their clients to their production sites will increase dramatically. All these trends will ease the ability of manufacturers to source locally. Western multinationals manufacturing in China will be able increasingly to reduce their production costs and increase flexibility in planning and manufacturing, essential if they are to adjust production to the varying demands of the international market.

## ACKNOWLEDGEMENTS

The writing of this case study would not have been possible without the kind support of various people. Many thanks to Alfred Kunz, managing director of Braun Electric (Shanghai) Co. Ltd, who opened all doors to key information, and who enabled me to ask thousands of questions, study helpful documents and observe the operations and transactions in and around the company. Thanks also to Dennis Yu, materials manager, who introduced me to key informants in planning, material purchasing, exporting, importing and local transportation. Thanks to Mr Scott Lu (Planning), Ms Jane Wang (Import), Ms Sharon Sha (Local Transport), Mr Frank Yang (Export) and Mr Bob Bei (Purchasing) for giving me the chance to attend meetings with current and potential local suppliers. Henry Chen (engineering), Roy Lin (manufacturing) and Mike Weber (moulding) were also extremely helpful. Finally, thanks to David Kirby, Mike Jones and Roger Strange for commenting on earlier versions.

## NOTES

1. For a review of key studies about investment in China see S. Kaiser, D.A. Kirby and Y. Fan, 'Foreign Direct Investment in China', *Asia Pacific Business Review*, Vol.2, No.3 (1996), pp.44–65.
2. The Regulations were promulgated by the State Council on 20 September 1983 and amended by the State Council on 15 January 1986.
3. (1) Those under planned distribution shall be brought into the supply plan of departments in charge of joint ventures and supplied by materials and commercial departments or production enterprises according to contract. (2) Those handled by materials and commercial departments shall be purchased from these departments. (3) Those freely circulating on the market shall be purchased from production enterprises or their sale or commission agencies.

(4) Those export items handled by foreign trade corporations shall be purchased from the appropriate foreign trade corporations.

4. The Equity Joint Venture Law was adopted on 1 July 1979 at the Second Session of the Fifth National People's Congress. It was revised in accordance with the decision of the National People's Congress regarding the revision of the 'Law of the People's Republic of China on Joint Ventures Using Chinese and Foreign Investment' adopted at the Third Session of the Seventh National People's Congress on 4 April 1990.

5. The Contractual Joint Venture Law was adopted on 13 April 1988 at the First Session of the Seventh National People's Congress.

6. The Wholly Foreign-Owned Enterprise Law was adopted on 12 April 1986, at the Fourth Session of the Sixth National People's Congress.

7. If, with the approval of the competent authorities, the enterprise markets its production in China and consequently experiences an imbalance in foreign exchange, the said authorities shall be responsible for helping it to eliminate the imbalance.

8. Braun, *Braun Products 1993/94: Reliability, Quality and Good Design* (Kronberg: 1993), p.2.

9. Braun, *Braun Aspekte*, June (Kronberg: 1995).

10. Braun, *Facts on Braun* (Kronberg: 1991).

11. Braun, *Braun Aspekte*.

12. Braun, *Facts on Braun*.

13. According to a Braun publication of 1991 (*Facts on Braun*) which sets the contribution of electric shavers to total sales at 48 per cent, the importance of the shaver business for Braun's corporate success has been declining.

14. Braun, *Braun Aspekte*.

15. Braun, *Facts on Braun*.

16. Braun, *Braun Products*, pp.5–8.

17. Braun, *Braun Aspekte*.

18. These Rules were approved by the State Council of the People's Republic of China on 28 October 1990 and promulgated by the Ministry of Foreign Economic Relations and Trade (MOFERT) on 12 December 1990.

19. Some special plastic parts are shipped over from Braun AG, Germany.

20. Braun, *Braun Aspekte*.

21. Although re-generated PC can be used to produce these parts, the robustness of the plastic cannot be guaranteed.

22. Braun uses mercury-, lead- and cadmium-free cells in all its rechargeable shavers.

23. The calculation is based on current costs; material and components priced in Japanese Yen (¥) are excluded from total material costs.

24. Based on a convenience sample of eight types, including subtypes, which were available to the author for study from BES's engineering department.

25. Name changed.

26. Braun, *Braun Products*, p.2.

27. Braun, *Braun Aspekte*.

28. Braun, *Facts on Braun*, p.34.

29. The remaining packaging material, such as the transport box and the shipping box, as well as instructions for all shaver products manufactured in Shanghai are sourced locally.

30. Name changed.

31. Name changed.

32. Type *Pocket* is a battery shaver and thus needs no PCB.

33. Name changed.

34. Name changed.

35. Name changed.

36. Name changed.

37. This was experienced by the personnel manager of BES enquiring about the possibility of involving a head-hunter when recruiting certain staff.

38. The survey report does not have a category for purchasing manager.

39. Or the equivalent of approximately £70–750.

40. Handelsblatt, *Mittelständler folgen Konzernen*, 14 June (1995), p.18.

## REFERENCES

Braun (1991), *Facts on Braun,* Kronberg.

Braun (1993), *Braun products 1993/94 – Reliability, Quality and Good Design,* Kronberg.

Braun (1995), *Braun Aspekte,* June, BM-C, Kronberg.

Brück, F. (1995), 'Make Versus Buy: the Wrong Decision Cost', *McKinsey Quarterly,* No.1, pp.28–47.

Campbell, N. (1989), *A Strategic Guide to Equity Joint Ventures in China.* Oxford.

Chu, B. and W. Dong (1987), *A Complete Guide to Foreign Direct Investment in China.* Beijing and Los Angeles.

Cohen, J.A. (1988), 'The Long-Awaited Cooperative Venture Law', *China Business Review,* Vol.15, No.4, pp.14–18.

Delegation of German Industry and Commerce (1996), *Umfrage zur Personalpolitik in Produktionunternehmen mit deustcher Beteiligung in Raum Shanghai für ortliche chinesische Mitarbeiter 1995.* Shanghai.

Duscha, W. (1987), *Technologietransfer in die Volksrepublik China durch Wirtschaftskooperation.* Hamburg.

Handelsblatt (1995) 'Mittelständler folgen Konzernen', 14 June, p.18.

Kaiser, S. (1995), 'German Direct Investment in China'. Conference on China's Foreign Trade and Investment, University of Abertay Dundee, 20 April 1995.

Kaiser, S., D.A. Kirby and Y. Fan (1996), 'Foreign Direct Investment in China', *Asia Pacific Business Review,* Vol.2, No.3, pp.44–65.

Mu, Y. (1995), 'The Dinosaur' in D. Bloodworth (ed.), *The Risks and Rewards of Investing in China.* Singapore.

Schneider, D.J.G., R Scheuble and A. Stolz (1987), *Exportmarketing für die Volksrepublik China.* Aichwald.

Schuchardt, C.A. (1994) *Deutsch-chinesische Joint Ventures. Erfolg und Partnerbeziehung,* München: R. Oldenbourg Verlag GmbH.

Trommsdorff, V., B. Wilpert, K. Jakubowski, S.Y. Scharpf and C.A. Schuchardt (1994), *Deutsch–chinesische Joint Ventures: Wirtschaft, Recht, Kultur.* Wiesbaden.

# The Selection of Distribution Channels in China

CHOO SIN TSENG, PAULA KWAN
and FANNY CHEUNG

China is an important market for many foreign companies, and the western media have given the economic development of China a great deal of publicity.[1] It has a population of 1.2 billion,[2] and is the third-largest economy in the world.[3] Recently, the average real growth of Gross National Product has been more than 10 per cent a year. This rapid economic growth has created a relatively affluent urban population, eager and able to pay much more for quality products. In his report to the Fourteenth Congress of the Chinese Communist Party (CCP) in October 1992, the General Secretary, Mr. Jiang Zemin, proclaimed China's intention to open further to the outside world and to attract foreign investment in accordance with its national industrial policy. In the Third Plenary Session of the 14th Central Committee of the Communist Party of China, held in November 1993, the decision was made to establish a socialist market economic structure and to speed up the reform of the system of economic relations abroad. The determination and eagerness of China to join the international trade system is fully assured. Local authorities in cities and autonomous regions can trade with foreign companies under a system of contractual obligation and self-responsibility for profit and loss. These regional trading companies act as agents looking after importation procedures and documentation.

Many foreign companies have taken this opportunity to venture into China. According to UNCTAD (1994), China was the second-largest recipient of foreign direct investment (FDI) after the United States in 1993, with investments flowing into mainland China amounting to US$26 billion. China's total investment was only slightly behind the US, which totaled $32 billion, and the mainland was expected to overtake the USA as the largest recipient of FDI within the following few years. When companies enter a new market, marketing channel decisions are among the most critical decisions facing management. A company's chosen channel intimately affects all other marketing decisions (Kotler, 1994). Channel decision involves a relatively long-term commitment, as channel choices, once made, are difficult to change for reasons of high costs and other factors. Hence, channel choice has a large and lasting impact on the success of a firm's international operations (Anderson and Coughlan, 1987). Inferior channel choice makes the entrant vulnerable to new competition (Caves and Porter,

Choo Sin Tseng, Paula Kwan and Fanny Cheung, City University of Hong Kong

1977). All products need competent distribution, and this is all the more true in the ever-changing Chinese market.

This study considers the question of the selection of distribution channel in China, where the distribution system is gradually changing from an hierarchical three-tier structure to a more free-market structure. The western literature on channel choice is briefly discussed in the next section, as is the limited literature on channel choice in China. Various factors of particular importance in the context of China in the mid-1990s are highlighted. The reforms in both the wholesale and retail distribution systems are outlined. Two case studies – one of the photocopier manufacturer, Rank Xerox, and one of a beverage manufacturer – are presented to illustrate some of the considerations associated with the appropriate choice of channel. Finally, various recent initiatives by the Chinese government to open further the distribution sector are noted.

## REVIEW OF THE LITERATURE

Most of the literature on distribution channel choice has focused on the west. The two principal choices available to companies when marketing abroad are direct selling or indirect selling (Onkvist and Shaw, 1989: 503–4): a choice between selling by the company sales force and distribution divisions, or primarily by independent intermediaries. The former option constitutes an integrated channel, and the latter a non-integrated, or independent, channel (Anderson and Coughlan, 1987). To the manager, this is the 'make or buy' issue: the integrated system being the 'make' option, and the independent channel the 'buy' alternative (Robinson, 1978). The decision is difficult and relates to the trade-off between the need for coordination and control and the costs and risks associated with the various institutional arrangements to operate in foreign markets (Porter, 1990).

Research documenting the actual practices of managers making these difficult decisions indicates that the decision-making process is often non-systematic and based on little information. An important reason for this is that managers operating outside their familiar domestic settings have few guidelines (Robinson, 1978). In the international business literature, the choice between internal/integrated channels and external/non-integrated channels is a decision based on the relative merits of internalization versus externalization. The choice thus depends on five main factors: the relative costs of each form of operation; the importance of market intelligence; the perceived needs of the manufacturer to control operations; host market infrastructure; and the distinct competencies of the firm (Buckley, Pass, and Prescott, 1990).

The empirical research in this area has taken two directions. The first has involved the examination of one or two factors in isolation (such as Coughlan, 1985). The second has adopted a multivariate approach (for example. Gronhaug and Kvitastein, 1993), and related channel choice to variables such as the firm's resource base, and its management and product

TABLE 1

THE DETERMINANTS OF THE CHOICE OF DISTRIBUTION CHANNEL

| FACTORS | DECISION | | AUTHOR(s) |
|---|---|---|---|
| | Internal/<br>Integrated<br>channel | External/<br>Non-integrated<br>channel | |
| **Product-related** | | | |
| • Maturity of product | Less | More | Davidson, 1982 |
| • Service Intensity | High | Low | Etgar, 1978;<br>Terpstra, 1983;<br>Keegan, 1984. |
| • Differentiation | More | Less<br>1983. | McGuire & Staelin, |
| • Closeness to the firm's<br>core business | More | Less | Davidson, 1982;<br>Davidson & McFetridge, 1985. |
| • Novelty & complexity | High | Low | Nelson, 1970. |
| **Market-related** | | | |
| • Geographical distance | Less | More | Thorelli, 1980. |
| • Cultural differences | More | Less | Davidson, 1982;<br>Terpstra, 1983;<br>Keegan, 1984. |
| • Following competitor's<br>make strategy | Yes | Not | Calvet, 1981 |
| • Power of agents | Low | High | Williamson, 1979 |
| • Legal restrictions | Less | More | Robinson, 1978 |
| **Company-related** | | | |
| • Experience with foreign<br>market | More | Less | Cavusgil & Nevin, 1981 |
| • Importance of brand<br>knowledge of salesman | More | Less | Anderson, 1985 |
| • Trade confidentiality | High | Low | Davidson, 1982;<br>Root, 1982;<br>Anderson, 1985. |
| • Existence of foreign<br>channel structure | Yes | No | Coughlan & Flaherty, 1983;<br>Davidson & McFetridge, 1985 |
| • Resources availability | High | Low<br><br><br>1988 | Porter, 1980;<br>Cavusgil & Nevin, 1981;<br>Bradley, 1987; 1991;<br>Jeannet & Hennesey, |
| • Risk taking willingness | High | Low | Ahmed, 1977;<br>Porter, 1990. |

offerings. Anderson and Coughlan (1987) modeled the impact of a number of factors on channel choice, and stated that researchers should avoid ignoring or holding constant a broad variety of influences on channel design. Table 1 categorizes the important factors for the channel-form decision identified in the literature into three categories: product-related, market-related and company-related.[4]

Most western theories were not readily applicable in China during the pre-reform period, because internalization of distribution channels was strictly prohibited. A review of the more recent, but still limited, literature on distribution channels in China shows that the majority of studies have focused on the retailing element instead of the distribution system. For example, Mun (1988) studied Chinese retailing in a changing environment, and Ho and Leigh (1994) reported on the retail revolution in China since the 1980s. Tseng *et al.* (1994) studied the centralized Chinese distribution system of consumer goods before the economic reform, considered the changes, and speculated about future trends in retailing. In a further study, Tseng *et al.* (1995) addressed the distribution problems and practices in China. Some primary work has also been done by Luk (1996) and by Yip (1995).

It is a truism to say that modification of their distribution strategies to meet different sets of circumstances is vital to the success of firms operating in a foreign environment (Luk, 1995). So what factors are of particular importance in the context of China in the mid-1990s? Although the restrictions on foreign investors have been gradually eased as China has moved from a centrally-planned economy to a market economy, the operation of distribution channels is still rather restricted in some industries (such as sugar and cigarettes). Moreover, regional protectionism is still prominent in some cities, and this will also hinder the internalization of distribution channels.

The nature of the product will also affect the choice of the distribution channel. For products that need frequent and extensive transportation or require large investment in transportation and warehousing facilities (such as beer or other drinks), companies may initially externalize the distribution function and then later internalize the operation by purchasing a fleet of trucks when the sales volume warrants it. Benefits derived from internalizing the distribution channel would include better collection of market information, and the ability to implement a service-oriented approach (as in door to door delivery) with a local presence. The poor infrastructure for transportation in China also favours the use of government agents, as the rail system is very unreliable, and priority is often given to goods that are still under tight government control (notably coal and agricultural products) or where producers need close connections with the relevant authorities.

Finally, the choice of an appropriate distributor is a vital factor for success. A joint venture in Shenzhen, involving a European electrical appliance manufacturer, appointed a collective distributor as its sole agent in Shanghai. As a result of this, the Shanghai Number One Department Store (the top wholesaler in Shanghai and distributor in China) felt insulted and refused to have any dealings with the collective distributor. The sales of the electrical appliances were greatly affected. The European manufacturer then had to make substantial efforts to mend the relationship with the Shanghai Number One Department Store, and eventually concluded a special arrangement whereby the store would take direct delivery from the manufacturer.

## THE STRUCTURE OF DISTRIBUTION IN CHINA

### The Pre-Reform Structure

Shortly after the founding of the People's Republic, several measures were introduced by the central authorities to discredit and abolish the practice of individual commerce in China. Private wholesalers were largely replaced by either state or collectively-owned wholesale agencies. In parallel with the above changes, private retailers were transformed into either joint state-private commercial units or cooperative groups (Tung, 1982). The trading and distribution of consumer goods was thus monopolized by the government. Before the commencement of the series of reforms in 1978, the Ministry of Commerce held overall responsibility for regulating the supply of consumer goods, while the supply of industrial goods was under the sole control of the Ministry of Materials and Equipment. Under the Ministries there existed specialized corporations divided along product lines to handle specific categories or groups of goods. For instance, the distribution of household electrical appliances was under the control of the Metals, Transport, Electrical and Chemical Companies, a corporation under the Ministry of Commerce.[5]

At the local level, the distribution system for consumer goods in, for instance, Shanghai was a three-tier structure,[6] comprising First Level Purchasing and Supply Enterprises (FLPSEs), Second Level Purchasing and Supply Enterprises (SLPSEs), and Third Level Wholesalers (TLWs). The FLPSEs were located in three cities only, namely Tianjin, Shanghai and Guangzhou. Reporting to the Ministry of Commerce in Beijing and to the local Commercial Bureaux, the FLPSEs both purchased domestic goods from all over China and accepted imported goods, and then distributed them to the second tier of the system, the SLPSEs. The SLPSEs operated at the provincial level; each reported to the Commercial Bureau of the province and also to the local government department in charge of commercial matters. They were normally located in the capital cities of the provinces, and were responsible for the purchase of goods from FLPSEs, and then for the distribution of these goods to the TLWs in the various cities and counties, which, in turn, re-distributed the products to local retailers that were normally state-owned enterprises. The supply and distribution of goods in rural areas was under the control of the Supply and Marketing Cooperatives.

Regional protectionism was an important characteristic of this system. The retailers were only allowed to buy from wholesalers within the dictated region; supplies from elsewhere were brought in only as a very last resort. Theories regarding the choice of integrated channels were of no relevance to foreign investors selling in China, as they had no alternative but to use

FIGURE 1

PRE-REFORM DISTRIBUTION CHANNELS IN CHINA

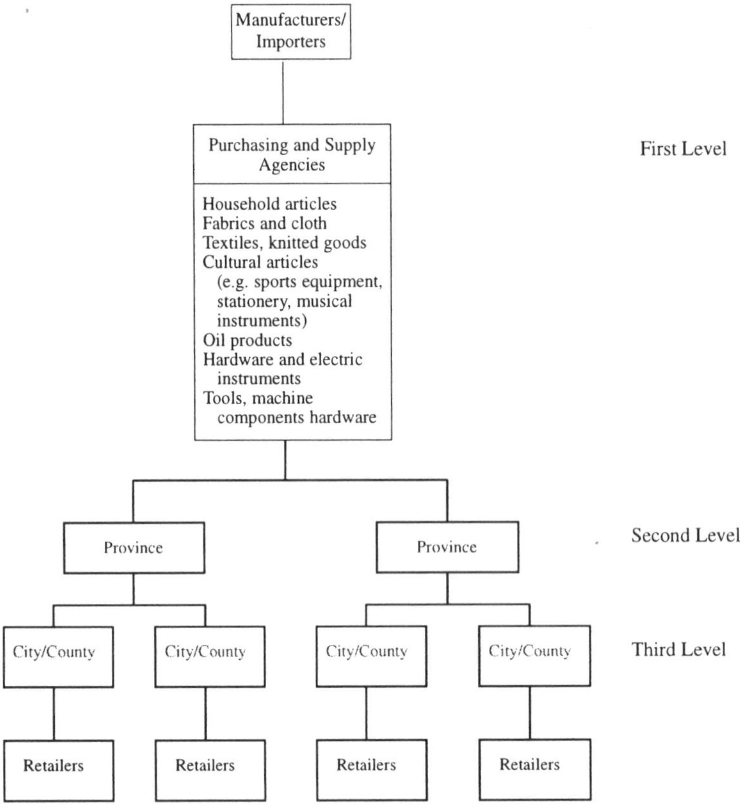

the 'external' channels in such a situation. Figure 1 shows the distribution structure before the reforms.

*Reforms to the Wholesale System*

Since 1979, China has gradually moved from a centrally-planned economy to a more market-oriented, decentralized economy. The establishment of the Special Economic Zones, the opening-up of the 14 coastal cities, and the preferential treatment given to foreign investors has resulted in a soaring number of foreign investments. Moreover, China has gradually loosened its controls over imports and foreign exchange paving the way for its re-admission to the World Trade Organization (WTO). All of these developments accelerated import trade, and increased the burden on the inherited distribution system until it could no longer cater to the market's needs in terms of both trade volume and commodity variety. Reform of the state distribution system started to take place with the state-owned monopolistic distribution system gradually breaking down. Now, instead of the distribution of goods being restricted to the three-tier system (central, provincial and county), private individuals, collectives, producers and other government units may buy and sell freely.[7] Even within the state commercial system, the distribution of certain types of goods is no longer restricted to the specialized corporations. For example, the distribution of television sets in Shanghai can be carried out by a corporation under the Bureau of Aquatic Products!

In February 1992, Deng Xiaoping's historic tour to Southern China reaffirmed the Government's intention to accelerate economic reform and opening-up to the outside world. The following June, the Central Committee of the China Communist Party and the State Council issued Document Number 5 which urged the faster development of tertiary industries and the service sector. Since then, foreign corporations have been permitted to set up joint venture department stores in the following eleven cities: Beijing, Shanghai, Tianjin, Dalian, Qingdao, Guangzhou, Shenzhen, Xiamen, Zhuhai, Shantou and Hainan. One of the objectives of the faster development of tertiary industries was to encourage state enterprises to set up service subsidiaries so that the excess staff and workers could be re-deployed. As a result, many newly-established tertiary industry organizations (TIOs) have entered the wholesale and distribution sector. Together with more and more collective and private players entering the industry, the distribution system in China is undergoing great changes. In a concomitant move to streamline the government structure, the Ministry of Materials and Equipment (in charge of the supply of raw materials and equipment to industrial organizations) and the Ministry of Commerce (in charge of the distribution of commodities to consumers) were combined to form the Ministry of Internal Trade in March 1993. Furthermore, in order to support the WTO application, a Ministry of Internal Trade official revealed in December 1993 that foreign investors would be given the green light to create wholesale businesses.[8] The present wholesale distribution system in China is shown in Figure 2.

The experiment of giving permission to foreign investors to set up joint venture department stores in 11 cities has speeded the development of the distribution system in these cities. In general, the reform has been faster in the south where private enterprises have played a major role, and slower in the north.[9] In Guangzhou, for instance, state enterprises play a diminishing role, but the traditional state commercial system still has great influence. Thus the state commercial system still accounts for 80 per cent of the market for the distribution of beer.[10] The roles played by the state-owned and private sectors vary across regions-cities and across products-industries. By way of an example, the present structure of the Guangzhou commercial system for the distribution of electrical appliances is shown in Figure 3.

FIGURE 2

THE PRESENT WHOLESALE DISTRIBUTION SYSTEM

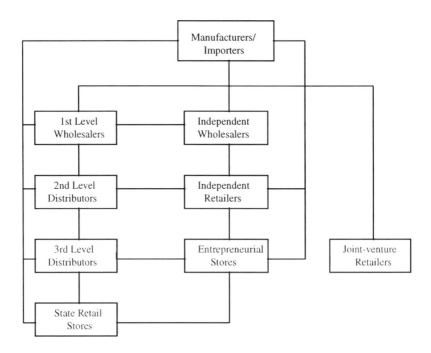

## Reforms to the Retail System

Three measures have been introduced to the retail system to accompany those in the wholesale system:

- Management reform in retail outlets. A contract responsibility system (*cheng bo zhi*) was implemented in many commercialized corporations. Staff may be rewarded according to their performance.
- Elimination of the fixed price policy. Retailers are allowed to vary the prices of most of the commodities within a certain range.
- Lifting of restrictions on retailing. Eleven cities have been opened for foreign investors to set up at most two joint venture retailers in each city on a trial basis. The joint ventures are allowed to sell a full range of merchandise, and enjoy import and export rights. They can import goods, limited to general merchandise, with value not exceeding 30 per cent of their annual total sales turnover, but they have to balance their foreign exchange needs. Department store projects under this scheme must be approved by the State Council.[11]

FIGURE 3

THE STRUCTURE OF THE COMMERCIAL SYSTEM FOR THE DISTRIBUTION
OF ELECTRICAL APPLIANCES IN GUANGZHOU

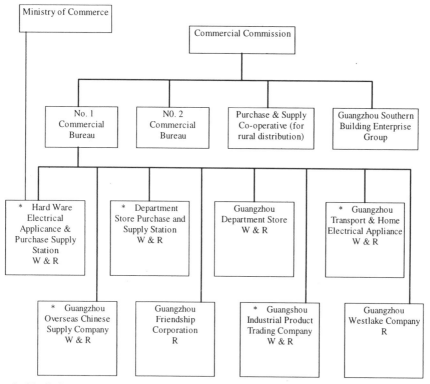

* Distribution network throughout China
W Wholesale
R Retail

*Source:* From relevant government officials

Under the scheme to encourage foreign investment, four department stores have been set up and are now in operation: the Beijing-Yansha Friendship Store; the Shanghai Oriental Department Store; the Shanghai First-Yaohan Department Store; and the Guangzhou Hualan Broadway Department Store. The development of joint venture retailers in China has been further accelerated by the flexible enforcement of the policies imposed on joint ventures. Often they are permitted to import more than the stipulated 30 per cent of turnover, as long as they can achieve their foreign exchange balance. Furthermore, local Foreign Trade Commissions can also approve retailing projects, without import and export rights, on a much smaller scale. For example, Yaohan Department Store – the Japanese retailing concern – set up a department store in Shenzhen with a local partner in 1991.[12] Yaohan made a total investment of US$1.25 million, and took 49 per cent of the shares in the venture – the first of its kind. Other subsequent examples of stores that have been approved by local Foreign Trade Commissions include the Sincere Department Store, the Shui Hing Department Store, the Carrefour Department Store, the Printemps Department Store and the Isetan Department Store in Shanghai, the Seibu Department Store in Shenzhen, and Park 'N' Shop in Shanghai and East China.

Table 2 shows the dramatic increase in retailing business under the reformed system up to the year 1992 as, from 1994 onwards, only figures on wholesale and retail trade combined are shown in the *Statistical Yearbook of China*. However, data from other sources reveal that the increases in subsequent years are even more substantial. According to Feng (1995), retail sales in 1994 and 1995 were Rmb1,600bn and Rmb1,900bn respectively. The figure for the first nine months of 1996 soared to Rmb1,732.7bn.[13]

TABLE 2

DEVELOPMENT OF THE RETAIL SECTOR IN CHINA

|  | 1978 | 1980 | 1985 | 1989 | 1990 | 1991 | 1992 |
|---|---|---|---|---|---|---|---|
| No. of retail outlets (000s) | 1,048 | 1,463 | 7,783 | 8,413 | 8,710 | 9,241 | 1,006 |
| Retail employment (million) | 4.47 | 6.37 | 17.96 | 20.33 | 20.91 | 21.98 | 24.34 |
| Total sales (Rmb billion) | 136.4 | 176.8 | 327.2 | 600.9 | 612.7 | 690.3 | 792.2 |

*Source*: *Statistical Yearbook of China 1993*, p.590 and p.613.

CASE STUDIES

Two case studies are presented below to illustrate how two different companies have resolved the issue of the selection of the most appropriate distribution channel for their products. The first case study is of the photocopier manufacturer, Rank Xerox, and of its efforts to establish a distribution network throughout China. The second case study concerns an anonymous beverage manufacturer intending to expand its business into the greater Shanghai area.

*Rank Xerox – Photocopier Manufacturer*

In 1987, Rank Xerox set up a manufacturing plant in the Minhang Economic Zone on the outskirts of Shanghai. Although the distribution system in Shanghai in 1987 was in transition, the influence of the three-tier system was still prevailing. The company decided to use the state distribution channels locally because the private distributors were not well developed. The distribution of photocopiers was under the control of the

Stationery and Sports Articles Company, which was a subsidiary of the Number One Commercial Bureau.

In other regions and cities, the company also had to choose between the state distribution system and collective-private distributors. In general, they found that state distributors possessed more working capital, but were more rigid and their staff less well motivated. In contrast, collective-private enterprises were found to be more flexible and their staff better motivated, but they were not so financially sound. In provinces and cities (such as Jiangsu, Zhejiang, Liaoning, Dalian) where private enterprises were comparatively not that well developed, the state distributor (the Stationery and Sports Articles Company) had to be used. But in both Shandong and Sichuan provinces, where the provincial governments were more open-minded, collective-private distributors were chosen.

Rank Xerox found it difficult breaking into the following three cities: Beijing, Hangzhou and Guangdong. In Beijing, the power of the appointed state distributor had been gradually eroded by private enterprises, and its sales had been affected. In Hangzhou, its rival Canon had set up a joint venture manufacturing plant and built up a strong local distribution network. Rank Xerox thus found it difficult to find a suitable and strong distributor for its products. In Guangdong, the sales of the company were heavily affected by the huge number of photocopiers smuggled across the border from Hong Kong. The unreliable transportation infrastructure in China also posed problems to the company. They found that their photocopiers were often accorded lower priority than goods that were still under tight government control, and that they also took second place behind producers with good connections with the relevant authorities. The company thus had to formulate contingency plans for the delivery of the products. If delivery fell behind schedule, Rank Xerox would transfer its products directly from Shanghai to nearby cities by its own fleet of trucks, and even had recourse to air freight for some urgent shipping.

## Beverage Manufacturer

The joint venture beverage manufacturer had a factory in Guangzhou, and had externalized its wholesale and distribution functions in Guangzhou by using a state enterprise under the commercial system. Following an increase in sales, the company decided to establish other distribution outlets elsewhere in Guangdong province. They accordingly carried out a detailed study in the course of which they identified four cities as potential candidates. The four cities were Foshan and Dongguan in the Pearl River Delta area, Shantou (East), and Zhanjiang, and one of the main criteria for selection was that local distributors should not be too influential. The company internalized their operations by establishing field warehouses in each location, and used their own trucks to deliver the product. The field warehouses also served as bottle collection and sorting centres (the return of good bottles to the factory via backhaul, and the sale of any remaining bottles to local beverage factories or collection centres). Among the other

FIGURE 4

THE DISTRIBUTION OF BEVERAGES IN THE SHANGHAI AREA

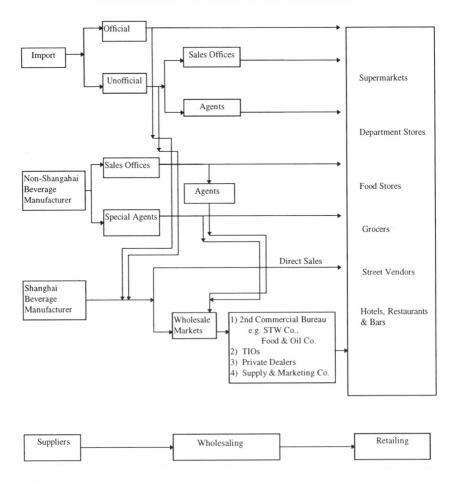

*Source*: Relevant government offices in China

benefits arising from the internalization of the wholesale and distribution functions were that direct distribution provided a high level of customer service through regular account interaction, better collection of market intelligence, and a perceived competitive edge over competitors who did not provide direct distribution.

The next stage in their expansion plan was to enter the market in the greater Shanghai area (which includes Shanghai itself, and Jiangsu and Zhejiang provinces). The company first examined the distribution channels existing in the greater Shanghai area, where they found three types of supplier: Shanghai beverage manufacturers (such as Shanghai Beer); non-Shanghai beverage manufacturers (such as Beck's and Qingtao); and imported beverage manufacturers (see Figure 4). The Shanghai beverage manufacturers were able to sell direct either to the retailers or to the wholesalers. Four types of wholesalers exist in the Shanghai beverage distribution system: corporations under the control of the Second Commercial Bureau (such as the Sugar, Tobacco and Wine Corporation, or the Food and Oil Corporation); the Tertiary Industry Organizations, the Supply and Marketing Company, and various private dealers. The non-Shanghai beverage manufacturers could either set up their own sales offices or distribute through the wholesale markets. And the imported beverage companies could either import their products through official channels by paying the standard tax rate, or through unofficial channels – 'converters' who have good relationships with the customs officers and are able to negotiate a lower tax rate.

Furthermore, the company discovered that it was rather difficult for joint-venture non-Shanghai manufacturers located in major cities to book train space for their products to Shanghai. It was, however, easier for joint-ventures located in remote cities to obtain space because of the lesser demand. Thus, for example, the German brewery Beck's, which had a joint venture factory in Fujian province, found it easier to book space to Shanghai than did the San Mugal brewery located in Guangzhou.

The company then went further to analyze the market structure in each of the three locations in the Shanghai area: Shanghai city, Jiangsu province, and Zhejiang province. In Shanghai city, the Food and Oil Corporation had the largest (40 per cent) share of the wholesale market, and also enjoyed an extensive bottle-serving capability, a vital factor for the beverage industry. The Sugar, Tobacco and Wine Corporation maintained an extensive network to supermarkets, department stores and street vendors but was highly dependent on canned beverages as a result of the shortage of bottle-serving capabilities. The Tertiary Industry Organizations were the results of the economic reform, and were service subsidiaries set up by state enterprises to absorb excess workers. Thus, they enjoyed easy access to workers within the same group of companies. A comparison of the different wholesale channels in Shanghai is shown in Table 3.

In the Jiangsu area – which includes Nanjing, Wuxi and Suzhou – the market shares held by The Sugar, Tobacco and Wine Corporation (STW) and the Tertiary Industry Organizations are more substantial than those in Shanghai (see Table 4). In Suzhou city, the STW accounts for 40 per cent of the wholesale market while the TIOs account for a further 25 per cent. In the Zhejiang area (see Table 5), the STW is again the largest wholesaler in the beverage market. In Ningbo, it accounts for the lion's share (70 per cent), with 20 per cent taken up by the TIOs. In Hangzhou, the combined share captured by the STW and the TIOs amounts to 80 per cent.

TABLE 3

A COMPARISON OF THE DIFFERENCE DISTRIBUTION CHANNELS IN SHANGHAI

| Channel | Number of Sales Offices | Number of Retailers within Network | Estimated share of the wholesale market | Comments |
|---|---|---|---|---|
| Food & Oil Corporation | more than 22 district offices and 60 district sub-offices | more than 300 | 40% | 1. largest wholesaler in beverage, processed flour and oil; 2. extensive network in suburban area of Shanghai; 3. extensive bottle serving capabilities. |
| Sugar, Tobacco & Wine Corporation (STW) | more than 22 district offices and 40 district sub-offices | more than 200 | 20% | 1. maintain extensive network to supermarkets, department stores, food stores, grocers, street vendors; 2. high dependence on canned beverage because shortage of bottle servicing capabilities. |
| Tertiary Industry Organisations (TIOs) | about 500 individual business units of state owned enterprises | N.A. | 20% | 1. trading subsidiaries of large state enterprises: easy access to workers within the same group of companies; 2. small to medium size players. |
| Private Wholesalers | about 3,000 individual companies | N.A. | 15% | 1. large number, mostly concentrated in wholesale maarket, e.g. Shiliupu; 2. small to medium players. |
| Others | N.A. | N.A. | 5% | small players. |

*Source*: Relevant government offices in Shanghai

We can see from the above that the Sugar, Tobacco and Wine Corporation and the Food and Oil Corporation (both under the Second Commercial Bureau), and the Tertiary Industry Organizations (the trading arms of large state enterprises) together account for the majority of the market share in all three areas. These findings reflect the fact that the state distribution systems still play an important role in greater Shanghai. Although Supply and Marketing Cooperatives also account for a significant market share, they are restricted to the rural areas. Consumers in these areas usually cannot afford the high-end beverages produced by foreign joint venture enterprises. In spite of the fact that the state distributors are not well-motivated and dare not commit a large volume of sales to foreign joint ventures, the foreign beverage manufacturer has no choice but to distribute

TABLE 4

A COMPARISON OF THE DIFFERENT DISTRIBUTION CHANNELS IN JIANGSU PROVINCE

| Channel | Estimated Share of Wholesale Market in each location | Estimated Number of Sales Offices | Comments |
|---|---|---|---|
| Sugar, Tobacco & Wine Co. (STW) | Nanjing – 25%<br>Wuxi– 35%<br>Suzhou – 40% | about 20<br>5<br>3 | Largest wholesaler |
| Tertiary Industry Organisations (TIOs) | Nanjing – 25%<br>Wuxi – 30%<br>Suzhou – 25% | about 200<br>about 30<br>about 20 | There are approximately 5–10 large TIOs in each city (e.g. Panda Electronic Group in Nanjing) |
| General Supplies Corporations | Nanjing – 20%<br>Wuxi – 15%<br>Suzhou – 15% | about 30<br>about 10<br>about 5 | Mainly limited to rural areas |
| Private Wholesalers | Nanjing – 30%<br>Wuxi – 20%<br>Suzhou – 20% | about 300<br>about 100<br>about 50 | Numerous small private players fragmented and usually middlemen who provide little service. |

*Source*: Relevant government offices in Jiangsu

TABLE 5

A COMPARISON OF THE DIFFERENT DISTRIBUTION CHANNELS IN ZHEJIANG PROVINCE

| Channel | Estimated Share of Wholesale Market in each location | Estimated Number of Sales Offices | Comments |
|---|---|---|---|
| Sugar, Tobacco & Wine Co. | Hangzhou – 40%<br>Jiaxing - 30%<br>Ningbo – 70%<br>Wenzhou – 30% | about 20<br>about 5<br>about 20<br>about 20 | Largest wholesaler |
| Tertiary Industry Organisations (TIOs) | Hangzhau – 40%<br>Jiaxing – 20%<br>Ningbo – 20%<br>Wenzhou – 30% | about 300<br>about 30<br>about 100<br>about 30 | There are approximately 5–10 TIOs in each city (e.g. Westlake Electronic Group in Hangzhou). |
| General Supplies Corporations | Hangzhau – 6%<br>Jiaxing – 30%<br>Ningbo – 0<br>Wenzhou – 0 | 0<br>about 20<br>0<br>0 | Mainly limited to rural areas. |
| Private Wholesalers | Hangzhou – 20%<br>Jiaxing – 20%<br>Ningbo – 10%<br>Wenzhou – 40% | about 300<br>about 100<br>about 300<br>about 100 | Numerous small private players fragmented and usually middlemen who provide little service. |

*Source:* Relevant government offices in Zhejiang

through the government channels. The company has thus adopted a dual distribution system in line with the prevailing systems in each area. In the Pearl River Delta areas in which the local distributors are not very influential, the company has chosen to 'internalize' its distribution system. In contrast, it has chosen to 'externalize' its distribution in the greater Shanghai area in order to capitalize on the existing structure.

## CONCLUSIONS

In order to pave the way for re-admission to the WTO, the Chinese Government is further opening up the retail sector to foreign investors. According to senior officials from the Ministry of Internal Trade, various cities in the central and western regions are being considered as permitted locations for foreign investors to establish joint venture retail businesses.[14] The 16 joint venture projects already approved by the State Council predominantly involve investors from Asian countries. The Chinese Government would now prefer large department stores from Europe, America and Japan as prospective investors: such stores are considered to possess the requisite expertise and knowledge in retailing.[15] In this regard, it is interesting to note that the Dutch firm, Makro, and the Japanese firm, Itochu, recently received approval from the State Council to operate a chain of stores in China.[16] Moreover, foreign investments in infrastructure in the distribution sector (warehouses, wholesale centres, packaging and goods distribution centres, and transportation) are also encouraged.[17] Furthermore, although foreign investment in wholesaling is still not allowed under Chinese law, foreign firms may engage in 'retailing in bulk quantity'. Examples of such outlets include the International Fashion Centre located in Panyu, Pearl River Delta, and organized by the Hong Kong Trade Development Council; the Industrial Park with distribution facilities developed by the Hong Kong company, Li and Fung Development (China) Ltd; and the International Merchandise Market, set up by Yaohan of Japan.[18]

China's growing affluence presents tremendous investment and expansion opportunities to foreign investors. However, the distribution system in China is in a state of flux, and foreign investors should realize the vital importance of continual monitoring and adjustment to the changing environment. The choice of an appropriate distribution channel is crucial to the success of the foreign firm. Initially, many firms have made use of external channels such as state, collective, or foreign distributors-retailers, with whom they have had a previous business relationship. Later, once they have accumulated sufficient knowledge of the Chinese market, they have considered making use of internal, integrated channels. It is likely that, as the business environment in China increasingly comes to resemble that in western countries, the factors that have been shown to influence the internalization versus externalization decision in the west will become more and more relevant in China.

## NOTES

1. See, for example, B.B. Conable and D.M. Lampton, 'China: the Coming Power', *Foreign Affairs*, First Quarter 1993, pp.133–49; 'China: the Next Superpower', *Time*, 10 May 1993, pp.14–45; 'China: the Making of an Economic Giant', *International Business Week*, 17 May 1993, pp.20–30.

2. State Statistical Bureau, *Statistical Yearbook of China 1993*, Beijing, State Statistical Bureau, 1993.

3. International Monetary Fund, *World Economic Outlook*, Washington DC, IMF, 1993. Reported in the *South China Morning Post*, 21 May 1993, Business Section p.4.

4. The references cited in Table 1 are as follows: A. Ahmed, 'Channel Control in International Markets', *European Journal of Marketing*, Vol.11, No.4, 1977, pp.327–36; E. Anderson, 'The Salesperson as Outside Agent or Employee: A Transaction Cost Analysis', *Marketing Science*, No.4, Summer 1985, pp.234–54; M.F. Bradley, 'Nature and Significance of International Marketing: A Review', *Journal of Business Research*, Vol.15, 1987, pp.205–19; M.F. Bradley,*International Marketing Strategies*, New York, Prentice Hall, 1991; A.L. Calvet, 'A Synthesis of Foreign Direct Investment Theories and Theories of the Multinational Firm', *Journal of International Business* Studies, No.12, Spring–Summer 1981, pp.43–59; S.T. Cavusgil and J.R. Nevin, 'Internal Determinants of Export Marketing Behaviour: an Empirical Investigation', *Journal of Marketing Research*, Vol.88, February 1981, pp.114–19; W.H. Davidson, *Global Strategic Management*, New York, John Wiley, 1982; W.H. Davidson and D.G. McFetridge, 'International Technology Transactions and the Theory of the Firm', *Journal of Industrial* Economics, Vol.32, March 1984, pp.253–64; M. Etgar, 'The Effects of Forward Vertical Integration on Service Performance of a Distributive Industry', *Journal of Industrial Economics*, No.26, March 1978, pp.249–55; J.P. Jeannet and H.D. Hennesey, *International Marketing Management, Strategies and Cases*, New York, Houghton Mifflin, 1988; W.J. Keegan, *Multinational Marketing* Management, Englewood Cliffs NJ, Prentice Hall, 1984; W.T. McGuire and R. Staelin, 'An Industry Equilibrium Analysis of Downstream Vertical Integration', *Marketing* Research, No.6, May 1983, pp.156–63; P. Nelson, 'Advertising as Information', *Journal of Political Economy*, Vol.81, July–August 1970, pp.729–54; M.E. Porter, *Competition Strategy*, New York, The Free Press, 1980; M.E. Porter, *The Competitive Advantages of Nations*; R.C. Robinson, *International Business Management: A Guide to Decision Making*; F.J. Root, *Foreign Market Entry Strategies*, New York, AMACON, 1982; H. Thorelli, 'International Marketing: An Ecologic View', in H. Thorelli and H. Becker (eds) *International Marketing Strategy (revised edition)*, New York, Pergamon, 1980, pp.5–20; V. Terpstra, *International Marketing, Third Edition*, New York, The Dryden Press, 1993; O. Williamson, 'Transaction Cost Economics: the Governance of Contractual Relations',*Journal of Law and Economics*, Vol.22, October 1979, pp.233–62.

5. China Handbook Editorial Committee, *Economy*, Beijing, Foreign Language Press, 1984.

6. This description of the pre-reform distribution system in Shanghai is based on information collected by one of the authors during interviews with government officials in Shanghai in early 1993.

7. *Almanac of China's Economy*, Beijing, Economic Management Press, 1985, pp.15–16.

8. *China Daily: Business Weekly*, 11–17 December 1993, p.1.

9. C.S. Tseng, P. Kwan and F. Cheung, 'The Distribution System in China – Past, Present and Future'; S.T.F. Luk, 'The Reform of the Distribution System in China and its Implications for Channel Design'.

10. *Hong Kong Economic Journal*, 6 January 1995, p.10.

11. *China Business Review*, September–October 1992, p.4.

12. Hong Kong Trade Development Council, *Chinese Consumer Goods Market*, February 1992.

13. *Hong Kong Commercial Daily*, 24 October 1996.

14. *Ming Pao Daily*, 29 October 1996.

15. *Jiefang Daily*, 21 October 1996.

16. *Wen Wei Po*, 21 May 1996.

17. *Wen Wei Po*, 8 April 1996 and 29 May 1996.

18. C.S. Tseng, 'Foreign Investment in Retail Sector in People's Republic of China', in Sally Stewart and Anne Carver (eds) *Coming of Age: Development in Sino–Foreign Joint Ventures*, Advances in Chinese Industrial Studies Vol.5, Greenwich CN, JAI Press, 1997.

## REFERENCES

Anderson, E. and A. Coughlan (1987), 'International Market Entry and Expansion via Independent or Integrated Channels of Distribution', *Journal of Marketing*, Vol.51, pp.71–82.

Buckley, P.J., C.L. Pass, and K. Prescott (1990), 'Foreign Market Servicing by Multinationals: An Integrated Treatment', *International Marketing Review*, Vol.7, No.4, pp.25–40.

Caves, R. and M.E. Porter (1977) 'From Entry Barriers to Mobility Barriers: Conjectural Decisions and Contrived Deterrence to New Competition', *Quarterly Journal of Economics*, No.91, pp.241–61.

Coughlan, A.T. (1985), 'Competition and Cooperation in Marketing Channel Choice: Theory and Application', *Marketing Science*, Vol.4, No.2, pp.110–29.

Feng, M.M. (1995), 'Grasp the Opportunity, Mutual Development'. Paper presented at the Chinese Retail Conference, 7 November.

Gronhaug, K. and O. Kvitastein (1993), 'Distributional Involvement in International Strategic Business Units', *International Business Review*, Vol.2, No.1, pp.1–14.

Ho, D. and N. Leigh (1994), 'Retail Revolution', *The China Business Review*, January–February.

IMF (1993), *World Economic Outlook*. Washington DC: IMF.

Kotler, P. (1994), *Marketing Management*. Eaglewood Cliffs, NJ: Prentice-Hall.

Luk, S.T.F. (1995), 'The Reform of the Distribution System in China and Its Implications for Channel Design' in H.Davies (ed.), *China Business: Context & Issues*. Hong Kong: Longman Asia.

Luk, S.T.F, Y.Z. Xu and W.C. Ye (1996), 'Evolution of China's Wholesale System: Review and Marketing Implications'. Paper submitted for presentation at the Second Conference on East Asia-EU Business, King's College London, April.

Mun, K.C. (1988), 'Chinese Retailing in a Changing Environment' in *Transnational Retailing*. Berlin: Walter de Gruyter.

Onkvist, S. and J. Shaw (1989), *International Marketing: Analysis and Strategy*. Merrill Publishing.

Porter, M.E. (1990), *The Competitive Advantage of Nations*. New York: Free Press.

Robinson, R.C. (1978), *International Business Management: a Guide to Decision Making*. Dryden Press.

Tseng, C.S. (1997), 'Foreign Investment in Retail Sector in People's Republic of China' in S. Stewart and A. Carver (eds), *Coming of Age: Development in Sino–Foreign Joint Ventures*, Advances in Chinese Industrial Studies, Vol.5, Greenwich, CN: JAI Press.

Tseng C.S., P. Kwan and F. Cheung (1994), 'The Distribution System in China – Past, Present and Future'. Paper presented at the INSEAD Euro–Asia Centre, France.

Tseng, C.S., P. Kwan and F. Cheung (1995), 'Distribution in China – a Guide through the Maze', *Long Range Planning*, Vol.28, No.1, pp.81–91.

Tung, R.I. (1982), *Chinese Industrial Society after Mao*. Toronto: Lexington Books.

UNCTAD (1994), *World Investment Report 1994: Transnational Corporations, Employment and the Workplace*. New York: UN.

Yip, L.S.C. (1995), 'The Emergence of a Retail Market in China' in H.Davies (ed.), *China Business: Context & Issues*. Hong Kong: Longman Asia.

# Marketing in an Emerging Consumer Society: Character Images in China's Consumer Magazine Advertising

NAN ZHOU and LINMING MENG

Advertising is mainly a business tool for promoting products, but it is also an ideal means for observing how the logic of the commodity form expresses itself culturally and socially (Goldman, 1992). In particular, human images in advertising, like people in family albums, 'tell us in miniature a great deal about an entire civilisation, its actual material life and interlocking collective fantasies' (Atwan et al., 1979). Some advertising historians even consider human characters used in advertising, when taken as a whole, as expressions of national character (Goodrum and Dalrymple, 1990).

When an economy is in the developing stage, it is in an 'era of market fragmentation' because most sellers are in the process of developing national markets for branded products (Tedlow, 1990). As these sellers are not well known in the marketplace, they may feel it necessary to inform potential customers about who they are, in addition to providing product information. Therefore, they often present a seller's image in their advertising. Some characters in advertisements are, in fact, the advertisers themselves (Pope, 1983). But the advertisers may decide that it is more important to portray a buyer's image in their advertising, so as to appeal to potential buyers. This may entail the use of professional models with a 'sterilised' better-than-life look, which appeals to potential consumers' ideal self-image (Brown, 1981), with which real or 'typical' customers may easily identify. Alternatively, 'likeable' people such as celebrities are used. Because of their referent power, these characters could serve as guideposts for potential buyers' personal and social identities.

In this contribution we report the results of a preliminary study of human characters in advertising in China, one of the world's fastest developing economies. Advertising was cursed as a western capitalist evil and forbidden during the Cultural Revolution of 1966–76. However, it has been 'resurrected' under the policy of *gaige kaifang* (reform and opening) since 1978, and has grown into a large industry, becoming an increasingly important part of the country's economic and social life (Tse *et al.*, 1989). In our study, we first describe in what sense Chinese advertising is relational and contextual in economic and socio-cultural terms under the reform policy. Within this framework, we then present the findings of a content

Nan Zhou, City University of Hong Kong; Linming Meng, Xiamen University analysis of human images in Chinese consumer magazine advertising. Finally, based on our findings, we discuss the prospects of advertising in China and the implications for advertisers.

## THE ADVERTISING ENVIRONMENT IN CHINA

### Economic Reform

After the founding of the Communist government in 1949, for 30 years China followed the Soviet model of developing a plan-based economy (Xue, 1981). The sectors relating to the improvement of the people's standard of living were low on the development priority list. There was a shortage of supply of consumer goods. Average citizens were called on by the government to maintain 'selfless dedication and self sacrifice as well as a willingness to forego private material gain and personal comfort' (Wang, 1977). The 'government shops' did not need to be market- or customer-oriented (Mun, 1984). They simply carried out production and 'circulation' (distribution) functions and used little commercial promotion (Xu, 1990).

Reform was introduced in 1978 to transfer the economy to a 'Chinese-Style Socialist Market Economy', according to Deng Xiaoping's thinking that it does not matter whether a cat is white or black, as long as it catches mice. Many steps have been taken to allow market forces to play an increasingly greater role in the economy. This has helped turn the country into one of the world's fastest-growing economies (Kotler et al., 1996). As the country is undergoing a momentous transition from a subsistence society to a consumer society, material desires are growing, a middle class is emerging, and there is a gradual change in the supply and demand balance of the marketplace (Taylor, 1995). In some areas, a buyer's market has emerged. Some major indicators of China's consumer market are shown in Table 1.

For businesses to reach and influence the increasingly affluent consumers, an advertising infrastructure is being developed (Semenik, 1986). National advertising expenditure has grown at an average annual rate of over 30 per cent (Liang and Jacobs, 1993). In the early 1980s, industrial goods made up 70–80 per cent of the goods advertised. The percentage diminished to around 50 per cent by the mid-1980s and became even smaller towards the end of the decade. The 1990s has been predicted to be the decade of consumer advertising.[1] Unlike highly buyer-oriented advertising in the west, which focuses on the satisfaction of buyers' needs, Chinese advertising is still to a large extent seller-oriented, and often emphasizes the introduction of the seller to potential customers and the provision of information to the customer about the existence of the product. This emphasis is reflected in surveys of managers (Semenik et al., 1986), and in Chinese marketing textbooks.[2] It is also found in content-analysis-based studies of advertising which report a high level of product information (Rice and Liu, 1988; Tse et al., 1989).

TABLE 1

PROFILE OF CHINA'S CONSUMER MARKET, 1994

| Major Indicators | | | |
| --- | --- | --- | --- |
| Year-end population (10,000 persons) | | | 119,850 |
| Gross national product (GNP) (100,000,000 yuan) | | | 44,918 |
| Gross domestic product (GDP) (100,000,000 yuan) | | | 45,006 |
| Total wages of staff and workers (100,000,000 yuan) | | | 6,656.4 |
| Average annual wage of staff and workers (yuan) | | | 4,538 |
| Per capita annual consumption (yuan) | | | 1,737 |
| Total value of retail sales (100,000,000 yuan) | | | 16,264.7 |
| Saving deposit balance of rural and urban residents (year-end) (100,000,000 yuan) | | | 21,518.8 |
| Per capita living floor space (sample survey) (sq. m) | | | 20.2 |
| | | | |
| Basic Indicators of Urban Households | | | |
| Average persons per household (persons) | | | 3.28 |
| Average employees per household (persons) | | | 1.88 |
| Annual income per capita (yuan) | | | 3,502.31 |
| | | | |
| Urban Household Ownership of Major Consumer Durable Per 100 Households | | | |
| Bicycles | 192.00 | Colour television sets | 86.21 |
| Sewing machines | 64.38 | Stereo recorders | 28.65 |
| Washing machines | 87.29 | Cameras | 29.83 |
| Refrigerators | 62.10 | | |

*Source*: State Statistical Bureau, *China Statistical Yearbook 1995* (Beijing: China Statistical Publishing House, 1995).

At the same time, various 'modern' advertising approaches and techniques have been 'imported' from the west by multinational corporations and both foreign and Chinese advertising agencies. They have a strong influence on Chinese advertising and are helping the mass media 'nurture ... a more consumption-oriented public' (Sklair, 1991). He also observes that, for Chinese advertisers in this early-learning stage of foreign advertising methods, '[i]n the short term, ... the socialist purpose of advertising is [often] lost in the rush to master techniques' (Ibid.: 201).

## Cultural Transformation

The impact and consequence of the policy of 'reform and opening' is as significant to Chinese culture as it is to the economy. China has a long history as a patriarchal culture. Men and older people have traditionally occupied much higher ascribed status in the social hierarchy than women and younger people (Yau, 1988). The constitution, however, stipulates that women enjoy the same rights as men. Growing numbers of women have paying jobs and occupy important positions comparable to those held by men. According to a politically correct expression in China, this is because 'women hold up half of the sky'. But gender inequality still favours men with respect to broad occupational categories (Bauer *et al.*, 1992; Tuan and Zhao, 1993). Some factories refuse to employ women over the age of 40, and others do not hire pregnant women or mothers until their children are seven years old.[3]

The threat to old cultural values and ways of life also comes from the outside world. Before the reforms, China's government isolated its people from many things 'foreign'. Now these things are infiltrating the country almost with impunity (Schell, 1988).[4] The country is said to be 'anointed as the mecca for multinational marketers.'[5] Foreign companies have set up operations in various parts of the country. Advertisements promoting foreign consumer goods and brands can be seen everywhere (Sklair, 1991; Stewart and Campbell, 1986).[6] Some people, especially younger ones, are very much *chongyang meiwai* (worshipping and having a blind faith of things foreign). To them, foreign things represent superiority, prestige and modernization. Some of them buy products simply because they have foreign words on the package.[7] Some also consider Chinese advertising designs to be inferior to foreign designs (Pollay et al., 1990). While many companies are interested in including a foreign flavour in their advertisements, it is difficult for them to portray foreign people in Chinese advertising because they are not only hard to find but also expensive to hire. Language barriers also prevent them from working effectively with their Chinese counterparts.

## METHOD

Consumer magazine advertisements were used in the study. As was found in previous studies (Rice and Lu, 1988; Stewart and Campbell, 1986), systematic data on magazine circulation and syndicated audience measures were unavailable. To insure a broad base of magazine advertisements, 130 nationally distributed, non-duplicated consumer magazine issues published during April–July 1992 were purchased in three large cities: Guangzhou, Shenzhen and Xiamen. All consumer magazines believed to have the largest circulations in the country were included. No regional editions could be identified. Only advertisements containing analysable human character photographs (photographs in advertisements with clear, complete or large close-up shots of people) that promoted Chinese products were retained. Advertisements promoting imported or Sino–foreign joint-venture products were eliminated because they would distort the results of a study of Chinese advertisements. We found that most of the magazines only carried one advertisement that included a human photograph on one of the covers. The resultant sample consisted of 161 advertisements from the magazines, which contained 325 analysable characters. Tables 2 and 3 provide analysis of the 161 advertisements by type of magazine and type of product respectively.

Four coding categories for each character's socio-demographic characteristics were adopted after a literature review and a pilot study. The categories are ethnicity, gender, age and occupation (see Table 4). Two trained Chinese coders, each with a university-level educational background, content-analysed the data independently under the supervision of one of the researchers. Discrepancies between the coders were resolved through discussion between themselves and consultation with the

TABLE 2

ADVERTISEMENTS BY MAGAZINE CATEGORY

| Category | n | % |
|---|---|---|
| Family Life | 45 | 28.0 |
| General Readership | 28 | 17.4 |
| Women | 24 | 14.9 |
| Youth | 17 | 10.6 |
| Pastime/Entertainment | 14 | 8.7 |
| Others | 33 | 20.4 |
| Total | 161 | 100.0 |

TABLE 3

ADVERTISEMENTS BY PRODUCT CATEGORY

| Category | n | % |
|---|---|---|
| Medicine/Health Products | 47 | 29.2 |
| Cosmetics and Skin Care | 21 | 13.0 |
| Textiles/Clothing | 18 | 11.2 |
| Electronic Appliances | 17 | 10.6 |
| Others | 58 | 36.0 |
| Total | 161 | 100.0 |

TABLE 4

CATEGORIES OF ANALYSIS

| Category | Subcategories |
|---|---|
| Ethnicity[1] | Mainland Chinese; Non-mainland Chinese; Non-Chinese. |
| Gender | Male; Female. |
| Age | 15 or under (child, juvenile), 16 - 35 (youth), 36 - 59 (middle-aged), 60 or older (retiree, old-aged). |
| Occupation[2] | Advertisement sponsoring company employee: top level manager, middle level manager/technical expert, low level worker; Non-employee: celebrity, professional model, customer. |

*Notes*: 1. Non-Mainland Chinese: Chinese known to come from Taiwan or Hong Kong.
2. A character was first classified as a sponsoring company's employee (presenting a seller's image) or non-employee (presenting a buyer's image); the character was then further classified based on his/her actual occupation (for an employee) or occupational role in the advertisement (for a non-employee).

researchers. Inter-coder reliability coefficients, calculated using Perreault and Leigh's method (Perreault and Leigh, 1989), were as follows: ethnicity -1.0; gender -1.0; age -0.95; and occupation -0.96.

Given the preliminary nature of this study, no formal hypotheses were formulated. Nevertheless, four propositions regarding advertisements created for Chinese companies may be put forward based on the foregoing discussion.

- **P1**: Chinese companies would use Chinese characters in their advertisements more often than foreign characters.
- **P2**: Chinese companies would use male characters more often than female characters in their advertisements.
- **P3**: Chinese companies would use older characters more often than younger characters in their advertisements.
- **P4**: Chinese companies would use a seller's image more often than a buyer's image in their advertisements.

## RESULTS

*Sample Composition by Ethnicity, Gender, Age and Occupation*

Table 5 reveals that Chinese and non-Chinese characters accounted for 87.1 per cent and 12.9 per cent of the sample respectively ($Z = 19.94$, $p < 0.01$). This finding confirms proposition P1 that advertisements created for Chinese companies would use Chinese characters more often than foreign characters. Of the 283 Chinese characters, 54.1 per cent were female and 45.9 per cent were male ($Z = -1.37$, $p < 0.01$), while of the 42 foreign characters, 90.5 per cent were female and 9.5 per cent were male ($Z = -8.94$, $p < 0.01$). These findings do not confirm proposition P2 ($Z = -3.21$, $p < 0.01$) that Chinese companies would use male characters more often than female characters in their advertisements.

Proposition P3, which states that Chinese companies would use older characters more often than younger characters in their advertisements, is also not confirmed ($Z = -5.01$, $p < 0.01$). Over half (59.0 per cent) ($Z = -3.09$, $p < 0.01$) of the Chinese characters and most (92.9 per cent) ($Z = -10.80$, $p < 0.01$) of the foreign characters were in the age groups of 35 or under.

More than half (62.5 per cent) ($Z = -6.68$, $p < 0.01$) of the Chinese characters and all of the foreign characters were portrayed in the buyers' occupations as models or customers. This finding contradicts proposition P4, which states that Chinese companies would use a seller's image more often than a buyer's image in their advertisements.

Thus three of the four propositions put forward are not suppoted on the basis of the advertisements collected in the sample. The reasons for these findings are discussed in more detail below.

TABLE 5

CHARACTER COMPOSITION BY ETHNICITY, AGE, AND GENDER

|  | Age | | | | Total | |
|---|---|---|---|---|---|---|
|  | 0 – 15 | 16 – 35 | 36 – 59 | 60 or + | n | % |
| Chinese |  |  |  |  |  |  |
| Male | 1 | 40 | 84 | 5 | 130 | 45.9 |
| Female | 7 | 119 | 27 | – | 153 | 54.1 |
| Total |  |  |  |  |  |  |
| n | 8 | 159 | 111 | 5 | 283 |  |
| % | 2.8 | 56.2 | 39.2 | 1.8 |  | 100.0 |
| Non-Chinese |  |  |  |  |  |  |
| Male | 1 | 2 | 1 | – | 4 | 9.5 |
| Female | – | 36 | 2 | – | 38 | 90.5 |
| Total |  |  |  |  |  |  |
| n | 1 | 38 | 3 | – | 42 |  |
| % | 2.4 | 90.5 | 7.1 | – |  | 100.0 |

TABLE 6

CHINESE MALE CHARACTER'S OCCUPATION

|  | Age | | | | Total | |
|---|---|---|---|---|---|---|
|  | 0 – 15 | 16 – 35 | 36 – 59 | 60 or + | n | % |
| Seller-oriented Occupation |  |  |  |  |  |  |
| Manager | – | 3 | 55 | – | 58 | 44.6 |
| Middle level manager / |  |  |  |  |  |  |
| technical expert | – | 5 | 11 | – | 16 | 12.3 |
| Worker | – | – | 3 | – | 3 | 2.3 |
| Buyer-oriented Occupation |  |  |  |  |  |  |
| PRC celebrity | – | 4 | 3 | – | 7 | 5.4 |
| Hong Kong or Taiwan |  |  |  |  |  |  |
| celebrity | – | 2 | – | – | 2 | 1.5 |
| Model | – | 7 | 1 | – | 8 | 6.2 |
| Customer | 1 | 19 | 11 | 5 | 36 | 27.7 |
| Total |  |  |  |  |  |  |
| n | 1 | 40 | 84 | 5 | 130 |  |
| % | 0.8 | 30.8 | 64.6 | 3.8 |  | 100.0 |

## Images of Chinese Characters

There were significant differences in the portrayal of Chinese male and female characters ($\chi^2 = 86.14$, $p < 0.01$). Male characters were mainly in the 36–59 age group (64.6 per cent) and were usually portrayed in sellers' occupations (59.2 per cent), most frequently as top-level managers in the company (44.6 per cent) (see Table 6). In contrast, Chinese women were mainly in the 16–35 age group (77.8 per cent) and were often portrayed as either customers (39.9 per cent) or professional models (30.1 per cent) (see

TABLE 7
CHINESE FEMALE CHARACTER'S OCCUPATION

| | Age | | | Total | |
|---|---|---|---|---|---|
| | 0 –15 | 16 – 35 | 36 – 59 | n | % |
| Seller-oriented Occupation | | | | | |
| Manager | – | – | 8 | 8 | 5.2 |
| Middle level manager / technical expert | – | 3 | 3 | 6 | 3.9 |
| Worker | – | 12 | 3 | 15 | 9.8 |
| Buyer-oriented Occupation | | | | | |
| PRC celebrity | – | 9 | – | 9 | 5.9 |
| Hong Kong or Taiwan celebrity | – | 7 | 1 | 8 | 5.2 |
| Model | 3 | 43 | – | 46 | 30.1 |
| Customer | 4 | 45 | 12 | 61 | 39.9 |
| Total | | | | | |
| n | 7 | 119 | 27 | 153 | |
| % | 4.6 | 77.8 | 17.6 | | 100.0 |

TABLE 8
NON-CHINESE CHARACTER'S OCCUPATION

| | Age | | | Total | |
|---|---|---|---|---|---|
| | 0 – 15 | 16 – 35 | 36 – 59 | n | % |
| Male | | | | | |
| Model | – | 2 | – | 2 | 4.8 |
| Customer | 1 | – | 1 | 2 | 4.8 |
| Female | | | | | |
| Model | – | 33 | 1 | 34 | 81.0 |
| Customer | – | 3 | 1 | 4 | 9.4 |
| Total | | | | | |
| n | 1 | 38 | 3 | 42 | |
| % | 2.4 | 90.5 | 7.1 | | 100.0 |

Table 7). Five men (3.8 per cent) were in the retirement age group (60 or older) and all of them were the advertisers' customers, but there were no women in the retirement age group.

Sixteen Mainland Chinese celebrities were included in the advertisements. Seven were male and nine were female (see Tables 6 and 7). They were actors, musicians or sports stars, and were mostly in the 16–35 age group. In comparison, there were ten non-Mainland Chinese celebrities. The two male celebrities were from Hong Kong and the eight female celebrities were from Hong Kong or Taiwan. All were well-known entertainers in the 16–35 age group, except one Hong Kong female television programme hostess in the 36–59 age group.

*Images of Non-Chinese Characters*

Thirty-six (85.7 per cent) of the 42 non-Chinese characters were professional models. All except one of the models were in the 16–35 age group, and 34 (80.1 per cent) of them were female (Table 8). The other six of these characters (14.3 per cent) were the advertisers' customers shown in photos in the advertisements. There was only one black character; the other 41 were Caucasians.

## DISCUSSION AND CONCLUSIONS

Human images in China's advertising, as reported in this study, are a mix of older, authoritative, seller-oriented male figures and younger, good-looking, buyer-oriented female faces and bodies; they are also a mix of traditional Chinese and 'imported' images. To a certain extent, these portrayals are consistent with the sex roles prescribed in the Confucian tradition. While a direct comparison with the results of studies in other countries cannot be made due to differences in categories of analysis used, these portrayals are similar to gender role images in advertising in the west in general, in that men are more often portrayed in 'working' roles and women in 'non-working' roles (Wiles, Wiles and Tjernlund, 1995).

The majority of Chinese businesses are run by men in the 36–59 age group. Using these people's images to represent the seller in advertisements appears to be the favourite choice for many companies in our study. On the other hand, female characters were mainly in the 16–35 age group, and were mostly models and customers. It is probably true that Chinese women do more household shopping than men. Thus advertisers who are learning to become customer-oriented would often want to portray them in advertisements. But any sensible reasoning for the high frequency of young female characters in advertisements would conclude that Chinese advertisers are interested in using sex appeal to attract audience attention. At the same time, the lower frequency of female employees used as company spokespeople and their lower occupational status relative to male employees point to the reality that both employment opportunities and importance in the corporate hierarchy are still unfavourable to women. The 'half of the sky' that Chinese women hold up, as reflected in advertising, is clearly less important than the other half that men hold up in terms of occupational role and capacity.

The status of retirees is declining in China in general and in the family in particular.[8] They are still in name regarded as *niangao-deshao* (of venerable ages and eminent virtue) according to the tradition. But their decline in status and influence is evident in their lack of power in areas such as their children's mate selection, shared decision-making power within the household, and the unwillingness of children to care for them according to tradition and the Constitution, largely because older people's incomes are reduced. For the same reason, advertisers ignore older people, as shown in our study. This finding is similar to that of a recent study on images of older characters in Canadian consumer magazine advertisements (Zhou and Chen, 1992).

It is not surprising that eight per cent of the characters in the sample (16 Mainland Chinese and ten non-Mainland Chinese) were well-known entertainers or sports stars. In the pre-reform era when personal consumption was restricted, and in the pursuit of social control, government propaganda machines heavily promoted *mofan renwu* (exemplary personages) who negated material life and devoted themselves to working for the collective good. These people's pictures and stories were often seen in mass news media and billboards. Now that the country is moving towards a consumer society, different 'heroes' – the nouveau riche – have a high profile (Belk and Zhou, 1987). The well-known entertainers and sports stars who belong to this rich and famous group attract many admirers and followers, and their conspicuous consumption habits make them potentially very effective spokespeople for advertisers.[9]

Our results support previous findings about the Chinese interest in using foreign appeals in advertising (Tse, Belk and Zhou, 1987). Considering that the target audience for the advertisements in this sample was virtually all Mainland Chinese and the products promoted in these advertisements were all made by Chinese firms, the proportion of 'foreign' (that is, non-Mainland Chinese and non-Chinese) characters found in the advertisements (16.0 per cent) was probably higher than one would expect. Using 'foreign' characters potentially gives a product a higher quality image as well as a western lifestyle image. Average consumers cannot afford foreign products, but they can still envy and yearn for the higher standard of living in foreign countries. Advertisements using 'foreign' characters exploit this fascination for foreign places and things, as they promote the (mis)conception that ownership of these products equates with the better lifestyle of foreigners. Thus to use celebrities from Hong Kong and Taiwan who are known in the Mainland may, as mentioned previously, also create a higher level of advertising recall and product recognition than the use of Chinese celebrities.

The findings of our study may be considered to provide a realistic reflection both of China's socio-economic reality and of the consequences of the economic reforms and the open door policy. Whether or not a readily identifiable Chinese 'national character' can be found in advertisements, – one which is said by advertising historians to exist – the images reported here seem to support the notion that advertising is a manifestation of the mental structure of a people in their appreciation of the world; in so being, advertising appeal and styles are designed to fulfil marketing roles as defined by the marketing environment and to fit present consumer needs and consumer desires for a better life in the future (Pope, 1983).

Clearly China's economic and cultural developments are both at a crossroads. Looking to the future, China is expected to follow a path similar to that pursued by once underdeveloped or developing, and now developed economies (Overholt, 1994). As the seller-oriented market makes way for a more buyer-oriented market, China will soon enter an 'era of market segmentation' which is characterized by increasing competition (Pope, 1983; Tedlow, 1990). The use of buyer's images in advertising may be expected to increase significantly.

However, we do not expect any improvement in the portrayal of retired people in the foreseeable future. While the economic objective and functions of advertising are obvious and substantial, the socio-cultural impact of advertising is unfortunately largely unrecognized in China. Since the primary motive of advertisers is to sell goods, they will continue to focus on the younger population segments that have greater spending power (Zhou and Chen, 1992).

However, it is essential for advertisers to recognize that while the use of sex appeal, celebrities and foreign faces may help to sell products, their role could be limited. As Pollay, *et al.* (1990), advertisers, including those from foreign countries, should prepare for a more critical perspective that could be just around the corner. This could happen once Chinese consumers and the government gain more experience with advertising. Some of the new cultural values and lifestyles, and the approaches in advertising that they are now enthusiastically learning and embracing so as to function in a consumer society, may soon become alien. For example, a survey of consumers from three large cities reported that the respondents preferred advertisements that portray 'simple' and 'hard-working' lifestyles. Some of the respondents were disinclined towards the use of celebrities and the portrayal of affluent lifestyles, and some noticed and disapproved of the growing use of sex appeal in advertising (Pollay *et al.*, 1990).

Foreign companies interested in advertising in China should ensure that imagery and meanings transmitted through foreign characters are transformed and grounded in deeply-rooted Chinese cultural values and social and economic practices that the government considers non-threatening. Mueller's study of the level of westernization in advertising in Japan (1992), another East Asian culture, may be telling here. Although English words and western models were often found in advertisements, several common western techniques (such as hard-sell appeals) made only a rare appearance. Mueller's review of the relevant literature suggests that signs of westernization may be superficial as far as their impact on matters of the Japanese heart and mind; and concludes that the Japanese fascination with the west may not last. So too could that of the Chinese.

## ACKNOWLEDGEMENTS

The authors gratefully acknowledge the financial support of the Council of Maritime Premiers under the program 'Fostering International Business Research and Networks in the Maritime Provinces', which is administered by the Centre for International Business Studies, Dalhousie University, Halifax, Nova Scotia, Canada; and of the Social Sciences and Humanities Research Council of Canada Small University Grant Programme, Acadia University, Wolfville, Nova Scotia, Canada.

## NOTES

1. J. Yu, 'Nowadays, Advertising Industry is Booming', *Economic Reporter*, No.5, 1993, pp.6–8.
2. See, for example, X. Peng, *Shi Chang Ying Xiao Xue* (Marketing), Beijing, Zhong Guo Cai Zhen Jing Ji Chu Ban She, 1990; K. Xiao, *Shi Chang Xue Gai Lun (An Introduction to Marketing)*, Shanghai, Shanghai She Hui Ke Xue Yuan Chu Ban She, 1990; X. Yang, *Shi Chang Xue Jiao Cheng (Marketing)*, Beijing, Zhong Yang Guang Bo Dian Shi Da Xue Chu Ban She, 1989.
3. 'When the Sky Falls on Women', The Economist, 13 March 1993, p.41.
4. L. Kraar, 'China after Marx: Open for Business', Fortune, 18 February 1985, pp.28–33.
5. C. Miller, 'China Emerges as Latest Battleground for Marketing Researchers', Marketing News, 14 February 1994, pp.1–2.
6. J. Kahn, 'P&G Marketing Army Conquers China', *The Asian Wall Street Journal*, 13 September 1995.
7. S. WuDunn, 'Cosmetics from the West Help to Change the Face of China', *New York Times*, 6 May 1990.
8. M.Y.T. Chen, 'Status of the Elderly in Urban China', Society, Vol.15, No.1, 1991, pp.16–24; S. Zeng, 'China's Senior Citizens', *China Reconstructs*, Vol.32, No.1, 1983, pp.9–15.
9. J. Barlow, 'More than Just Another Pretty Face', *Asia Advertising and Media*, 22 March 1996, p.14.

## REFERENCES

Atwan, R., D. McQuade and J.W. Wright (1979), *Edsels, Luckies, and Frigidaires: Advertising the American Way*. New York: Dell.

Bauer, J., F. Wang,, N.E. Riley and X. Zhao (1992), 'Gender Inequity in Urban China – Education and Employment', *Modern China*, Vol.18, No.3, pp.333–70.

Belk, R.W. and N. Zhou (1987), 'Learning to Want Things' in M. Wallendorf and P. Anderson (eds), *Advances in Consumer Research*, Vol.14, pp.478–81

Brown, B.W. (1981), *Images of Family Life in Magazine Advertising: 1920–1978*. New York: Praeger.

Chen, M.Y.T. (1991), 'Status of the Elderly in Urban China', *Society*, Vol.15, No.1, pp.16–24.

Goldman, R. (1992), *Reading Ads Socially*. New York: Routledge.

Goodrum, C. and H. Dalrymple (1990), *Advertising in America: The First Two Hundred Years*. New York: Harry N. Abrams.

Kotler, P., S.H. Ang, S.M. Leong and C.T. Tan (1996), *Marketing Management: An Asian Perspective*. Singapore: Prentice Hall.

Liang, K. and L. Jacobs (1993), 'China's Advertising: Education and Research is the Key', *International Journal of Advertising*, Vol.12, No.2, pp.181–5.

Mueller, B.B. (1992), 'Standardization vs. Specialization: An Examination of Westernization in Japanese Advertising', *Journal of Advertising Research*, Vol.32, No.1, pp.15–24.

Mun, K.C. (1984), 'Marketing in the PRC' in E. Kaynak and R. Savitt (eds), *Comparative Marketing*. New York: Praeger, pp.247–60.

Overholt, W.H. (1994), *The Rise of China: How Economic Reform is Creating a New Superpower*. New York: Norton.

Perreault, W.D. and L.E. Leigh,. (1989), 'Reliability of Nominal Data Based on Qualitative Judgments', *Journal of Marketing Research*, Vol.26, No.2, pp.135–48.

Pollay, R.W., D.K. Tse and Z.Y Wang (1990), 'Advertising, Propaganda, and Value Change in Economic Development: The New Cultural Revolution in China and Attitudes toward Advertising', *Journal of Business Research*, Vol.20, No.1, pp.83–95.

Pope, D. (1983), *The Making of Modern Advertising*. New York: Basic Books.

Rice, M.D. and Z. Liu (1988), 'A Content Analysis of Chinese Magazine Advertisements', *Journal of Advertising*, Vol.17, No.4, pp.43–8.

Schell, O. (1988), *Discos and Democracy: China in the Throes of Reform*. New York: Pantheon.

Semenik, R.J., N. Zhou and W.L. Moore (1986), 'Chinese Managers' Attitudes Toward Advertising in China', *Journal of Advertising*, Vol.15, No.4, pp.56–62.

Sklair, L. (1991), *Sociology of the Global System*. Baltimore: Johns Hopkins University.

Stewart, S. and N. Campbell (1986), 'Advertising in Mainland China: A Preliminary Study', *International Journal of Advertising*, Vol.5, No.4, pp.317–23.

Taylor, R. (1995), 'The Emergence of a Consumer Market in China', *Asia Pacific Business Review*, Vol.2, No.1, pp.37–49.

Tedlow, R.S. (1990), *New and Improved: The Story of Mass Marketing in America*. New York: Basic Books.

Tse, D.K, R.W. Belk and N. Zhou (1989), 'Becoming a Consumer Society: A Longitudinal and Cross-Cultural Content Analysis of Print Ads from Hong Kong, the People's Republic of China, and Taiwan', *Journal of Consumer Research*, Vol.15, No.4, pp.457–72.

Tuan, C.H. and X. Zhao (1993), 'Contemporary Chinese Women's Status and Problems', *Hong Kong Journal of Social Sciences*, Vol.1, No.1, pp.35–59.

Wang, J.C.F. (1977), 'Values of the Cultural Revolution', *Journal of Communication*, Vol.27, No.3, pp.41–6.

Wiles, J.A., C.R. Wiles and A. Tjernlund (1995), 'A Comparison of Gender Role Portrayals in Magazine Advertising', *European Journal of Marketing*, Vol.29, No.11, pp.35–49.

Xu, B.Y. (1990), *Marketing to China: One Billion New Customers*. Lincolnwood, Illinois: NTC.

Xue, M. (1981), *China's Socialist Economy*. Beijing: Foreign Language Press.

Yau, O.H.M. (1988), 'Chinese Cultural Values: their Dimensions and Marketing Implications', *European Journal of Marketing*, Vol.22, No.5, pp.44–57.

Zeng, S. (1983), 'China's Senior Citizens', *China Reconstructs*, Vol.32, No.1, pp.9–15.

Zhou, N. and M.Y.T Chen,. (1992), 'Marginal Life after 49: A Preliminary Study of the Portayal of Older People in Canadian Consumer Magazine Advertising', *International Journal of Advertising*, Vol.11, No.4, pp.343–54.

# What to Learn from the Japanese? The Process of Japanese-Style Management Transfer to China

## ZAIXIN MA

Sino–Japanese business has developed gradually since China and Japan resumed diplomatic relations based on the joint communiqué of September 1972. Japanese Direct Investment (JDI) in China was limited through the mid-1980s, but more recently there has been an ever-increasing influx of Japanese investment. JDI to China was US$1.07bn in 1992, and this figure rose to US$2.57bn in 1994, and to US$4.15bn in 1995.[1] By the end of 1995, there were 12,447 Japanese-funded enterprises in China (including equity joint ventures, contractual joint ventures, and Japanese wholly-owned enterprises), accounting for six per cent of the total of foreign-funded enterprises.[2] Japanese Funded Enterprises (JFEs) have played an important role in the process of industrialization in China, and have helped to raise not only production levels, but also productivity, in many industries. Yet their contribution is still below the level hoped for by the Chinese, and there are many unresolved problems in Sino–Japanese economic co-operation.

One of these problems is the transfer of management skills (Fukuda, 1993; Beechler and Yang, 1994; Yamashita, 1991; Kaplinsky and Posthuma, 1994; Sasaki, 1990; Taylor, 1994; Elger and Smith, 1994; Chen, 1992; Zheng, 1993).[3] World interest in Japanese-style management skills essentially began in the late 1970s, after the Japanese economy and Japan's major companies had proved themselves highly resilient to, and apparently unaffected by, the oil crises and other significant international developments. Literature on Japanese management proliferated in the 1980s as managers and scholars became engrossed in learning exactly what had led to Japan's phenomenal industrial success (Appana, 1995). The answer to the question 'Why has Japan succeeded?' is that, to a certain degree, its success has been attributable to political and economic factors, but also that business management has been key factor, much influenced by the Japanese culture.

What is Japanese-style management and what are its characteristics? It is difficult to give a comprehensive definition for Japanese-style management but, through examining it in practice, it is possible to identify the following strengths: stability of employment; attention to human resources as the most important factor in the organization; co-operation between labour and management; co-operation between various levels of

Xaixin Ma, Durham University

suppliers based on a reliable long-term relationship; training and re-educating of employees; flexibility of the workforce through job rotation; and strong internal identification.[4] Lifetime employment and seniority systems, and enterprise unions are among the main characteristics of Japanese-style management, together with co-operative industrial relations and *ringi*-type decision-making systems. A collective orientation is often highlighted as the basic principle of Japanese-style management (Kawabe and Kimbara, 1991).

It also appears that it is easier to transfer Japanese-style management methods to Asian countries than to western countries. Many Asian JFEs have successfully adopted Quality Control Circle (QCC) and Total Quality Control (TQC) approaches in their enterprises. This is revealed by QCC-adoption rates for Asian JFEs as follows: South Korea, 91 per cent; Taiwan, 79 per cent; the Philippines, 85 per cent; Indonesia, 73 per cent; Malaysia, 50 per cent; Singapore, 50 per cent; Thailand, 44 per cent; and Hong Kong, 30 per cent. In contrast JFEs in the United States, Western Europe, Australia, and New Zealand have used TQC and QCC either to a very limited extent, or not at all (Zheng, 1993). As a further example, a senior American Vice-President of a Japanese bank in New York stated that his firm was adopting an American HRM system because Japanese-style HRM practices were found to be unsuitable for the financial industry.[5]

Why are Japanese-style management methods more readily transferable to Asian areas? One of the main reasons is that the traditional culture of these countries is very close to that of Japan. It appears that the lower the cultural distance between the Japanese parent company and the overseas labour pool, the more likely it is that the JFE will adopt Japanese-style management overseas (Beechler and Yang, 1994). However, even within the same Asian region, the extent of QCC adoption varies considerably: Korea, the Philippines and Taiwan show the highest rates,[6] while Malaysia, Singapore, Thailand and Hong Kong show the lowest. Why do such discrepancies exist? Here it should be noted the British influence on Malaysia and Singapore as members of the Commonwealth, and on Hong Kong under British colonial control, as a result of which they have adopted many British-style management features. For example, Singapore is a society strongly influenced by western culture, and Singaporeans are said to be as individualistic and economically pragmatic as are people in western countries. In contrast, Asian countries belonging to the Confucian cultural tradition – particularly Korea, Japan, Taiwan and China – and are all members of the 'chopsticks culture'.

Many Chinese and Japanese believe that Japanese-style management methods are a vital factor in establishing the international competitiveness of JFEs, and both sides thus favour the transfer of such methods to China. This study considers three basic questions about the process of this transfer: what kind of Japanese-style management methods have been transferred to China, how has this transfer been effected, and what problems have hindered the transfer? The next section will consider the issue of cultural communication between China and Japan, and show that many ideas in Japanese-style management draw upon material from ancient China. A detailed case study is then presented of a Sino–Japanese joint venture in the fashion industry in Beijing. The venture's management skills training programme is outlined in some depth, both to show the kinds of methods which are being introduced and how this introduction is being handled. Finally, there is a brief discussion of the difficulties of assimilating Japanese-style management methods in China, which highlights the importance (for the Chinese) of learning the 'essence' of Japanese management.

## CULTURAL COMMUNICATION BETWEEN CHINA AND JAPAN

Fukuda (1993) has reported that Japanese executives working in East Asia often assume that geographical proximity and cultural similarity would automatically make their fellow Asians think and behave very much like themselves. In particular, he found that management practices in Japanese subsidiaries in South Korea, Taiwan and Singapore were generally quite similar to those implemented in Japan. However, his survey of Japanese subsidiaries in Hong Kong also showed that only 13 per cent of the respondents, when asked to state a view on the transferability of Japanese-style management to Hong Kong, expressed a strong conviction that it could be transferred. About 20 per cent had a negative view, while the majority (67 per cent) were uncertain. The overall view was thus neither very positive nor very negative. As noted above, Hong Kong has prospered under British rule for over 150 years, and HK firms have adopted many British-style management features.

What should one expect of Japanese-style management practices in China? We might expect much, since Chinese culture is itself the source for much of Japanese culture. Up until now, researchers have lacked data in this field, and have not explored in detail the similarities in management ideology between China and Japan through history. It is significant that many management books in China today are translations from Japanese but, if we look at them closely, we find that many of the ideas that constitute Japanese-style management draw upon material from ancient China. Works such as 'Strategies of the Warring States' (*Zhan guo ce*), 'Garden of Anecdotes' (*Shuo yuan*), 'A Comprehensive Mirror for Aid in Government' (*Zi zhi tong jian*), 'Main Politics of Zhen Guan' (*Zhen Guan Zheng Yao*), 'An Expanded Supplement to the Wisdom Sack' (*Zeng guang zhi nang bu*), and 'The Art of War' (*Sun Zi Bing Fa*) contain an inexhaustible wealth of material, which forms the basis for so-called 'Chinese-style management'.[7]

Chinese culture and production technology began to be transferred to Japan around 2000 years ago. Cultural communication developed between China and Japan gradually from 200 BC to 600 AD. The period between 600 AD and 1000 AD was a golden age of ancient Sino–Japanese cultural communication. During these centuries the Japanese government sent delegations and students to China on 23 occasions (Wang, 1992). They learned about Chinese politics, law, arts, Confucian studies, building technology and traditional social customs. From the tenth century to the nineteenth century, Sino–Japanese cultural communication continued uninterrupted and included not only culture, arts and Confucian thought, but also Chinese-style management ideology. For example, the Chinese military strategist, Sun Tzu (spelt Sun Zi under the *pinyin* version currently used in China), wrote his book *The Art of War* about 2500 years ago. In 734 AD, a Japanese student took it back to Japan and, since then, over 170 pieces of research concerning *The Art of War* have been published in Japan.[8] Much of Sun Tzu's strategic management thought has been used in modern Japanese-style management practice. Even the Japanese word for management has Chinese origins. In Chinese, the word for 'management' is *guanli; guan* – to manage and control – has a meaning used by Chinese scholars in the Han Dynasty (206 BC to 220 AD).[9] In Japanese, 'management' is termed *kanri*; the word's meaning, pronunciation and concept were thus all transferred from China to Japan over a thousand years ago.

It is not the intention to discuss here in detail traditional Chinese concepts of management, but one example may still be given. One day, Wen – the Marquis of Wei who reigned from 446 BC to 397 BC – heard the Imperial Ensemble playing in the palace and said, 'The pitch on the left is too high.' A scholar named Tian Zifang laughed and said: 'A Head of State doesn't need to understand music. All he needs to know is how to appoint the right conductor. If you pay too much attention to music, I worry that you will have problems appointing the conductors' (Liu, 1978). Scholar Tian's view that a head of state needed only to know how to appoint the right conductor so as to have a good orchestra holds true today. The production manager who has been promoted to general manager yet still meddles in production is making the same mistake as the Marquis of Wei. That will be detrimental in a company where there are many departments (such as personnel, finance, and marketing) for which the general manager is supposed to be responsible. His job is to choose the right people to head them up, not to involve himself in their day-to-day running. Many such ideas were transferred to Japan from Chinese traditional culture.

This kind of example is not intended to imply that all Japanese-style management ideas came from China, rather that some of the basic principles did. For many native Chinese, it is said that Chinese-style management was exported overseas and is now coming back. The Chinese had valuable ideas which they were not using, and the Japanese took them, digested them and then sold them back to China at a high price.[10] However, it is also said that, even though the Japanese borrowed three ancient doctrines (Confucianism, Taoism and Buddhism) from China in the sixth century, they have since effectively combined and modified them to suit their own conditions and needs. These have, in turn, become the important cultural underpinnings of Japanese management (Fukuda, 1993).

Now it appears that both Chinese and Japanese are in favour of

TABLE 1

WHY DID THE CHINESE CHOOSE THE JAPANESE AS THEIR PARTNER?

| Reason | Cited by % of respondents |
| --- | --- |
| Technology and equipment | 65% |
| Management skills | 47% |
| Marketing | 38% |
| Strong reputation in business sector | 33% |
| Financial/economic strength | 25% |
| Possession of patent rights & trade marks | 15% |
| Others | 9% |
| Access to key materials | 4% |

*Note*: Responses to a 1995 survey of the Chinese partners in 81 Japanese-funded enterprises in China. Multiple responses were permitted.

transferring Japanese-style management methods to JFEs in China. In 1995, the author undertook a survey of 81 JFEs in China and posed the question: 'Why did the Chinese choose the Japanese as their partner?'. The responses are shown in Table 1, and it is interesting to note that management skills were the second most cited response, and were cited by almost half the sample. Furthermore, and as already noted above, 85 per cent of the respondents had actually adopted Japanese-style management methods.

AN ILLUSTRATIVE CASE STUDY

Since a large amount of Japanese direct investment in China has been concentrated in the textile and clothing industries, a Japanese-Funded Enterprise in the fashion industry in Beijing was chosen for an in-depth case study. This Sino–Japanese joint venture was established in September 1992. Its total investment was 1.3bn yen (approximately equivalent to US$13m), and the registered capital was 0.7bn yen (about US $7m). The Chinese side invested 30 per cent, and the Japanese side (several partners) 70 per cent of the total. There are 900 employees, an annual output of 510,000 garments of all kinds, and 65 per cent of the total production is exported. The company is an integrated business which includes technology, production, marketing and trade, and has a fashion factory and a shop. The aim of the company is, through Sino–Japanese economic and technical co-operation, to establish and develop the production base and marketing network, and thereby produce profits through the utilization of the advanced production technology, management know-how and marketing experience of the various partners. To achieve this aim, it intends to produce and sell high quality products at fair prices and provide good service so as to increase the competitiveness of the company in the world market, and thus to expand overseas trade and reap good returns.

    The Chinese partner in this joint venture was established in 1961, and is the largest fashion company in the Beijing fashion industry with 176 factories and 48,000 employees. Not only does it lead in size, but is also regarded as a leader in design, production, research, education and marketing in the fashion industry. Its annual output is about 40m garments of all kinds. The Chinese partner is one of the best-known fashion companies in China, has rich experience of the fashion business, and is noted for its exquisite workmanship, and its many factories have enjoyed a long history of fashion production. There are a number of Japanese partners in the joint venture, including well-known companies such as C.Itoh Commerce Co. Ltd.' But the main Japanese partner is a leading company in Japanese fashion circles and a large commercial group which markets many famous labels around the world. It has 500 factories and shops in Japan and many subsidiary companies overseas.

## The Research Methodology

Six people from the top management level of the joint venture were interviewed. Two were Japanese (the Managing Director of the company and the Director of the factory), and four were Chinese (the Deputy Director of the company, the Head of the Affairs Office, the Assistant Director of the factory, and a Sales Manager in the fashion shop). Altogether, the researcher visited the company on five occasions: twice to the main office for interviews totalling about six hours; once to the factory for an interview of about three hours; once to the workshop for a tour while speaking to various managers and workers; and once to the fashion shop for another tour while speaking to managers and saleswomen. In addition, documents were examined, including the Annual Report, a company guide, regulations concerning labour and wages, and plans for and reports of management skills training.[11]

### THE JAPANESE-STYLE MANAGEMENT SKILLS
### TRAINING PROGRAMME

The joint venture had already been in business for three years at the time of the case study, and had employed Japanese-style management skills from the inception. These skills have been codified through the company's 'Japanese-style Management Skills Training Programme', and the discussion which now follows has been derived from responses obtained from the Managing Director, the Deputy Director, and other managers in the company.

## The Objective of the Training Programme

The objective of the programme was to train and develop the skills of the managers and workers in the company so as to allow them be able to operate and manage the company independently from the third year after start-up. The first stage was to set up a training tutor group, to transfer Japanese management skills. This group consisted of members of both the Chinese and Japanese staff, and its task was to promote the implementation of the training plan and to assess those staff who were involved in the training course. Next came the training of 30 managers from the joint venture using the tutor training group. Finally those 30 managers were, in turn, to train all relevant staff. The membership of the training group was four Japanese and three Chinese tutors.

The programme itself involved *inter alia* training in the following four areas: Japanese language education; 'basic management knowledge', labour management, and production management. A brief overview of the content of the programme with respect to each of these areas, and of the learning methods used, is given below. Other areas for which training was also provided, but which are not discussed here, were materials management, equipment management, safety management, project management, and quality management.

## Japanese Language Education

All members of the training course were required to learn basic Japanese, and to be able to use a language handbook of corresponding terms. Learning first involved simple conversation, and then moved on to daily morning and evening meetings and general conferences.

## Basic Management Knowledge

The principal area for the transfer of Japanese-style management skills through the training course was the study of the issues listed below, which were considered by the Japanese to represent 'basic management knowledge'.

- Promoting methods of management
- Enterprise organization and organizational structure
- Organization function
- Faults produced
- Accident prevention and first aid
- Standardization, simplification and specialization
- Promoting methods of improving management
- Activities to improve and raise management skill
- Developing initiative

It is not appropriate here to cover all these issues in detail, but a selective expansion will give a clearer view of some of the questions underlying these key issues. Thus, for example, the section of training with regard to 'promoting methods of management' considered the following questions and areas of concern:

- What is active management?
- What are the responsibilities of the manager?
- What is on-the-spot management, and what are its five main tasks? (Quality, output, cost, discipline, and safety) How to grasp problems on the spot? How to explain problems on the spot to workers? How to

strengthen the commitment to quality?
* Analysis of the main areas of management
* Definitions of management terminology
* Assignment and acceptance of instructions
* Reports, contact, and discussion.

The training with regard to the section on 'promoting methods of *improving* management' was concerned chiefly with the idea that improvements must start from an awareness of the problems and would comprise the elements of investigation, analysis, discussion, testing and examination. In contrast, the section on 'activities to improve and raise management *skill*' was concerned with key *tools* such as 3S, 4S, 5S (Arrange, Rectify, Eliminate, Clear and Cultivation, so-called 5S because these five words in Japanese all begin with 'S'); ZD movement ( Movement of Zero Defects); and QC (Quality Control).

*Labour Management*

Labour management is often cited as one of the most important elements in Japanese-style management. In this area, the training course gave some general pointers to the managers with regard to the following: the purpose of labour management, and its ideal organization; personnel matters; testing and assessment; the labour management of enterprise; aspects of general dissatisfaction on the site; labour policies; and education through QC activities, suggestion and commendation systems, and production bonuses.

Once again, a detailed discussion of each of these sections is not appropriate but some further information on some of the concerns raised may illustrate the nature and extent of the training process. Thus, for example, the section on 'the ideal organization of labour management' highlighted the trinity of operator, production line, and workers (see Figure 1). It is interesting to note that the Japanese tutors made extensive use of such diagrams to help engender a sound understanding by the managers.

The section on the 'labour management of enterprise' included training on the nature of personnel matters; ways of creating good personnel relations; methods for controlling the commendation and criticism of subordinates; methods for educating subordinates; raising the level of leadership; raising the independent decision-making of subordinates; enterprise discipline; social morality; and the determination of pay increases.

The section on 'aspects of general dissatisfaction on the site' considered four sources of dissatisfaction: treatment by management (salary, working conditions); management failure to recognize labour contribution (achievement, value, personal disparities); lack of information; and dissatisfaction arising as a result of a lack of understanding of site conditions (personnel problems, equipment and machinery problems, environmental problems). And the section on 'labour policies' included investigation, analysis and discussion of how pay affects the consciousness

FIGURE 1

THE IDEAL ORGANIZATION OF LABOUR MANAGEMENT

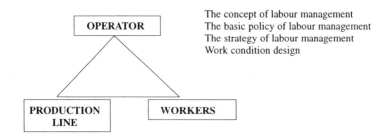

The concept of labour management
The basic policy of labour management
The strategy of labour management
Work condition design

Labour management on the spot
(Putting plans into practice)
(The evaluation of subordinates)

Regulation; Plan project; Labour affairs;
Special service for production lines;
Safety and sanitation; Testing.

of workers, and dealt with how to establish a long-term policy based on these findings.

*Production Management*

Production management is usually considered, together with labour management, one of the main elements in Japanese-style management. Here the training programme focused initially on the position of production management in the organization, and on understanding the system and main functions of production management. The Japanese tutors characterized the production management system as the control system and structure for establishing, issuing and carrying out the corporate plan, and for recording the results and making necessary adjustments. The key functions of the system were considered to be the following:

- Planning product type and amount
- Making plans for affiliated equipment
- Planning equipment, staff and production patterns
- Establishing project order, standard time, quality and cost etc.
- Planning ordering of goods
- Checking material stocks and initiating the purchase of merchandise
- Planning the project schedule
- Preparing and publishing documents on production techniques and types
- Quality control, progress control, equipment management and safety management
- Adjusting the relationship between operation, design and material
- Determing and recording results
- Settling difference between practice and plan
- Evaluating production result

- Organization & function of management
- Labour policies (initiative, education and training)
- Promoting ZD movement and QC activities

In addition, the programme provided training on the organization and function of management (including factors which might hamper effective functioning); the preparation of monthly and annual plans, and the relevant documentation; methods for promoting production (recording in ledgers, the collation of statistics, booking and delivery management); and the management of costs. As regards this latter section, attention was given to the preparation of both planned and realized cost schedules regarding both fixed and variable costs.

## DISCUSSION

We have described in some detail parts of the training programme used to effect the transfer of Japanese-style management methods to the fashion company in Beijing. The parts highlighted have covered the provision of Japanese language education, and training on basic management knowledge, labour management, and production management. Furthermore, it has been pointed out that it is these latter two areas that typically exhibit the distinctive elements of the Japanese-management system. What is immediately apparent from the case study is how systematic, meticulous and well thought out is the training programme, and this is in a relatively low-technology (compared to an electronics firm, for example) clothing company.

It has been possible to catalogue the Japanese-style management methods which have been transferred to the joint venture without as yet being clear as to which methods were difficult to transfer, and why. According to the Chinese Deputy Director:

> Some of the most difficult methods to be transferred are in personnel and financial management, because of the big difference between China's and Japan's economic and social systems. If the company is using the Japanese system, it will be difficult to relate to local systems in China. On the other hand, language problems influenced the Chinese staff's ability to understand Japanese-style management.

The Japanese Director of the joint venture's factory commented:

> There is no disparity of learning in management skills as between the Chinese and Japanese staff, but there are many disparities of *spirit* between the Chinese and the Japanese. Some Chinese staff lack a sense of responsibility, some will not observe discipline, and they tend not to use Japanese-style management methods in the way that Japanese staff do. And also, sometimes Chinese staff do not work together as a unit, so that collectively they are not as effective. Therefore, they cannot fully employ the principles of Japanese-style management.

TABLE 2

DIFFERENCES BETWEEN THE POLITICAL, ECONOMIC AND SOCIAL SYSTEMS
OF CHINA AND JAPAN

|         | Politics   | Economy          | Society                                               |
|---------|------------|------------------|-------------------------------------------------------|
| China   | socialist  | socialist market | family, clan group blood-relationship society        |
| Japan   | capitalist | free market      | family, local group geographical-relationship society |

These quotes draw attention to some underlying differences between China and Japan which, in turn, have given rise to difficulties in transferring Japanese-style management methods. The first quote, from the Chinese Deputy Director, emphasizes 'external' factors: the differences in the social and economic systems. There are indeed significant differences in the political, economic and social systems of China and Japan, and these are summarized in Table 2.

The problems of transferring Japanese-style management methods have certainly been exacerbated by these differences between the systems, but it is unlikely that these differences are the essential cause. Furthermore, as the Chinese political and economic reforms progress and as Chinese society changes, the difficulties associated with these differences will tend to diminish.

The quote from the Japanese Director, on the other hand, emphasizes differences in 'internal' factors, such as the sense of responsibility and attitude to discipline. These differences are perhaps more deep-seated. What are the essential differences in these 'internal' factors between China and Japan? China, Japan, and other Asian countries all belong to the Confucian cultural circle. In contrast to western societies which emphasize individualism, East Asian societies generally stress collectivism. However, there are still many differences in the collective orientation of Chinese and Japanese societies – see Table 3.

TABLE 3

CHARACTERISTICS OF COLLECTIVE ORIENTATION
IN CHINESE AND JAPANESE SOCIETIES

|          | Orientation                                                                      | Characteristics of collective orientation                                                                          |
|----------|----------------------------------------------------------------------------------|-------------------------------------------------------------------------------------------------------------------|
| Chinese  | family-oriented; not society-oriented; society is 'like a tray of loose sand'*    | orientation is one of clan-type collectivity, normally replaced by individual orientation at workplace             |
| Japanese | family-oriented; society-oriented; society is 'together like a piece of granite'* | a traditional household of related members, and in an artificial group of unrelated members such as a business enterprise |

Note : * Y.T. Lin, *My Country and My People*, London, Heinemann, 1962.

Whereas Chinese society is a blood-relationship society, Japanese society is a geographical-relationship society, and certain differences follow. In Chinese society, people always consider the 'family relationship' (*jiazu guanxi*); in a group, the 'collective spirit' is not very strong. People put themselves and their family first. The Chinese like to live together, but they usually do not like to be united as one. The same situation occurs not only in Mainland China, but also in Overseas Chinese groups. In contrast, the Japanese appear to have a stronger 'collective spirit', are less concerned about things outside their group, and more concerned about what happens within their group. This kind of Japanese spirit arises from the Japanese geographical-relationship society. Japanese workforces call their company *uchi no kaisha*. *Uchi no* means 'our' or 'homes'; *kaisha* means 'company'. Thus the Japanese staff regard the company as home, and themselves as a member of a family within that home. They therefore have a stronger sense that this is 'my company', and work hard to make it the best. Chinese people lack this orientation.

## CONCLUSIONS

This essay has involved an inquiry into cultural communication between China and Japan, and has considered some of the problems of transferring Japanese-style management to China in order to better understand how this process takes place. Some similarities in management ideology have been identified, arising from historical contacts between the two countries up to 2000 years ago and, on this basis, there is reason to believe that some Japanese-style management methods should be relatively easy to transfer to China. This perspective has not been fully brought out in previous studies.

The process of transfer has been investigated using an in-depth case study of a joint venture company in the fashion industry. The conclusions are threefold. First, as China continues to reform and open up to the outside world, many of the (external) impediments hindering learning from advanced countries should disappear of their own accord. Second, the Chinese are adopting many Japanese-style management methods which involve not only learning management skills but also the essence of Japanese management (internal factors). This 'essence' involves a certain attitude towards the company, towards responsibility, and towards the implementation of the adopted management methods. In the words of Akio Morita, the former Chairman of the Sony Corporation,

> No (economic) theory or plan or government policy will make a business a success; that can only be done by people... The most important mission for a Japanese manager is to develop a healthy relationship with his employees, to create a family-like feeling within the corporation.... (Morita, 1987).[12]

In the transfer of Japanese-style management methods, learning this essence is rather more important than coming to terms with the external factors.

Third, the Chinese need to develop an appreciation of the contribution of *Chinese-style* management ideas from their own history, so as to gain fresh self-confidence and be able to contribute more to the learning of advanced foreign management methods, especially those adopted from the Japanese.

ACKNOWLEDGEMENTS

Help in preparing this contribution was received from Peter Manly and John Ritchie at Durham University Business School.

NOTES

1. The data are provided by the Japanese Ministry of Finance.
2. The data are provided by the Chinese State Administration Bureau for Industry and Commerce.
3. For a review, see N. Kawabe and T. Kimbara, 'Review of Studies on Japanese-style Management', in S. Yamashita (ed.) *Transfer of Japanese Technology and Management to the ASEAN countries*, Hirojima: Hirojima University Press, 1991, pp.123–34.
4. T. Kimbara, 'Localization and Performance of Japanese Operations in Malaysia and Singapore', in S. Yamashita (ed.) *Transfer of Japanese Technology and Management to the ASEAN countries*, Hirojima: Hirojima University Press, 1991, pp.153–68.
5. S. Beechler and J.Z. Yang, 'The Transfer of Japanese-style Management to American Subsidiaries: Contingencies, Constraints and Competencies'. *Journal of International Business Studies,* 3rd Quarter 1994, pp.467–91.
6. No statistics are available for China but, according to a questionnaire survey undertaken by the author, 85% of JFEs in China have adopted Japanese-style management methods.
7. G. Zhu, 'Looking at Leadership through History', *Sinorama*, November 1992, pp.110–12.
8. W. Lu, 'The Discover Notes of *The Art of War*', *The Press Digest*, Beijing, Beijing BIKE Electronics Tech. Co. Ltd., October 1996.
9. *A Chinese Dictionary*, Chengdu: Sichuan Lexicographic Work Press, 1993, p.1245.
10. G. Zhu, 'Looking at Leadership through History'.
11. In addition to the transfer of management methods, the following issues were also covered in the interviews: the motivation and background to the investment; the reasons for the choice of partners and details of the negotiations; main points of co-operation; production and marketing; labour and training; operation, decision and performance; interference by local government; conflicts arising from cultural and organizational differences.
12. A. Morita, *Made in Japan:* Akio Morita and Sony, London: Collins, 1987.

REFERENCES

Apana, S. (1995) 'Japanese-style Operations Management,' *The Japan Foundation Newsletter,* pp.15–22.
Beechler, S. and J.Z. Yang (1994), 'The Transfer of Japanese-style Management to American Subsidiaries: Contingencies, Constraints and Competencies', *Journal of International Business Studies*, Vol.25, No.3, pp.467–91.
Chen, J. (1992), 'Japanese Firms with Direct Investments in China and Their Local Management' in S. Tokunaga (ed.) (1994), *Japan's Foreign Investment and Asian Economic Interdependence*. Tokyo: University of Tokyo Press, pp.257–71.
Elger, T. and C. Smith (eds) (1994), *Global Japanization?* London: Routledge.
Fukuda, K.J. (1993), *Japanese Management in East Asia and Beyond*. Hong Kong: The Chinese University Press.
Kaplinsky, R. and A. Posthuma (1994), *Easternisation*. London: Frank Cass.
Kawabe, N. and T. Kimbara (1991), 'Review of Studies on Japanese-style Management' in S. Yamashita (ed.), *Transfer of Japanese Technology and Management to the ASEAN Countries*. Hirojima: Hirojima University Press, pp.123–34.
Kimbara, T. (1991), 'Localization and Performance of Japanese Operations in Malaysia and

Singapore' in S. Yamashita (ed.), *Transfer of Japanese Technology and Management to the ASEAN Countries*. Hirojima: Hirojima University Press, pp.153–68.

Liu, X. (1978), *Strategies of the Warring State*. Shanghai: Shanghai Ancient Books Press.

Morita, A. (1987), *Made in Japan: Akio Morita and Sony*. London: Collins.

Sasaki, N. (1990), *Management and Industrial Structure in Japan*. Oxford: Pergamon Press.

Taylor, R. (1994), 'Japan's Role in China's Economic Transformation since 1978', *Journal of Far Eastern Business*, Vol.1, No.2, pp.13–33.

Wang, X. (1992), *The History of Modern Sino–Japanese Culture Communication*. Beijing: Zhong Hua Press.

Yamashita, S. (ed.) (1991), *Transfer of Japanese Technology and Management to the ASEAN Countries*. Hirojima: Hirojima University Press.

Zheng, C. (1993), 'The Operational Management Characteristics of Japanese Supranational Corporations', *Japan Research*, No.1, 1993, pp.1–6.

# Evolving China Strategies:
# How the Japanese Compare

## JOHN RITCHIE

Both eastern and western sources forecast rising prospects for the Chinese economy ahead. As a recently re-invented global factory-cum-marketplace, China accordingly gains widespread attention. This raises questions about how international trade and business approaches towards China compare. Almost inevitably, differing cultural lenses naively bias whatever picture results. On another wavelength from neighbouring Japan and Korea, many western cultural lenses find China difficult. Since these classically imagined only Europe inspiring industrialization in China, any self-generated Chinese economic breakthrough first stayed far from view. Now, many false starts and dead ends later, China seemingly verges upon that breakthrough, and in ways that make Japan and the United States look better placed to capitalize than Western Europe.

Future economic development trajectories in China are difficult to predict. Both Lardy (1996) and Wall (1996), among others, anticipate that exports might approach Japanese levels by the turn of the century; yet, in 1994, China was not among the top ten largest exporters in the world, even though its trade amounted to 40 per cent of its GDP and contributed around 15 per cent of world trade growth through that year. Continuing Chinese concern about over-dependence upon Japan and the United States as suppliers, markets and sources of investment could favour Western European partners as counterweights, though China also seeks other alternatives. China's status as a leading 'developing country' recipient of (often high export generating) inward investment is well-documented, and it is now increasingly a provider of outward investment.

Earlier speculative waves about Chinese economic prospects appear almost forgotten now. Some even overlook how the rising intra-Asian trade that has supposedly spurred the breakthrough once depended upon classic Chinese trading networks that also embraced Japan, long before the currently fashionable ideas about Greater China added further embellishment (Taylor, 1996). Far from evolving entirely separately, early western trading power approaches were imposed upon both China and Japan, whatever the so-called service-sector-led 'gentlemanly capitalism' ideal might prescribe (Akita, 1996). Now any prospective Chinese global factory-cum marketplace could press upon international high strategy once again. Within Western Europe, this certainly touches upon first German,

John Ritchie, Durham University

then French, Italian and British interests particularly, while the European Union itself deliberates between regarding China as a developing country or as a non-market economy. At the very least, more forward thinking might result from first seeing how other possible trade and business approaches towards China compare.

Despite other rising speculation about Japan's prospective 're-Asianization' (Steven, 1996), any putative 'Japan-rides-the-Chinese-tiger' thesis should also consider national security considerations. However, building bridges that will help understand the two together may well encounter problems. China and Japan have long been studied apart and, while their cultural differences still intellectually puzzle (Boisot, 1995), their respective intelligentsia have found dialogue difficult. Why their historic economic development paths originally diverged still provokes classic debates (Moulder, 1977). Statistically major economic differences divide them still (Minami, 1994). Some accordingly advise that China should time-lag anything learned from how the Japanese economy has developed (Nafiziger, 1995). Others take speculative leaps forward towards the next century when any Chinese global factory-cum-marketplace might eventually displace recent Japanese industrial strength. Whatever happens, the further development paths of China and Japan must inevitably cross, with far-reaching consequences for both (Johnson, 1991).

Historical changes in Japanese approaches to trade and business with China have carried major consequences not just within China but also outside, and potentially will do so again in the future. Purely contemporary accounts lack the timespan and complexity needed for tracking how these approaches have evolved. Much history lies behind how Japan became China's most important trading partner, and more lies behind its role as the predominant donor of official aid – which still dwarfs the flows of private Japanese direct investment – to China. Only through deciphering the longer-term meta-strategies can the distinguishing features of each Japanese approach finally become clear. What follows therefore theoretically reconstructs these meta-strategies in order to understand and predict them better.

Those already persuaded of 'global Japanization' may assume that the Japanese have evolved a grand model approach towards neighbouring China. Some claim that Japanese business 'success' in China has arisen particularly from highly-transferable organizational and management practices (Campbell, 1994). By combining different perspectives, this study finds such claims premature. Instead, four evolving Japanese meta-strategies towards China are proposed, thus giving the problem more theoretical bearing, and moreover outlining a conceivable sea-change ahead. As this sea-change is only just emerging, the detail of the new meta-strategy still remains provisional upon the realization of its full scope and potential. However, the new approach presupposes rising Japanese strategic intent, and corresponding Chinese support, for going beyond bilateral trade towards growing organization for, increasing direct investment to, and better management within China itself, thereby transforming rather than just up-scaling whatever went before. Any further appreciation, however, requires a long enough timespan for seeing how the different approaches have evolved, while also recognizing contemporary complexities.

HOW JAPANESE APPROACHES HAVE EVOLVED

Table 1 outlines the main features of the four historically-evolving Japanese approaches here postulated, including the emergent strategic-managerial mode. As deliberate abstractions, such meta-strategies do not arise from any one single regime, institution, or organization alone, but rather constitute their collective direction. As ideal-typical constructs, these approaches smooth over some empirical fine detail wherever they extrapolate ahead. Granted, however, that they are not therefore exact empirical replicas, critical differences between the different approaches should become theoretically clear by specifying their dominant forms along systematically comparable lines.

In principle, each mode compositely reproduces trade and business its own particular way. So long as that mode dominates, trade and business will follow its particular circuit, absorbing customary fluctuations without changing character along the way. Only rare historic breakthroughs therefore bring about decisive switchovers between, rather than routine realignments within, the configurations outlined here. Their immediate circuit-breaking effects meanwhile ensure that certain hybrid forms temporarily dominate middling transitions between. Otherwise each theoretically 'pure' mode is an ideal-typical approximation with certain inbuilt limitations. For example, classic trader-merchant networks date back very much further, and remain more deeply ingrained, than anything the other modes, and indeed much formal history, immediately recognizes. Long after its first surges, the imperial-militarist mode likewise left its mark upon the civil-nationalist approach, while also bearing upon Chinese collective memory today. Set against that, any strategic-managerial mode would itself appear only partly emergent at the present time. By considering this mode in three ways – in purely stand-alone form, then compared against the other three modes, and finally matched against emergent trends – one may nevertheless weigh its prospects better. Since any sea-change would still carry many past complications before it, this examination starts from past trade and business platforms beginning with historic Sino–Japanese trader-merchanting.

### The Trader-Merchant Mode

A consideration of the trader-merchant mode should ideally help benchmark where subsequent Japanese approaches have changed, and illuminate the problematic history of Sino–Japanese relations. What exact angle that history should take, how far and how deep it might reasonably go, by what means trade and business have become traditionalized, and how

FIGURE 1
JAPANESE APPROACHES TOWARDS CHINA COMPARED

| | Trader-Merchant Mode | Imperial-Militarist Mode | Civil-Nationalist Mode | Strategic-Managerial Mode |
|---|---|---|---|---|
| Original Context | Agrarian Economic Frontiership | Extraterritorial Domination | Inter-State Separatism | Market-Reformism |
| Prime Movers | Stranger-Outsider Minorities | Quasi-Militarised Movements | Individual Interest Brokers | Business Groups |
| Focal objects | Private/Tributary Trade | Preferment/Imposition | 'Coarse' Plan Amelioration | Capital-Technology Transfer |
| Model Organization | Segmentary Trade Networks | 'Informal Empire' | 'Red Factory' Campaign | 'Enterprise Culture' |
| Authority Figures | Trader-Merchant Compradors | Occupier-Overlords | Specialists-Officials | Joint Managers |
| Labour process | Customary Compliance | Appropriated Compliance | 'Organized Dependency' | Factor Resource |
| Control | Petty Equivalence | Occupier Prerogative | Political-Ideological | Market-Corporate |
| Payoff | Tribute-Exchange | Surplus Expropriation | Leveraged Reapprochement | Production-Consumption |
| Dilemma | Traders' Dilemma | Occupiers' Dilemma | Modernizers' Dilemma | Business Dilemma |

such culturally 'inherited scripts' bear upon action today are all difficult questions. Indeed, considering these questions in retrospect while bringing other agendas to bear, some outsiders have assumed that the early western trading powers helped trigger developments in Sino–Japanese bilateral relations. In simple terms, this purported historic 'modernization' thesis rather naively considers the west itself 'developed', with Japan later 'developing' in its light, thereafter constituting China as 'underdeveloped' by comparison.

Yet, recent Eastern histories alternatively maintain that Japanese industrialization also drew upon Chinese influence (Latham and Kawakatsu, 1994; Post, 1994). After once being regarded like piratical smugglers more concerned with brigandage, the Japanese developed import-substituting industries in the production of raw silk, silk textiles, sugar – all formerly major imports from China, while also re-customizing certain incoming western small wares within China (Tsuoyama, 1994). Such marginalized trader-merchanting was, however, hardly transformative, scarcely penetrating either heartland, staying small scale, and being informally networked throughout. At the frontiers of an agrarian economy, this would mean working across customary social and geographic boundaries and, as with other segmentary societies, this was prompted by certain stranger-outsider minorities. Elsewhere the Chinese state sought trading under licence in return for tribute, even though the very idea of individually raising 'fortunes' in this way seemed inimical and illicit. Having long accentuated what Dieter-Evans has termed the classic 'trader's dilemma' of perpetual marginality, imperial-militarist intervention interposed instead (Dieter-Evans, 1994).

## The Imperial-Militarist Mode

In principle, this mode overturns original trade reciprocity, whatever the form taken. When force compels more aggressive and/or defensive postures, expropriation displaces purely voluntary economic exchange and, bearing injunctions about other possible hostilities and warfare besides, economic power changes face accordingly. Past history would suggest China and Japan appreciate this better than most. Long regarded as a 'nation army', former Japanese slogans about 'rich country/strong military' appear particularly emblematic. Erstwhile Chinese combat traditions are likewise cited among more aggressively conceived western corporate strategy texts today. Both nations have constituted 'commerce as warfare' which, along with other evocative mutual stereotypes like *Shina* and *Nippon*, sensitizes economic exchange accordingly.

Fifty years after Japan surrendered, certain past transgressions appear ingrained. In consequence, this mode is difficult to periodize yet it changed the entire trade context. Even though the classic Sinocentric worldview considered the Japanese like some unruly tributary of 'island barbarians', some believe that Japan was more aggressively imperial than China in this respect. Western trading powers also influenced this too, having originally compelled the opening of selected national treaty ports. Despite that, Japan verged upon sub-imperial power status within China following the Opium Wars and the introduction of the unequal system of treaty ports. British and German interests subsequently encountered more direct competition, once the Japanese had side-stepped hitherto customary Chinese compradores (Allen and Donnisthorne, 1954).

Other imperial powers might have considered the great river and seaport concessions enough. Western classic social science likewise never considered that China had very much future where trade and commerce were concerned. Sino–Japanese warring and then the First World War, however, necessitated realignments which meant that, having been ceded what were originally German interests, Japan's Chinese involvements then grew just when those of other nations plateaued (Steeds and Rush, 1977). Although more privately owned, and also more geographically concentrated, than certain others, it is not clear how these Japanese ventures were managed and organized, for the resident Japanese typically kept themselves very much apart. Since this expansionist 'informal empire' approach placed political and military ambition uppermost (Duus, Myers and Peattie, 1989), Japanese targets thereafter extended beyond Shanghai and the treaty ports towards the more resource-laden parts of North-East China. In so doing, Japan also conducted preliminary economic and industrial experiments within ceded Manchuria. With aspirations towards a longer term 'enclave economy', these experiments envisaged the forging of links between Japan, Manchuria, and North China, focusing upon mines, minerals, transportation, communication networks, and services ranging from schools to research institutes (Myers, 1995). Such imperial state-initiated economic development planning arose before wider ideas about some 'Greater East Asia Co-prosperity Sphere' finally told hold, although Ahlers has dismissed this as a diversionary smokescreen (Ahlers, 1940). Japanese economic imperialism has also appeared highly contentious in other ways (Eng, 1986; Osterhammel, 1986). Yet some Chinese consider this a 'golden rice-bowl' period, in contrast to their later experience of the state 'iron rice-bowl' (Warner, 1995). With state support, the Japanese pursued the 'Maeda tripod' of trading house/banking/industrial collaboration, while using trade and investment expansion to learn about foreign ventures, develop markets, and adapt to local conditions: the archetypal image is of the Mitsui soya bean buyer traversing rutted Manchurian roads, progressing slowly, but never giving up (Howe, 1996). Other imperial-militarist rituals apart, some such learning about China from inside could have informed later initiatives, but the costliness of the Second World War, and the civil-nationalist trade and business mode that followed, postponed their development.

*The Civil-Nationalist Mode*

In principle, this mode subjects trade and business to wider forces including, in particular, economic nationalism. Being more 'governed' than 'managed', it thereby institutionalizes forms of trade and business where subordinate organizations have limited free play. The aftershocks from prior Japanese imperial-militarist incursions clearly took considerable working through. Any associated separatism accordingly constrained trade and business while America occupied Japan, Nationalist China went Communist, and the Korean War brought trade embargoes. Under these circumstances, the remaining trade might have gone underground, bypassing official channels altogether. Already very dependent upon top-level individual brokering (Radtke, 1990), the gradual reclassification of the so-called 'friendship' trade, first as 'memorandum' trade, and then as 'official' trade, marked this mode's progress until China's purported 'Sovietization' finally faltered during the early 1960s (Whiting, 1989). Before then Sino–Soviet trade had enjoyed high priority, while the Sovietization of (hitherto smaller scale) urban Chinese workplace management assumed quasi-military proportions with slogans like 'machines are our weapons, factories are our battlefields', epitomizing what Kaple terms the 'dream of a red factory' (Kaple, 1994).

Once this process finally faltered it ironically created some residual role for Japanese expertise to ameliorate its adverse consequences. In China's steelmaking industry, in particular, Japanese-style 'human relations' approaches reportedly suited Chinese labour's 'organized dependency' (Walder, 1986) better than Soviet-style technological preoccupations (Chung, 1980). Furthermore, the way that the Japanese had standardized organizational structures across *inter alia* certain Chinese railways, mills, and breweries was still regarded as model practice (Warner, 1995).

The way civil-nationalist priorities thereby skewed trade and business relationships continued after Japan replaced the Soviet Union as China's leading trade partner during the 1960s. As rapprochement developed, the way Sino–Soviet relations deteriorated might just have presented Japan with fresh Chinese investment opportunities once its own domestic capital controls were finally relaxed. But with relatively fewer, smaller, and less managerially sophisticated multinational businesses than its rivals, Japan's outward manufacturing investment first scattered elsewhere across Asia (Ozawa, 1979).

As Sino–Japanese relations became 'normalized' during the 1970s, less mutual distancing prevailed. Both the 1978 Treaty of Peace and Friendship Treaty, and the Sino–Japanese Long-Term Trade Agreement indeed implied that civil-nationalist priorities had virtually peaked. A new 'economic diplomacy' thereafter emerged, which Lee (1984) saw being fuelled by rising 'China fever' among Japanese businesses. Considering what the Japanese might have learnt from their previous incursions into China, anything 'fevered' seems surprising indeed. All the more since those Japanese firms with particular South Korean, Taiwanese, and USA connections were dismissed by the Chinese authorities from the direct negotiations envisaged by the Long-Term Trade Agreement (Kazuo, 1979).

With the 'open door' reforms already rising, China's own purported modernization plans then assumed fresh significance. Notably successful Japanese bidding for newly-dispensed Chinese large-scale plant contracts – especially concerning steel and petrochemicals – suggested that Sino–Japanese relations had finally turned the corner, with further business breakthroughs pending. Among these contracts, those associated with the construction of the Baoshan Steel complex near Shanghai were held up as showpiece examples of just what further collaboration might achieve. Once serious implementation problems arose, however, earlier doubts and reservations resurfaced among the respective parties about each other and about the project's feasibility. With the first of its two phases thwarted, the entire project then fell foul of the Chinese authorities' abrupt cancellation of many large-scale plant contracts. At first surprised and perplexed, then subsequently dependent upon state intercession for alleviating their predicament, the resulting 'Baoshan Shock' soon punctured the rising 'China fever' of Japanese business, and showed how civil-nationalist priorities ultimately overshadowed everything. Any further business breakthrough therefore depended upon moving towards the more strategic-managerial mode.

## The Strategic-Managerial Mode

Any peaceable breakthrough from historic segmentary trading networks, through these other modes, towards more business-led, rather than just state-led, investment and management in China required Japan to rise above any Baoshan-type shockwaves while also signalling some prospective sea-change in Sino–Japanese economic relations. In principle, this implies that rising Japanese approaches become much more corporate strategic and managerially organized than before. Even those who, like Steven (1996), suspect that some other Japanese 'imperialism' lies behind such 're-Asianization', and who have accordingly labelled Japan's prospective 'second invasion', apparently concur. Steven further maintains that the Japanese would target certain regional and industrial sectors for direct investment. To actually bring this about, however, wider contextual change would seem essential, and any full changeover to the strategic-managerial mode will hardly progress otherwise. Despite several bursts of investment, many Japanese firms never progressed much beyond exporting to China right through into the 1980s. When further production-related direct investment again surged in 1988, China was officially critical about supposed Japanese investment reticence (Zhang, 1995). Even then other Japanese aid, assistance, and indirect investment overshadowed direct investment anyway (Taylor, 1994), although there are many problems accounting for such (Matsuoka and Rose, 1994). With its post-war 'full set industrial structure' under increasing competitive pressure, some internationalist Japanese even advocated its partial dismantling and 'export' to China with concomitant benefits to both parties (Mitsuhiro, 1994).

However much this context changed, investment could only produce further payoffs through purposeful management. Indeed, this whole mode presumes such management and cannot otherwise fully materialize. Conventional investment equations nevertheless play management down. Despite past historical affinities, diverging Japanese and Chinese organizational preferences still present problems (Komiya, 1990). One cannot therefore simply take willing Sino–Japanese organizational coupling for granted. The very way that some Chinese authorities have expressly commended Japanese-style 'enterprise culture' and 'enterprise groups', implies that many Chinese still have much to learn as joint-venture partners (Chan, 1995). For all the significance commonly accorded Japanese ownership elsewhere, associated 'vintage effects' have varied over time (Mason and Encarnation, 1994).

Furthermore, any westernized assumption that enterprises operate autonomously through internal hierarchies might well not hold up under Chinese circumstances. To appreciate this better means closely observing what organizational and managerial forms actually arise, along with workplace labour processes. Currently lower Chinese labour costs supposedly rank high – if not the highest – among many incoming investors' assumed motives. Under the full strategic-managerial mode, employees are not only economic 'costs' but, going beyond that, developing 'human resources' co-responsible for initiating organizational successes. Warner suggests these inevitably become 'human resources' with Chinese characteristics (Warner, 1995), while others still consider Chinese 'labour markets' underdeveloped. Interestingly, Warner observes more 'labour market' development within North-East China in general, and in Dalian in particular, where Japanese examples have been particularly evident.

A further issue concerns whether the Japanese input into emerging ventures raises their managerial profile as much as Campbell (1994) and Taylor (1996) suggest. As more Sino–Japanese ventures emerge, their control could become another issue. Some, like Komiya (1990) suggest that few Chinese organizations are 'firms' in any western sense, while many Chinese State-Owned Enterprises appear to be 'total institutions' and 'mini-states'. Any emerging payoffs might therefore present problems when matched against whatever the respective power holders expect. That alone raises dilemmas over how ventures might best grow, collaborate, stabilize, or decline over time, particularly once more mutual organizational learning takes place and former trade and business modes unravel.

## EMERGING STRATEGIC-MANAGERIAL TRENDS

The essential differences between trade and business under the four modes may be summarized as follows: under the trader-merchant mode, they appeared peripherally segmented; under the imperial-militarist mode more forcibly appropriated; under the civil-nationalist mode attenuated unto other priorities; but, under the strategic-managerial mode, they become a guiding issue for economic meta-strategy, requiring better management accordingly. New issues could potentially arise across every front, ranging from the context through which its new prime movers operate, through changing trade and business objectives and their further managerial organization and control, towards whatever payoffs eventually materialize. Given that the full mode will only arise once various intermediate stages have been experienced, emerging strategic-managerial trends are now considered.

In principle, this mode envisages another context which reprioritizes trade and business, opens further channels, and frees subordinate organizations, enabling better technology and expertise transfer than before. In the process, simply acquiring, experimenting with, and then operationally 'bedding down' new plant and technology investment alone cannot suffice, for corresponding human organization building is also required. Elsewhere labelled 'enterprise culture', such building confers particular power and authority upon managers to pursue 'human resource' policies and practices, depending upon how their ventures are controlled and what payoffs result. Further trend-seeking inquiries might specifically ask questions such as:

- Is the emerging context really more enabling?
- Which organizations mobilize most?
- What actually transfers into emerging ventures?
- Are more 'enterprise cultures' arising?
- How might their management hierarchies work?
- Do human resource policies and practices apply?
- What official corporate control gets exerted?
- What payoffs are expected and/or materialize?
- Will further dilemmas arise?

In so far as changes occur simultaneously across this many fronts, particular changes could prove difficult to isolate except over considerable periods of time. From the Japanese angle, Yabuki (1995) details how the gross value of recorded Sino–Japanese trade increased sevenfold after the early 1970s. By 1992, Japanese customs statistics indicated that imports from China ranked second only to the United States, whereas China only ranked ninth as a destination for Japanese exports, down from second in 1985, representing less than 3 per cent of total exports. However, the changing scale of trade alone cannot signal rising sea-changes, because aid, investment and management also enter this equation. During this period, Japan itself completed the transition from being the leading regional aid-receiver to the leading aid-donor instead. By 1993, it arguably supplied half of China's official aid, raising sensitive questions about how this might privilege Japanese business itself (Taylor, 1996). Against this backdrop of more aid and yen loans, any gathering momentum towards more direct investment also took into account wider global and regional factors. Although the total amount of Japanese investment into Asia was less than that of the United States, the former provided the largest number of individual manufacturing investment projects, particularly by smaller-scale firms. Building on its experience of establishing bases in the Asian Newly Industrializing Countries and in ASEAN, the Japanese would have gained knowledge about new business entry and development costs which would have been relevant in China. Although precise accounting for the extent of this organizational learning remains difficult wherever cross-ownership, reinvestment, invisible assets, and similar problems obscure the way, 'organizational intelligence' gained through Hong Kong service connections, for example, could well have guided moves towards particular Chinese investment targets (Naughton, 1995).

By whatever process the Japanese have learnt which particular business entry and development routes suited them best, their approaches towards China appear more contingent thereafter. In some respects, they have re-mapped China into a federation of several semi-separate zones each requiring separately customized sub-approaches. Here Masuda (1994) differentiates the Dalian, Shanghai, Guangdong, and Beijing sub-approaches particularly. Of course, some Japanese already knew Dalian and its surrounds since the Imperial Army was once headquartered there. Now this area attracts higher-value industrial processing and assembly investment under what Masuda considers an originally ASEAN-filtered management model. In contrast, the Shanghai sub-approach is more concerned with commercial, distribution, and consumption-related investments, and appears to be managed under some originally Taiwanese-filtered model instead. A more specifically Chinese model has arisen around Guangdong using, in particular, 'back door' connections with Overseas Chinese outward processing operations. Finally, yet another variant has arisen in Beijing which was more concerned with trade, banking, and service sector interfaces with official Chinese state agencies, thus using instead a Socialist China management model. All such customization implies increasing Japanese focus, even when that entails alliances with outsiders. Elsewhere around the so-called Yellow Sea Economic Zone spanning North East China, West Korea and Japan's Kyushu coastal regions where trade and migration have traditionally been cross-border, still more functional economic complementarity also seems possible (Grunsven, Wang and Kim, 1995).

More focused sub-approaches like these suggest what some Japanese call more 'soft landings' in China, based upon better organizational intelligence about what business entry and development requires. Some such intelligence could well arise from their unique 'triple-teaming' of trading houses, banks, and enterprises together, itself going back some time before, but yielding further advantages now. Wider intelligence networks likewise embrace joint Japan–China economic and trade advisory groupings, while other educational 'cultural' exchanges may also provide support. Aid-loan giving apart, the Japanese state itself appears to keep some distance from direct investment-related activity, compared with the various Chinese state agencies that appear actively involved. These include inter alia Chinese State-Owned Enterprises, 'investment corporations', banks, and particular provincial and local agencies, together concerned with first attracting and then controlling investment flows. Research suggests that the Japanese obtain some competitive advantage from being better able/willing to accommodate whatever complications are created by these Chinese inter-organizational relationships (Pan, 1994).

Any switchover to the strategic-managerial mode would grant particular organizational networks more free play over both making and realizing investments. Although not easily defined and identified, the way many small and medium-scale Japanese enterprises and industries have developed new joint-venture-type connections helps explain the limited value of capital and technology transfer thus far. A few exceptions apart, many leading Japanese corporations – in particular, the high-profile automobile businesses – doubted China's real development potential during the 1980s. Recent JETRO studies suggest that, of the top 100 foreign firms in China as ranked by 1993 sales value, only 14 were Japanese-affiliated, and they were largely concentrated in the electrical, transportation, and general machinery sectors. Much more numerous were the smaller-scale operators, particularly in the textile and clothing sectors.[1] In short, many small and, perhaps increasingly, medium-scale Japanese enterprises have pathfinded neighbouring Asia generally, and China particularly (Fujita, 1995), creating particular technological profiles accordingly. To some Japanese, the value of any know-how and expertise thus 'transferred' almost equates with that of the physical assets (Harris, 1991). Such 'capability transfer' counters other high-ranking Chinese criticisms about sharp practice over more sophisticated 'hard' technology transfers – technology which some Japanese have long feared might 'leak'.

Other research suggests that, compared with their American counterparts, the Japanese may adopt less individualistic go-it-alone approaches, prepare more, network together better, negotiate longer, are less impressed with gross market size, and manage over longer time horizons, without this making them distinctive *per se* (Grow, 1991). At the very least, this implies growing concern for 'human resources', bearing in mind that the Chinese alone assumed responsibility for labour affairs among earlier 'friendship ventures'. Recent Japanese 'positive commitment' policies espouse joint control principles instead. In practice, issues associated with equal treatment, meritocratic progression, and residency and welfare rights, for example, complicate the picture making some observers predict possible industrial relations problems ahead.[2] Few Japanese firms yet assume 'full responsibility' for such matters, while the smaller and medium-scale incomers could hardly transfer 'lifetime employment' practices from Japan given that they hardly practised them there anyway. Whatever else the Chinese authorities consider they might learn from the Japanese, it is still difficult to determine what other organizational changes will occur later, although Shaw and Meier (1993) report the emergence of 'second generation' variants.

The assumption of management responsibility for joint ventures has never been straightforward. A decade ago, China only gradually afforded individual ventures more autonomy (Pearson, 1991). Few outsiders could ever observe if and how Japanese and Chinese managers worked together, and what knowledge and skills were thereby 'transferred'. In situations like negotiating and bargaining with Chinese local authorities, their customary division into 'two sides' might mislead (Roehrig, 1994). As to their hierarchical ranking, Masuda suggests that the allocation of the chairmanship, board membership, presidency, and functional/departmental responsibilities are closely associated with whether an ASEAN, Taiwanese, or specifically Chinese-derived management model applies.[3]

Apart from often treating internal organizational workings as isolated factors (Chou, 1994; Chen, 1992), much investment-related research also underrates how such workings impact upon eventual payoffs. Such payoffs are not straightforward, however, since intra-firm transfers, re-exports, and 'invisible assets' (including 'capability transfers') for example pose complications. Among the non-economic payoffs, those Japanese who practice 'learning by monitoring' through regarding these initiatives like selected field experiments might regard them like 'insurance' for subsequent, substantial developments. On balance, other Japanese firms' rising interest in China in the immediate future would itself suggest that, having first gone full circuit, trade and business could well become further transformed through this mode; these firms having learnt along the way and deployed their growing 'organizational intelligence'.[4]


## SUMMARY AND CONCLUSIONS

The very re-invention of China like some would-be global factory-cum-marketplace that might better suit the prevailing world order, clearly poses vital questions about both. At the very least, observers interested in the future should increasingly question how differing international trade and business approaches towards China might evolve and compare given the changed prospects ahead. More evolutionary issues concern the way historically decisive changes might predictably come about. Overlaying them come other issues about how particular approaches specifically compare. All this should certainly concern Western Europe because, as currently re-invented, the rising Chinese economic trajectory apparently favours Japanese and US interests, whatever other Asia-Pacific trends materialize.

Partly for cultural-competitive reasons, the passage and conduct of Japanese trade and business across the Asia-Pacific in general has never been that clearly visible before. Where they still bear upon collective memory, former imperial-militarist incursions provide further controversy to this day. Isolated anti-Japanese outbursts and boycotts can still erupt even now. Any new appreciation of Japanese trade and business with China should therefore be grounded upon what has transpired thus far, rather than on forward speculation alone. To that end, this study has proposed its own four-fold typology of evolving Japanese approaches towards China, which latterly conceives a rising strategic-managerial alternative that would represent another sea-change were it ever realized.

Although drawn from limited sources, such ideal-typical extrapolations particularly specify how this approach differs from what went before. In terms of time alone, this mode has not yet continued long enough for all its intended features and full outcomes to be made clear. In line with current global-regional business thinking, this approach nevertheless emphasizes how the Japanese seek and deploy organizational learning and intelligence and refocus further initiatives accordingly. If it is not yet time for the more dramatic business developments that certain Japanese domestic surveys would indicate – and Japanese business does, after all, lack certain Overseas Chinese connections – it is nevertheless clear that steps already taken should help pave the way. Granted that 'triple teaming' arrangements surround them, many small and medium-scale Japanese enterprises have been notable pathfinders thus far. This cautious approach has the strategic advantage of limiting possible losses (though also possible gains), while bolstering further learning before more substantial ventures commit themselves. Japanese commercial interests in Hong Kong may likewise gather 'offshore' intelligence from non-manufacturing targets within China.

In short, it is not just the relative volume of aid, trade and business which might henceforward differentiate Japanese from Western European approaches towards China, but their growing organizational coupling and managerial sustainability. Western European interests might particularly observe how, as well as what, Japanese firms learn about China, and also from each other there, and thereby better prepare the way for major changes ahead.

## NOTES

1. S. Imai, 'Comparison of Western, Overseas Chinese and Japanese Ventures', *JETRO China Newsletter*, No.119, 1995, pp.15–24.
2. M. Seki, 'Japanese Ventures in China – a Status Report', *JETRO China Newsletter*, No.111, 1994, pp.2–7; S. Sonoda, 'Growth Processes of Japanese Ventures in China', *JETRO China Newsletter*, No.111, 1994, pp.8–11.
3. T. Masuda, 'Pointers on Investment in the Chinese Market', *JETRO China Newsletter*, 7 No.111, 1994, pp.12–18.
4. As expressed in the domestic surveys cited by Taylor, Steven and others.

## REFERENCES

Ahlers, J. (1940), *Japan Closing the 'Open Door' in China*. Shanghai: Kelly & Walsh.
Akita, S. (1996), 'Gentlemanly Capitalism, Intra-Asian Trade and Japanese Industrialisation at the Turn of the Last Century', *Japan Forum*, Vol.8, No.1, pp.51–65.
Allen, G. and Donnisthorne, A. (1954), *Western Enterprise in Far Eastern Economic Development*. London: Allen & Unwin.
Boisot, M. (1995), *Information Space*. London: Routledge.
Campbell, N. (1994), 'Japan's Success in China', in M. Schutte (ed.) *The Global Competitiveness of the Asian Firm*. Basingstoke: Macmillan, pp.129–37.
Chan, A. (1995), 'Chinese Enterprise Reforms: Convergence with the Japanese Model', *Industrial & Corporate Change*, Vol.4, No.2, pp.449–70.
Chen, J. (1992), 'Japanese Firms with Direct Investments in China and their Local Management' in S. Tokunaga (ed.), *Japanese Foreign Direct Investment and Asian Economic Interdependence*. Tokyo: University of Tokyo Press, pp.257–72.

Chung, C. (1980), *Maoism and Development*. Seoul: National University Press.

Chou, Y. (1994), 'Japanese Joint Ventures in China: a Profile Analysis' in N. Campbell and S. Stewart (eds), *Advances in Chinese Industrial Studies*. Greenwich CN: JAI Press, pp.199–210.

Dieter-Evans, H. (1994), 'The Trader's Dilemma' in H. Dieter-Evans and H. Scrader (eds), *The Moral Economy of Trade*. London: Routledge.

Duus, P., R. Myers and M. Peattie (eds) (1989), *The Japanese Informal Empire in China 1895–1937*. Princeton: Princeton University Press.

Eng, R. (1986), *Economic Imperialism in China*. Berkeley: Institute of Asian Studies, University of California.

Fujita, M. (1995), 'Small and Medium Sized Transnational Corporations: Trends and Patterns of Foreign Direct Investment', *Small Business Economics*, No.7, pp.193–204.

Grow, R. (1991), Comparing Japanese and American Technology Transfer in China' in T. Agmon and M.A. von Glinow (eds), *Technology Transfer in International Business*. Oxford: Oxford University Press, pp.193–222.

Grunsven, L., S. Wang and W. Kim (eds) (1995), 'State, Investment and Territory: Regional Economic Zones and Emerging Industrial Landscapes' in R. Heron and S. Park (eds), *The Asian Pacific Rim and Globalization*. Aldershot: Avebury, pp.151–78.

Harris, M. (1991), 'Technology Transfer and Sino–Japanese Relations' in T. Agmon and M.A. von Glinow (eds), *Technology Transfer in International Business*. Oxford: Oxford University Press, pp.143–58.

Howe, C. (ed.) (1996), *China and Japan: History, Trends and Prospects*. Oxford: Clarendon Press.

Howe, C. (ed.) (1996), *The Origins of Japanese Trade Supremacy*. London: Hurst & Co.

Johnson, C. (1991), 'Where does Mainland China fit in the World organised into Pacific, North American and European Regions', *Issues and Studies*, Vol.27, No.8, pp.1–16.

Kazuo, O. (1979), 'How the 'Inscrutables' Negotiate with the 'Inscrutables': Chinese Negotiating Tactics vis-a-vis the Japanese', *The China Quarterly*, No.79, pp.529–552.

Kaple, D. (1994), *Dream of a Red Factory*. Oxford: Oxford University Press.

Komiya, R. (1990), 'Japanese Firms, Chinese Firms' in *The Japanese Economy: Trade, Industry and Government*. Tokyo: Tokyo University Press, pp.193–232.

Latham A. and H Kawakatsu,. (eds) (1994), *Japanese Industrialization and the Asian Economy*. London: Routledge.

Lardy, N. (1996), 'Chinese Foreign Trade' in R. Ash and Y. Kueh (eds), *The Chinese Economy under Deng Xiaoping*. Oxford: Clarendon Press, pp.217–46.

Lee, C. (1984), *China and Japan: New Economic Diplomacy*. Stanford: Hoover Institution Press.

Mason, M. and D. Encarnation (eds) (1994), *Does Ownership Matter? Japanese Multinationals in Europe*. Oxford: Clarendon Press.

Matsuoka, M. and B. Rose (1994), *The DIR Guide to Japanese Economic Statistics*. Oxford: Oxford University Press.

Minami, R. (1994), *The Economic Development of China*. Basingstoke: Macmillan.

Mitsuhiro, S. (1994), *Beyond the Full Set Industrial Structure*. Tokyo: LTCB Library Foundation.

Moulder, F. (1977), *Japan, China and the Modern World Economy*. New York: Cambridge University Press.

Myers, R. (1995), 'Creating a Modern Enclave Economy: the Economic Integration of Japan, Manchuria and North China 1932–1945' in R. Duus, R. Myers and S.M. Peattie (eds), *The Japanese Wartime Empire 1931–1945*. Princeton: Princeton University Press.

Nafziger, W. (1995), *Learning from the Japanese*. New York: M.E. Sharpe.

Naughton, B. (1995), *Growing Out of the Plan*. Cambridge: Cambridge University Press.

Osterhammel, J. (1986), 'Semi-Colonialism and Informal Empire in Twentieth Centure China – Towards a Framework of Analysis' in W. Mommsen and J. Osterhammel (eds), *Imperialism and After*. London: Allen & Unwin, pp.292–314.

Ozawa, T. (1979), *Multinationalism, Japanese Style*. Princeton: Princeton University Press.

Pan, Y. (1994), 'Entering China through Equity Joint Ventures: a Comparison of Japanese, US, European & Hong Kong Approaches', *Journal of Asian Business*, Vol.10, No.2, pp.81–93.

Pearson, M. (1991), *Joint Ventures in the People's Republic of China*. Princeton: Princeton University Press.

Post, P. (1994), 'Chinese Business Networks and Japanese Capital in South East Asia' in R. Brown (ed.), *Chinese Business Enterprise in Asia*. London: Routledge, pp.154–76.

Radtke, K. (1990), *China's Relations with Japan 1945–1983*. Manchester: Manchester University Press.

Roehrig, M. (1994), *Foreign Joint Ventures in Contemporary China*. New York: St. Martin's Press.

Shaw, S. and J Meier,. (1993), 'Second Generation MNC's in China', *The McKinsey Quarterly*, No.4, pp.3–16.

Sideri, S. (1995) 'The Economic Relations of China and Asia-Pacific with Europe', *Development Policy Review*, Vol.13, pp.219–246.

Steeds, D. and I. Rush (1977), *China, Japan and Nineteenth Century Britain*. Dublin: Irish Academic Press.

Steven, R. (1996), *Japan and the New World Order*. Basingstoke: Macmillan.

Taylor, R. (1993), 'Japanese Investment, Strategy and Management Training in China: Lessons for British Investors', *Asian Affairs*, Vol.24, Part 3, pp.315–26.

Taylor, R. (1994), 'Japan's Role in China's Economic Transformation Since 1978', *Journal of Far Eastern Business*, Vol.1, No.3, pp.13–37.

Taylor, R. (1996), *Greater China and Japan*. London: Routledge.

Tsunoyama, S. (1994), 'Sino–Japanese Trade and Japanese Industrialization' in A.Latham and H. Kawakatsu (eds), *Japanese Industrialization and the Asian Economy*. London: Routledge, pp.194–200.

Walder, A. (1986), *Communist Neo-Traditionalism, Work & Authority in Chinese Industry*. Berkeley: University of California Press.

Wall, D. (1996), 'China as a Trade Partner: Threat or Opportunity for the OECD', *International Affairs*, Vol.72, No.2, pp.329–44.

Warner, M. (1995), *The Management of Human Resources in Chinese Industry*. New York, St. Martin's Press.

Whiting, A. (1989), *China Eyes Japan*. Berkeley: University of California Press.

Yabuki, S. (1995), *China's New Political Economy: the Giant Awakes*. Boulder, The Westview Press.

Zhang, Z. (1995), 'International Trade and FDI: Further Evidence from China', *Asian Economic Journal*, Vol.9, No.2, pp.153–67.

# Abstracts

## Operating as a Foreign Company in China: Introduction and Overview
*by Roger Strange, Syed Kamall, and Hui Tan*

Since its government's dramatic shift in foreign and economic policy in 1978, China has been regarded as a lucrative target for foreign multinational enterprises and international business researchers alike. This essay reviews the distinctive features of the Chinese business environment and examines the empirical academic research on the management behaviour of foreign investors in China. The research addresses the issues of the choice of entry mode; the selection of appropriate partners for joint ventures; negotiations with Chinese partners and authorities; corporate governance; human resource management; the implementation of knowledge transfer between the foreign parent and the Chinese affiliate; and the problems and opportunities for successful marketing in China. It is noted that finance questions have received little attention in the literature. Finally, an overview is provided of the succeeding papers and their conclusions.

## Chinese State Enterprises and Their Reform *by Athar Hussain and Juzhong Zhuang*

The far-reaching changes in the economic environment in China since the start of the reform period have directly affected enterprise behaviour and have important implications for future enterprise reform. The growth of market transactions has been accompanied by an increase in competition which has forced State-Owned Enterprises (SOEs) to cut costs and upgrade quality. The growing exposure of Chinese enterprises to international markets and foreign business practices has led to an upgrading of their organization and management structure. The multiplication of the sources of external funds for investment has facilitated the establishment of new enterprises and provided enterprises with wider opportunities for diversifying risk. And the rapid growth of the economy has provided room for the non-state sector to expand without a major contraction of the state sector. But many problems still remain, notably with regard to government interference in the day-to-day management of the SOEs, the development of appropriate and effective governance structures, the need for efficiency-enhancing industrial restructuring, and reform of employment relations and the social security system. This article considers these problems and makes recommendations regarding future reform initiatives particularly with regard to loss-making enterprises.

## A Study of Management Attitudes in Chinese State-Owned Enterprises, Collectives and Joint Ventures *by Weihwa Pan and David Parker*

Since 1978 China has introduced a series of reforms that has gradually moved its economy away from planning and towards more market-based resource allocation. State-Owned Enterprises (SOEs) have been permitted to set market prices, retain profits after tax and employ factors of production much more freely than before. Private-sector firms have been allowed, and joint ventures with foreign firms encouraged. At the same time, continued political intervention in the management of enterprises may be dulling incentives for management to operate commercially. This study reports the results of research based on structured interviews with senior managers in 16 corporatized and non-corporatized SOEs, collective enterprises and joint ventures in Shanghai and Nanjing. The fieldwork was undertaken between October and December 1995, to shed light on the extent to which management attitudes had changed in recent years following the reforms, and to confirm whether there were noticeable differences in attitudes between managements in the various types of enterprises. The research also considers the current relationship between plant management and government bureaus, and management attitudes towards privatization.

### Local Sourcing in China: the Case of Braun Electric (Shanghai) Co. Ltd
*by Stefan H. Kaiser*

Increasingly, multinational enterprises manufacture locally in China, for reasons of cheap labour or as a means of more efficiently penetrating the vast Chinese market. However, the literature suggests a range of problems associated with local manufacturing, such as the sourcing of locally produced components and materials. This study looks into the case of Braun Electric (Shanghai) Co Ltd., a wholly owned subsidiary of Braun AG of Germany, which produces electric foil shavers in China, examining its reasons for local sourcing, associated problems and resulting strategies. The case study is based on a two-week research visit to the company in January 1996.

### The Selection of Distribution Channels in China *by C.S. Tseng, Paula Kwan and Fanny Cheung*

This contribution first traces the development of the distribution system in China from state monopoly to one which permits the limited participation of foreign ventures, and examines the problems faced by foreign investors in managing the distribution channels under such a transitional economy. Due to China's abundance of linguistic, cultural and economic differences, combined with growing territorialism at the provincial level, different problems may be encountered in different cities/regions, and therefore foreign investors need to modify their distribution strategies accordingly. Detailed case studies are provided as illustrations.

### Marketing in An Emerging Consumer Society: Character Images in China's Consumer Magazine Advertising *by Nan Zhou and Linming Meng*

A content analysis of a sample of Chinese consumer advertisements shows a mixed image of seller and buyer, and of traditional Chinese and 'modern' and 'imported' images: older, authoritative Chinese male figures are blended with younger, good-looking female faces and bodies. In the foreseeable future, there will be more buyer and foreign images in advertising. However, advertisers, particularly those from foreign countries, should recognize the importance of not using portrayals that could be perceived to be incompatible with Chinese cultural values and government policies in their advertisements.

## What to Learn from the Japanese? The Process of Japanese-Style Management Transfer to China *by Zaixin Ma*

Many Chinese and Japanese believe that Japanese-style management methods are a vital factor in establishing the international competitiveness of 'Japanese-Funded Enterprises' in China, and both sides thus favour the transfer of such methods to China. This contribution considers three basic questions about the process of this transfer: what kind of Japanese-style management methods have been transferred to China, how has this transfer been effected, and what problems have hindered the transfer? It is argued that many ideas in Japanese-style management draw upon material from ancient China. A detailed case study is presented of a Sino-Japanese joint venture in the fashion industry in Beijing, outlining in some depth the venture's management skills training programme, both to show the kinds of methods which are being introduced and how this introduction is being handled. Finally, there is a brief discussion of the difficulties of assimilating Japanese-style management methods in China, which highlights the importance (for the Chinese) of learning the 'essence' of Japanese management.

## Evolving China Strategies: How the Japanese Compare *by John Ritchie*

The recent designation of China as a global factory-cum-marketplace that might better suit the prevailing world order poses vital questions about both. At the very least, observers should question how differing international trade and business approaches towards China might evolve and compare, given the prospects ahead. This study examines various historical Japanese approaches towards trade and business with China, and puts forward the following four-fold typology of modes: classic trader-merchanting, imperial-militarist, civil-nationalist, and strategic-managerial. It is argued that the strategic-managerial mode is still emerging but that it presupposes rising Japanese intent, and corresponding Chinese support, for going beyond bilateral trade towards increasing organization and direct investment to China and better management within the country. The detail of this emerging mode remains provisional upon the realization of its full scope and potential, but it may be differentiated from Western European approaches not just by the relative volumes of aid, trade and investment, but also through the extent of organizational coupling and managerial sustainability. Western European investors in particular might observe *how* Japanese firms learn from China, as well as *what*, and thereby better prepare themselves for major changes ahead.

# Index